THE RISE OF THE
EUROPEAN POWERS
1679–1793

To Liz

THE RISE OF THE EUROPEAN POWERS
1679–1793

JEREMY BLACK

Lecturer in History, University of Durham

Edward Arnold

A division of Hodder & Stoughton

LONDON NEW YORK MELBOURNE AUCKLAND

© 1990 Jeremy Black

First published in Great Britain 1990

Distributed in the USA by Routledge, Chapman and Hall, Inc.
29 West 35th Street, New York, NY 10001

British Library Cataloguing in Publication Data

Black, Jeremy
  The rise of the European powers 1679–1793.
  1. Europe. Foreign relations, history
  I. Title
  327′.094

  ISBN 0-7131-6537-5

Library of Congress Cataloging-in-Publication Data

Black, Jeremy.
    The rise of the European powers, 1679–1793 / Jeremy Black.
      p.   cm.
    Includes bibliographical references (p.   ).
    ISBN 0-7131-6537-5
      1. Europe – Politics and government – 1648–1715.   2. Europe –
– Politics and government – 18th century.   3. Europe – Foreign
relations.   I. Title
  D273.B57   1990
  327′.094′09033 – dc20   89-27594 CIP

Typeset in Linotron Meridien by Rowland Phototypesetting Limited,
Bury St Edmunds, Suffolk. Printed and bound in Great Britain for
Edward Arnold, the educational, academic and medical publishing
division of Hodder and Stoughton Limited, Mill Road, Dunton
Green, Sevenoaks, Kent TN13 2YD by Richard Clay Limited,
Bungay, Suffolk.

CONTENTS

IV   Practice and Theory in *Ancien Régime* International Relations

V   The Mechanics of International Relations

MAPS

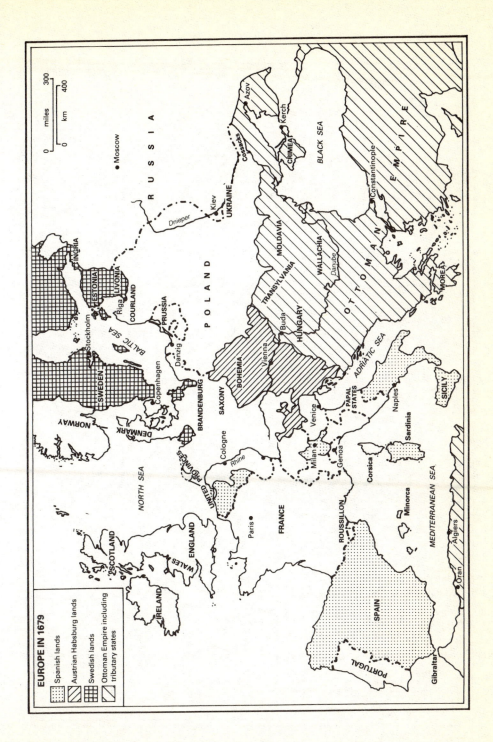

EUROPE IN 1679

Spanish lands
Austrian Habsburg lands
Swedish lands
Ottoman Empire including tributary states

RUSSIA

• Moscow

Dnieper

Kiev

UKRAINE

COSSACKS

Azov

Kerch

CRIMEA

BLACK SEA

Constantinople

OTTOMAN EMPIRE

MOREA

MOLDAVIA

TRANSYLVANIA

WALLACHIA

Danube

HUNGARY

Buda

ADRIATIC SEA

BOHEMIA

Vienna

POLAND

Danzig

PRUSSIA

BRANDENBURG

SAXONY

COURLAND

LIVONIA

Riga

ESTONIA

INGRIA

BALTIC SEA

Stockholm

SWEDEN

NORWAY

DENMARK

Copenhagen

Cologne

Rhine

UNITED PROVINCES

NORTH SEA

SCOTLAND

IRELAND

WALES

ENGLAND

Paris •

FRANCE

ROUSSILLON

Minorca

SPAIN

PORTUGAL

Gibraltar

Milan

Venice

Genoa

Corsica

Sardinia

PAPAL STATES

Naples

SICILY

MEDITERRANEAN SEA

Algiers

Oran

miles 300
0
km 400
0

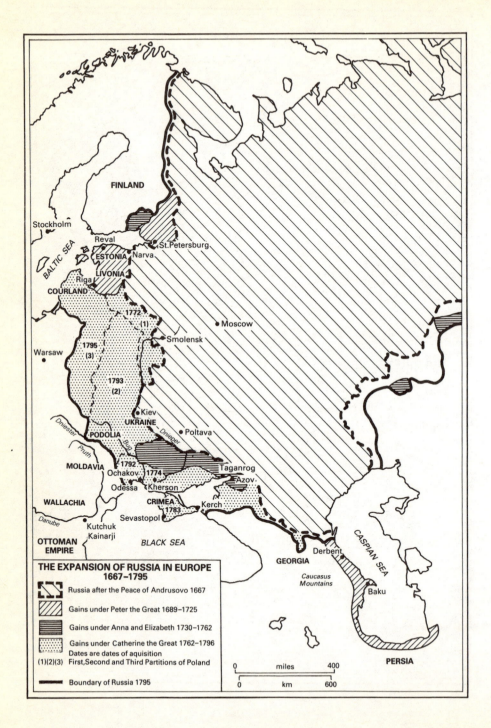

FINLAND

Stockholm

Reval

BALTIC SEA

St.Petersburg

ESTONIA Narva

LIVONIA

Riga

COURLAND

1772

(1)

Smolensk

Moscow

1795
(3)

Warsaw

1793

(2)

Kiev

UKRAINE

Poltava

Dniester

PODOLIA

Dnieper

Pruth

Bug

1792

Ochakov 1774

MOLDAVIA

Odessa Kherson

Taganrog

Azov

WALLACHIA

CRIMEA
1783

Kerch

Danube

Kutchuk
Kainarji

Sevastopol

BLACK SEA

Derbent

GEORGIA

CASPIAN SEA

OTTOMAN
EMPIRE

*Caucasus
Mountains*

Baku

PERSIA

THE EXPANSION OF RUSSIA IN EUROPE
1667–1795

Russia after the Peace of Andrusovo 1667

Gains under Peter the Great 1689–1725

Gains under Anna and Elizabeth 1730–1762

Gains under Catherine the Great 1762–1796

Dates are dates of aquisition

(1)(2)(3)   First, Second and Third Partitions of Poland

Boundary of Russia 1795

0   miles   400

0   km   600

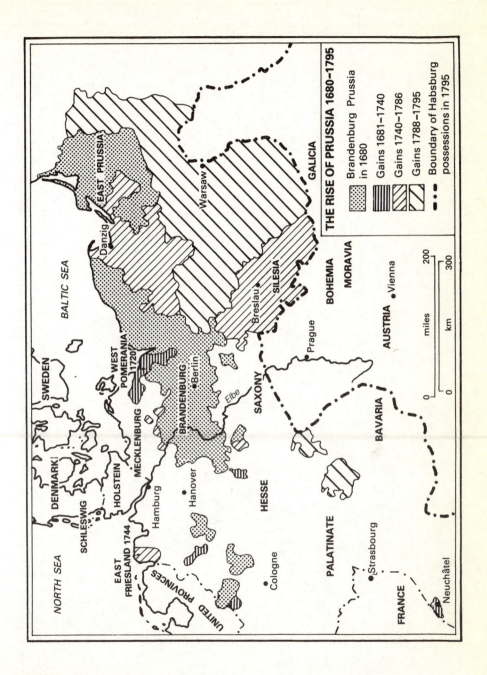

THE RISE OF PRUSSIA 1680–1795

Brandenburg Prussia
in 1680

Gains 1681–1740

Gains 1740–1786

Gains 1788–1795

Boundary of Habsburg
possessions in 1795

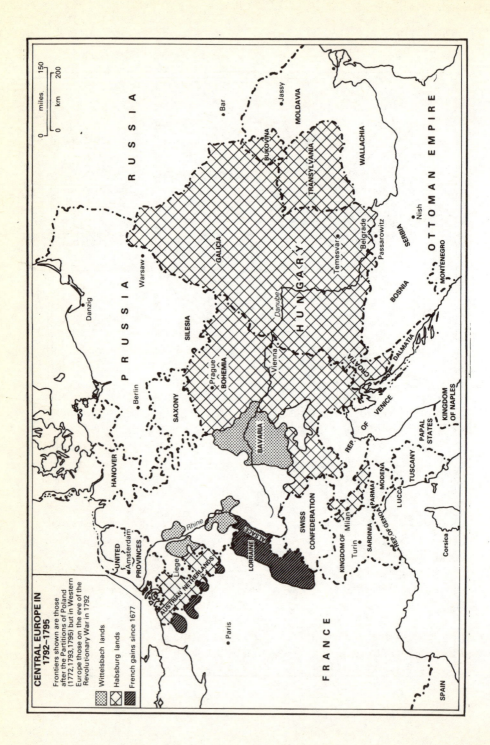

CENTRAL EUROPE IN 1792–1795

Frontiers shown are those
after the Partitions of Poland
(1772, 1793, 1795) but in Western
Europe those on the eve of the
Revolutionary War in 1792

Wittelsbach lands

Habsburg lands

French gains since 1677

miles 150
km 200
0

RUSSIA

PRUSSIA

Danzig

Berlin

Warsaw

Bar

Jassy

MOLDAVIA

BUKOVINA

TRANSYLVANIA

WALLACHIA

GALICIA

SILESIA

HUNGARY

Danube

SAXONY

Prague

BOHEMIA

Vienna

Temesvar

Belgrade

Passarowitz

Nish

SERBIA

BOSNIA

MONTENEGRO

DALMATIA

CROATIA

OTTOMAN EMPIRE

HANOVER

BAVARIA

VENICE

REP. OF

KINGDOM
OF NAPLES

PAPAL
STATES

UNITED
PROVINCES

Amsterdam

Rhine

Liege

AUSTRIAN NETHERLANDS

LORRAINE

ALSACE

SWISS
CONFEDERATION

Milan

MODENA

PARMA

LUCCA

TUSCANY

REP. OF GENOA

KINGDOM OF
SARDINIA

Turin

Corsica

Paris

FRANCE

SPAIN

PREFACE

International relations were central to state activity in the seventeenth and eighteenth centuries. They were the fundamental concern of monarchs and ministers who anxiously considered the strength and intentions of other powers. International relations were also of concern to peasants and artisans. The desire and apparent need of rulers for large military forces in order to protect their territories, maintain their reputation and underline their diplomatic demands led to enlistment and the recruitment systems that affected most of the adult male population, while the financial burdens of supporting these forces were the principal cause of higher taxes, which pressed hard on an economy that had few surpluses and experienced only limited growth. In wartime all these problems were exacerbated, and the consequences were generally savage in terms collectively of social disruption, economic hardship and financial strain, and individually of loss, injury, misery and despair. The demographic results of war could be serious while the psychological implications of uncertainty, loss and militarism were considerable.

The nature of international relations was a constant that helped to set the tone of society and to affect the lives of the people of Europe. However, international relations were far from static and they led to considerable change. Chance factors of birth and death played a major role in creating and affecting a diplomatic agenda in which dynastic considerations were often paramount. The nature of monarchical authority and power ensured that the often-changing and always unpredictable personal views of rulers were extremely important. The unpredictability of developments could not and cannot be disguised by terms such as balance of power and natural interests which imply that a hypothetical international system operated according to some rules. These terms may have reassured some contemporaries, though Puysieulx, the French foreign minister, noted in 1749 that the judicious assessments made by Frederick II (the Great) of Prussia did not prevent him from rapidly passing between fear and calm, and in the crisis of 1756 Frederick, as much as anyone else, misjudged the situation by supposing that there was something permanent about the opposition between France and Austria. Aside from the logical problem of arguing from a general theory, such as the balance of power, to individual governmental policies, it is apparent that these policies arose from particular and, therefore, changeable views and interests.

Europe did change considerably in the period, not in technological, economic, social or governmental terms, but at least in territorial and political matters. In 1679 Britain was a weak power, that had failed recently to defeat the Dutch in the Second and Third Anglo-Dutch wars (1665–7, 1672–4) and had watched with concern the French advance under Louis XIV into the Spanish Netherlands (modern Belgium) in the Dutch war (1672–8). The country had recently experienced in the most serious instance of the supposedly widespread European mid-seventeenth-century crisis, the civil wars of 1639–51, the consequences of the problems of religious differences, governmental financial weakness, constitutional divisions and, most seriously, monarchical rule over markedly different kingdoms. By 1793 Britain was again concerned about a French advance into Belgium, but in the meantime she had become the leading maritime and a leading imperial power, albeit one that had lost America, while domestically she was more united and a stronger state. Other major changes can be discerned readily and are discussed in this book. Louis XIV placed a grandson, Philip V, on the throne of Spain and kept him there in the face of a coalition of powers in the War of the Spanish Succession (1701–14), founding a ruling line, the Spanish Bourbons, that was to outlast the senior French branch. Russia became arguably the greatest European power, gaining Baltic and Black Sea coastlines in the Great Northern War (1700–21) and the Russo-Turkish war (1768–74) respectively, savaging the Swedish empire, defeating the Turks and being instrumental in the destruction of Poland. Austria and Prussia became major powers and the Turks were driven from Hungary. Poland, a state that in 1679 stretched from Riga to the Dniester and included the western Ukraine and much else of modern western Russia, was destroyed as an independent political unit in the partitions of 1772, 1793 and 1795.

This study stresses the unpredictability of developments in this period, the volatility of international relations. It argues that monarchs, ministers, diplomats and generals faced a hazardous and difficult international and domestic prospect. Information was difficult to obtain and often unreliable. Rulers were short of money, generals of trained men. Activities, whether military operations or the journeys of couriers, were dependent on weather and climate, the condition of the roads, the crops and the countryside. The study of international relations has evolved from an essentially narrow nineteenth-century view that concentrated on diplomatic activity and diplomatic archives into the more complex subject it is today. There is greater interest now in the mental world within which international relations were considered and conducted and a stronger and more sophisticated concern with the domestic causes and consequences of foreign policy. The study of the copious diplomatic archives of the period has to be set in the context of an awareness both of the weaknesses of these sources and of the role of domestic changes and pressures. The archives must be approached with caution. They are the carefully preserved records of a quasi-professional insider group, concerned with the minutiae of their trade, and especially alert to the details of intelligence, marriage proposals and treaty clauses. The ambiguities of diplomatic language have to be appreciated as, more generally, does the extent to which both change and continuity can be discerned in diplomatic activity and in the nature of international relations.

Reflecting a new, wider appreciation of the subject and advancing a powerful critique of those who propose an international system operating in accordance with implicit and explicit rules, this book is divided into two sections. The narrative chapters offer a survey that draws on several diplomatic archives and devotes equal weight to both western and eastern Europe and includes topics that it is easy to overlook, such as the Baltic after the Great Northern War. The colonial situation is also considered. The remainder of the book is devoted to an examination of the principal factors that affected the conceptualization, formulation, execution and discussion of foreign policy, ranging from the role of trade to the nature of the diplomatic corps. The two sections can be read separately, though it would be more profitable to consider them together. They offer a new approach to the study of international relations in this period, one that should also be of interest to those considering the subject across a wider timespan.

I am very grateful to David Aldridge, Leopold Auer, Marsha Frey, John Stoye and Philip Woodfine for commenting on earlier drafts of this book, and Janet and Gitte for word-processing them. As ever, Philip has offered very valuable intellectual and stylistic advice. I would like to thank the British Academy, the Wolfson Foundation and the Staff Travel and Research Fund for support in archival research.

This book was begun on one of those wonderful clear mornings that winter brings to Newcastle. It was finished at what must be one of the most beautiful spots on earth where jewels of sunlight speckled the deep lake and snow-crested peaks echoed the light, offering an infinity of peace and beauty. I have written several books but none has been so happy for me.

Jeremy Black
April 1989, Lake Como

ABBREVIATIONS

AE. CP.	Paris, Archives du Ministère des Affaires Etrangères
Ang.	Angleterre
AST. LM. Ing.	Turin, Archivio di Stato, Lettere Ministri, Inghilterra
BL. Add.	London, British Library, Additional Manuscripts
Bayr. Ges.	Bayr. Gesandtschaft
Bodl.	Oxford, Bodleian Library
CRO	County Record Office
HHStA	Vienna, Haus-, Hof-, und Staatsarchiv
KB	Kasten Blau
KS	Kasten Schwarz
MD	Mémoires et Documents
Munich	Munich, Hauptstaatsarchiv
n.a.f.	nouvelles acquisitions françaises
Politische Correspondenz	*Politische Correspondenz Friedrichs des Grossen* (46 vols., Berlin, 1879–1939).
PRO. SP.	London, Public Record Office, State Papers
SRO	Edinburgh, Scottish Record Office

Very deep reaches of policy exist in the page of history, much oftener than in real life: nations, like the individuals of which they are composed, act generally either from passion, or from contingent circumstances; seldom from long foresight and prescribed system.

Four letters to the Earl of Carlisle, From William Eden (1779)

INTRODUCTION: EUROPE IN 1679

The first requirement in considering Europe in the seventeenth century is the consultation of an historical atlas for though most of the states of the period can be given names that are the same as modern states their territorial extent was very different. As far as European possessions were concerned Portugal has essentially remained unchanged, but there were considerable differences in such cases as France, the United Provinces and Britain, while Poland, Russia, Spain, Denmark and Sweden were fundamentally different. The King of Denmark ruled Norway, his Swedish rival ruled Ingria, Estonia and Livonia (the Baltic provinces) and Finland, making a sizeable block of territory along the eastern Baltic, reaching down as far as Riga, with territories in northern Germany. Poland was a large state that included much that is modern Russia, including the western Ukraine, much of White Russia, Lithuania and Courland. Russia lacked not only a Baltic frontier but also one on the Black Sea though the Caspian had been reached. The king of Spain ruled half of Italy, the Spanish Netherlands (essentially modern Belgium and Luxemburg) and the largest overseas empire, including most of central America, all of South America, bar Portuguese-owned Brazil, and the Philippines. Geographically Germany, Italy and south-eastern Europe were most different. The Balkans were ruled by the Turkish or Ottoman empire, an Islamic monarchy based at Constantinople, that also ruled Egypt, the Near East and the northern shores of the Black Sea, including the Crimea. This empire had two principal rivals, the Islamic Persian empire with which it competed from the Caucasus to the Persian Gulf, and the Christian powers of eastern Europe, Russia, Poland and, especially, the Austrian Habsburgs. This dynasty, closely related to the Spanish Habsburgs, ruled a collection of territories that are collectively, though somewhat inaccurately, referred to as Austria. They included most of modern Austria, Silesia in modern south-west Poland, Bohemia and Moravia in modern Czechoslovakia and what they had been able to preserve of the kingdom of Hungary (modern Hungary, northern Yugoslavia and Slovakia) from the Turks.

For over 200 years the Austrian Habsburg ruler had also been elected Holy Roman Emperor, which provided him with a measure of authority, though less power, in Germany and northern Italy. In these areas sovereignty was divided and a large number of territorial princes, mostly lay but some ecclesiastical, and imperial free cities exercised effective power, within the loose bounds of an Imperial constitution.

Most of Europe was ruled by hereditary monarchs. The most important dynasty was the Habsburgs, who had interrelated Austrian and Spanish branches. Emperor Leopold I (1658–1705) was a brother-in-law of Charles II of Spain (1665–1700). Another brother-in-law of Charles was Louis XIV of France (1643–1715), the head of the Bourbon dynasty. The Stuarts ruled England, Ireland and Scotland in the person of Charles II (1660–85), the Vasa Sweden under Charles XI (1660–97) and the Romanovs Russia under Alexis (1645–76). The United Provinces (modern Netherlands), Venice and Genoa were the leading republics, dominated in practice by groups of wealthy oligarchs, while the Papacy, Poland, then ruled by John Sobieski (1674–96), and the Empire were elective monarchies. The single most distinctive feature of Europe was that almost everywhere wealth and prestige were based on the ownership of land, most of which was owned by a hereditary nobility, whose most powerful members constituted an aristocracy. Armies and central and local government were dominated by aristocrats, who were also extremely influential in the churches. Government worked best where the social elite could be persuaded to govern in accordance with the views of the monarch, and the most politically effective states were those where a consensus based on shared interests and views had developed. This consensus characterized a state such as France which has been misleadingly described simply as an absolutism. Domestically monarchs were most concerned with preserving order and maintaining law and the faith. Externally they sought to defend their possessions, maintain their reputation, exalt their dynasty, realize its pretensions, especially in succession disputes and matters of prestige, and watch for opportunities in a Europe of shifting alliances and unpredictable developments. They fulfilled these goals through diplomacy and war, two related means to achieve the success that was such an essential lubricant of domestic prestige, obedience and therefore order.

I

1679–1714

THE 1680s: A DECADE OF CHANGE

Periodization always entails difficulties since historical change is fluid, and does not show abrupt breaks corresponding to succeeding generations. Historical figures do not simultaneously all die conveniently or all discern new problems and opportunities or respond to a new diplomatic context. The balance of change and continuity that all at the time were aware of is difficult to delimit from our later standpoint. The changes of the 1680s had certainly been prefigured. Austrian hopes of Balkan conquests had featured in the thirteen-year Austro-Turkish war of 1593–1606. The armies of the Austrian ruler, Emperor Leopold I (1657–1705), and of his Turkish counterpart, Sultan Mehmed IV (1649–87) had already fought a brief war in 1663–4 over their conflicting views concerning Hungary and Transylvania, the buffer region where each had clashing aspirations and an insecure hold over his own possessions. Similarly, the outbreak of war in 1689 between France and a European coalition including England, soon after the successful combination of a Dutch invasion and a domestic conspiracy had delivered England to William III of Orange in the 'Glorious Revolution', had been prefigured in 1678. The Danby ministry of Charles II had threatened to join William and the anti-French camp and to send troops to fight the French in the Spanish Netherlands, a threat which led Louis XIV, king of France (1643–1715) to intervene in English politics in order to secure Danby's fall. Other elements of the pattern of the 1680s can be traced to earlier years. William's position as ruler of England (1689–1702), which he was to occupy alone after Mary's death in 1694, derived from his marriage to her in 1677. Azov, the Turkish base on the Sea of Azov and a gateway to the Black Sea, had been offered to Tsar Michael in 1641 by Don Cossacks who had temporarily captured it.

The Peace of Westphalia of 1648 is more commonly held to mark a major divide in European history. It is often seen as bringing to an end the Thirty Years' War (1618–48), and as marking the failure of the Habsburgs, the rulers of Austria and Spain, to achieve a position of hegemony in western and central Europe, and specifically of the Austrian Habsburgs to use their elective position as Holy Roman Emperors to dominate the Empire, the region that roughly corresponds to modern Germany, with the addition of Belgium, Lorraine, Austria, Silesia, Bohemia and most of northern Italy. However, it is equally appropriate to suggest that in so far as a major division can be seen in seventeenth-century European political history it should be located in the 1680s; that the previous decades can be regarded as in many respects a different period, one that marked a continuation of the group of major conflicts that began in the late 1610s and continued in the Thirty Years' War. The German and Dutch aspects of this war were substantially ended in 1648, but the Franco-Spanish conflict which, thanks to the far-flung nature of the Spanish formal and informal empire, entailed hostilities in Italy and along all France's frontiers, did not end until the Peace of the Pyrenees in 1659. However, this did not mark the end of the group of conflicts. The war between Portugal and Spain that had begun with the successful Portuguese rebellion of 1640 continued until the mid-1660s and the last stage of the war was the most intense. Philip IV (1621–65) made a major attempt to reconquer Portugal in the early 1660s, an attempt that was defeated with help from Charles II of England (1660–85) and Louis XIV, despite the French promise in 1659 to desist from helping Portugal.

In Baltic and eastern Europe the end by 1661 of the War of the North, a confused combination of Danish-Swedish, Polish-Swedish, Prusso-Swedish and Swedish-Russian conflicts, simply permitted the Russo-Polish war to flare more fiercely, though it was finally ended by the Peace of Andrusovo of 1667. This succession of conflicts ended in the 1660s, a decade when the Stuarts were restored in England (in 1660), Louis XIV's personal rule began in 1661 and the succession of the sickly and infertile Charles II of Spain (1665–1700) suggested that the Spanish Succession would soon become open. It would, however, be wrong to assume that in the years immediately after the Peace of the Pyrenees there emerged a new diplomatic agenda that could be described with reference to Louis XIV. This might appear to be the case if attention is devoted to the wars begun by Louis, the War of Devolution (1667–8) and the Dutch War (1672–8), and to the growing literature arguing that Louis and France represented a threat to Europe, the last an entity variously described and defined. Yet it would be foolish to ignore elements of continuity in this period. Wars were not followed by reconciliation. Franco-Habsburg confrontation remained as apparent as that between Poland and Russia. To a certain extent the French attack on the Spanish Netherlands (essentially modern Belgium and Luxemburg with bordering areas of France) in 1667 was Louis's contribution to the Thirty Years' War. England, which had already fought one war with the Dutch in 1652–4, was to fight another in 1665–7 and a third in 1672–4. France continued to fear the Habsburgs, a view that should not be dismissed as propaganda, for the Peace of the Pyrenees was a compromise, not a dictated, peace.

If continuity can therefore be stressed for the 1660s, change can be discerned in the 1680s. Open frontiers to the south were created by both

Austria and Russia. The failure of the Turkish siege of Vienna and the defeat of the besieging army in 1683, was followed by a generally successful Austrian advance across the plains of Hungary and into the Balkans. This advance was not without its setbacks, and the notion of Turkey as a power in decline, though already present, did not do justice to Turkish vitality and resilience, both during the course of the 1682–99 Austro-Turkish conflict and during subsequent wars in the following century. However, the end of the Turkish threat and the conquest of Hungary were major features of the rise of Austria to great power status. Though not complete until the challenges of the Spanish Succession war (1702–14), another Turkish war (1716–18) and a Hungarian revolt (1703–11) had been overcome, this rise was arguably the most impressive development in seventeenth-century European international relations. The Austrian Habsburgs had come a long way since the first two decades of the century when their territories had been affected by civil war, family rifts and religious heterodoxy. France had made a comparable transition but the challenge was more severe for the Habsburgs, whose lands were by comparison disjointed, and their foreign conquests greater.

If Austria was politically the great success story of the seventeenth century, Russia was to emerge most clearly as a great power in the following century. There are signs of a new departure in Russian policy in the 1680s. In 1686 Russia joined the Holy League, the alliance of Austria, Poland and Venice that had been created under the sponsorship of Pope Innocent XI to fight the Turks. In 1687 and 1689 unsuccessful attacks on the Khanate of the Crimea, a Turkish client state, were launched by the Russian chief minister, Prince Vasily Golitsyn. Hitherto, Russian interest to the south of the centres of Muscovite power had been largely devoted to the Ukraine, and not further south to Pontic Europe, the borderlands of the Black Sea. The Ukraine was part of the Republic of Poland-Lithuania and to a considerable extent Russian policy towards it was a function of Russo-Polish relations. Polish weakness helped to make the Ukraine a political vacuum, to destroy its value as a buffer-zone between Russia and Turkey and to attract Russian interest towards the south. This was to become a major theme of the 'Eastern Question', the term eventually used in the nineteenth century to discuss the fate of the Turkish empire. Although this Russian interest was associated with and at times, as in the 1700s, early 1730s and 1750s, obscured by westward Russian activity, it was to be a major theme, eventually, though not initially, influencing other European powers as much as Russian schemes in the Baltic.

The third major change in the 1680s was the British 'Glorious Revolution' and the consequent outbreak of an Anglo-French conflict that was to last from 1689 until 1697. William III's determination to resist Louis XIV helped to ensure that the hostilities that the French had begun in the Rhineland in 1688 became the major war that Louis had sought to avoid. The Revolution Settlement, the constitutional, political and administrative changes that followed William's coup, not without considerable controversy and not always in accordance with his wishes, helped to create a political and financial system that facilitated England's rise to great power status. The Bank of England and the funded National Debt could not ensure victory but they helped to allow England and, as she became after the Union of the Crowns of 1707, Britain to provide the sinews of war and to combine the maintenance of her position in Europe with increased prominence across the oceans.

Other changes can be noted in the 1680s. In 1684, on the ending of his mother's regency, Victor Amadeus II of Savoy-Piedmont (1675–1730) assumed power. His reign was to witness a successful exploitation of great-power rivalries that helped to make Savoy-Piedmont both an important second-rank power on the European scale and clearly the leading independent Italian state. Alongside change, however, was the continuance of the factors that constituted the context of international relations: proprietary dynasticism, the absence of any effective adjudicating agency, a widespread political willingness to consider the option of war, technologically limited military forces and a weak economic system that produced small and precarious surpluses. These factors helped to encourage tension and fighting, while restricting the possibility of decisive victory.

EUROPE AND THE OUTER WORLD PRE-1700

In terms of the future development of the world the most significant aspect of Europe's international relations in the sixteenth and seventeenth centuries was the conquest and sometimes settlement of large tracts of territory outside Europe that were eventually to give power, first to European states and secondly to European peoples. Russia vastly increased its territory. Ivan IV (the Terrible) conquered the Khanates of Kazan and Astrakhan in the 1550s, gaining control of the Volga and the route to the southern Urals. Fur trapping and the prospect of Oriental trade led the Russians across the Urals, through Siberia and to the Pacific, reached in 1648. The native peoples were brought under control and forts and trading posts founded, marking Russian progress eastwards: Tobolsk (1587), Tomsk (1604), Yakutsk (1632), Okhotsk (1649). Russia expanded up to Chinese territory. In south and east Asia first Portugal and then the Dutch became major trading and colonial powers, though prior to 1700 the political impact of the Europeans on the major Asian territories was limited. By 1600 the Portuguese were established in Malacca, Macao, coastal parts of Indonesia, Ceylon and India and in the Persian Gulf at Bahrain, Hormuz and Muscat. Many of these bases were subsequently lost to non-European powers and to the Dutch, who by 1680 had seized Ceylon and coastal areas of Indonesia, while the Spaniards ruled the Philippines and part of the western Pacific, the Mariana islands being acquired in 1668 and the

Carolines in 1696, and the English were establishing bases in India. Bombay, and Tangier in Morocco, had been gained in 1661 as part of the dowry of Charles II's Portuguese wife and the East India Company, the mercantile body that directed English interests in India, was to found a base at Calcutta in 1698.

There was restricted knowledge of the interiors of 'new' continents compared with their coasts. The most arid northern and western parts of Australia had been discovered but not settled. In 1696–7 the last major expedition launched by the Dutch East India Company to explore Australia explored its western coast and confirmed the uselessness of the 'Southland' as far as the Company were concerned. European penetration of Africa was slight; though Portuguese coastal mapping was very exact, the continent was largely unexplored. The Portuguese ruled coastal areas in Angola and Mozambique, and on the route to India the French had settled the island of Réunion in 1642 and the Dutch Cape Town a decade later. The European presence in Africa was mostly restricted to coastal bases, from many of which slaves were exported to the New World. Ambitious Portuguese schemes for the area of modern Zimbabwe were unsuccessful. Central America and the Caribbean were mostly under Spanish rule though at Belize and on the Mosquito Coast (the Caribbean coast of modern Nicaragua) England had a mainland presence, and a number of islands belonged to other European powers including England (Barbados, Jamaica, Bahama), France (Guadeloupe, St Domingue, Martinique), the United Provinces and Denmark. Most of coastal South America belonged to Spain or to the Portuguese colony of Brazil, though Patagonia, southern Chile and most of modern Uruguay were unsettled, and the last was becoming an area of conflict between the two powers. After the Dutch had been driven out of Brazil in the 1650s, the English, Dutch and French presence in South America was restricted to the Guiana Coast. In North America most of the eastern seaboard was settled by the English, while Canada was occupied by the French and Florida by Spain. Quebec was founded in 1608, Boston in 1630. The Delaware valley colony of New Sweden had been acquired by the Dutch colony of New Netherland in 1655 and that in turn had been seized by the English, New Amsterdam becoming New York. Earlier French exploration in and territorial claims to the Mississippi valley were followed in 1699 by a major expedition to Louisiana. All these developments were of great importance for the future, but one must not exaggerate the role of trans-oceanic concerns in European diplomacy. Struggles between European powers were essentially neither wars of overseas expansion nor wars of trade, though clearly both elements were crucial in the conflicts between the United Provinces and both England and Portugal. Europe was insulated to a degree from the wider world, partly because several of the major European powers were not maritime states, but also because of the nature of policy in this period. Far from being controlled by 'middle class' groups concerned to maximize their profits by increasing national wealth, the countries of the period were overwhelmingly monarchical. Those states where trade played a greater role in policy, Genoa, Venice, the United Provinces and England under the Rump Parliament, were maritime republics, countries that were exceptions to the general rules of political organization. Though several monarchs sponsored colonial and trans-oceanic commercial activities, most of the impetus and finance for such activities came from mercantile sources. In the 1680s the merchants of St Malo developed an international trade that linked the Newfoundland fisheries to Mediterranean commerce. In the following decades they exploited the commercial possibilities of trade to Spanish America and the southern seas, only to find their interests abandoned by Louis XIV at Utrecht. However, aside from the clash between commercial and political interests, mercantile views did not always coincide. In the 1640s the Zeeland interests who had supported the conquest of Brazil received little support from the province of Holland, which preferred the profits of its peaceful trade with Portugal or from William II of Orange who did not wish to anger Portugal's French ally.

Towards the end of the seventeenth century the increased prominence of the Spanish succession in European diplomacy helped to direct political attention to the fate of the Spanish colonies. In the negotiations for the Partition treaties William III expressed interest in territorial gains, though Louis XIV argued in 1698 that Spain would be of little value without the Indies and that she could never be called the master of the Indies if she had to share her position with the Maritime Powers.[1] The latter wished to prevent France from gaining control of the trade of Spanish America and once the War of the Spanish Succession had begun the relationship between the commercial and the political challenges posed by Louis could be clearly stated. Queen Anne told Parliament in October 1705, 'Nothing can be more evident than if the French king continues master of the Spanish monarchy, the balance of power in Europe is utterly destroyed; and he will be able in a short time to engross the trade and wealth of the world'. The English navy was used to try to stop the flow of wealth from Spanish America to the Bourbons. Though the Spanish Succession helped to push colonial issues to the front of political attention, the colonies played little role in the war and were not the essential topic of the peace negotiations. In addition, colonial disputes could be settled, neglected or exacerbated in order to facilitate diplomacy centred on European issues. Such disputes could contradict or reflect European rivalries. Dutch troops aided Portugal in the war of independence against Spain in the 1640s at the same time as the two powers fought in Angola and Brazil. Conversely France and Portugal reached agreement in their 1697–1700 dispute over the area of Maranhao – Brazil north of the Amazon – only after the problem of the Spanish Succession came to the fore and it is possible that French territorial claims for an Amazon frontier for their colony at Cayenne were designed to make Portugal more pliable over the Spanish Succession.[2]

---

[1] AE. CP. Angleterre 174 f. 164.
[2] A. S. Szarka, *Portugal, France, and the coming of the War of the Spanish Succession* (Ohio State, Ph.D. 1975) p. 125.

However, if the Spanish Succession raised political interest in the New World, there was no continuous curve of rising interest culminating in the major trans-oceanic struggles of the Seven Years' War (1756–63) and the War of American Independence. Late-seventeenth-century interest was separated from these conflicts by the relatively quiescent period of 1713–37 when alliances or understandings between the major maritime powers, especially the Anglo-French alliance of 1716–31, helped to keep the peace or to reduce tension. Nevertheless, during that period interest in colonial trade and possessions was more widely disseminated, particularly in Britain, but not only there, and, as a result, the colonial and commercial disputes of the period from 1738 onwards took place in a more highly charged political atmosphere.

THE DEFEAT OF THE TURKS

Whilst the western European powers founded great trading and colonial empires in the early-modern period the states of central and eastern Europe were involved in a bitter fight for survival. The struggle between European society and the powers to their east has been a major theme in the history of the last millenium. The century between 1650 and 1750 was a crucial one in this struggle. It saw the definitive stemming of the Turkish tide and the establishment of Russian hegemony in eastern Europe. The Turkish empire was an aggressive Islamic state with its capital at Constantinople (Byzantium, Istanbul), the former capital of eastern (Orthodox) Christendom which had been captured in 1453. The fifteenth century had also brought the acquisition of the Crimea, Wallachia (southern Romania), Albania, the Morea (Peloponnese), Serbia, Bosnia and Herzegovina (southern Yugoslavia). At the battle of Mohacs in 1526 the Hungarians had been defeated and in 1529 Vienna had been besieged. The sixteenth century brought the Turks Syria, Egypt, Iraq, Yemen and much of Hungary with suzerainty over the rest of North Africa bar Morocco, Moldavia and Transylvania (Northern Romania). If the Turkish advance had essentially stopped in Europe in the mid-sixteenth century it had not been reversed and it was not surprising that Christian Europe was in awe of the Turks.

The idea that *ancien régime* warfare was essentially inconsequential is particularly inappropriate in eastern Europe. The Austro-Turkish war of 1682–99 was a major struggle and, though it left the Turks in control of the Balkans, it ended their threat to central Europe. The causes of the war were various but it is symptomatic of the threat that the Turks posed that the war began in a Turkish act of aggression despite Leopold I's wish to maintain the peace. Leopold was concerned above all by Louis XIV's *réunion* policy, his employment of dubious legal claims in order to seize territory on his German frontier. As a result, Leopold failed adequately to consider changes in Turkish policy and the state of his Hungarian frontier and he disregarded intelligence reports of an impending Turkish attack. Seeking to distract Leopold, Louis resumed his policy of sending aid to those in the section of Hungary ruled by Leopold as king of Hungary (essentially modern Slovakia and parts of western Hungary), who were opposed to his Catholicizing and Germanizing policies. Because of the undesirability of being seen to support rebels, this was a particularly sensitive example of a French ploy common in the seventeenth and early eighteenth centuries, namely the attempt to put pressure on Austria, or on the Empire in general, by enlisting the support of Baltic and eastern European powers. The campaigns of the Swedes in the Empire during the Thirty Years' War represented possibly the most successful example of this policy, though the Swedes proved, like most useful allies, to be difficult to influence. Louis XIV had less success. With the Peace of Westphalia France had lost the benefit of Dutch and Swedish support against Spain. Louis found the German princes unreliable allies who were most consistent in their demands for money. He was angry with Sweden's opposition to his territorial gains in the late 1660s, when she helped form the Triple Alliance (1668), while in the following decade she proved of little military value as an ally during the Dutch war. The Russo-Polish peace of 1667 led Louis to hope for assistance from these powers against Austria but they were necessarily more concerned about the Turks.

For Louis there was an advantage in having as allies the Hungarian malcontents and the prince of Transylvania (a Turkish client state in modern north-west Romania ruled by Protestant Hungarians): they could be relied upon to oppose the Habsburgs. In 1677 he signed an alliance with them, which led to French financial help and the assistance of a French-paid Polish force, and in December 1681 Louis promised a subsidy to the Hungarian leader, Imre Thököly, if in the spring he would resume the military operations he had begun that September. These developments helped to direct the attention of Mehmed IV (1649–87) and his grand vizier Kara Mustafa (1676–83) to Hungary, though weight must also be placed on the bellicose nature of the Turkish state, exacerbated by the reciprocal relationship between the new provincial ruling class and governmental military adventurism, and Mustafa's need for money and prestige in order to maintain his power.[3] In the first half of the century the Turks had been heavily engaged in conflict with Persia (modern Iran) but the end of this conflict enabled Mehmed IV, and the energetic grand viziers of the Köprülü family whom he appointed, to direct their attention to their Christian neighbours. The war with Venice, begun in 1646, was brought to a successful conclusion with the fall of Crete in 1669. Turkish authority in Transylvania was made more effective as a result of a war in 1658–61. Austrian intervention led to a

[3]T. M. Barker, 'New Perspectives on the Historical Significance of the "Year of the Turk"' *Austrian History Yearbook* 19–20 (1983–4) p. 4.

Turkish declaration of war on Leopold in 1663 and a brief war marked in 1664 by an important Austrian victory at St Gotthard and the Peace of Vasvar. This treaty reflected Leopold's lack of confidence about any forward policy in Hungary. The Austrian army was clearly capable of defensive operations but there was doubt about the ability of both Austria and its army to sustain a major war. The Turks were left in complete control of Transylvania and Leopold agreed to pay a tribute.

Further Turkish pressure on Leopold would have inhibited the latter's participation in the Dutch war (1672–8), but in 1671 the Turks attacked Poland. As a result Montecuccoli, the victorious general at St Gotthard, was able to devote his energies in 1673 to outmanoeuvring French forces in the Rhineland. Initially very successful, the Turks were hampered by stronger Polish resistance when John Sobieski was elected king (1674–96) but the peace of Žuravno (1676) still saw them emerge with the gain of Podolia, a large territory stretching from the Dniester to the Dnieper which increased their ability to intervene in Poland and the Ukraine. The disturbed state of the latter encouraged the Turks to attack Russia (1677–81), but the war brought them no gains.

Hungarian disaffection seemed to offer a better prospect and in 1682 the Turks decided to help Thököly and to make him king of Hungary under Turkish protection. Thököly agreed to be a vassal of the sultan. On 6 August 1682 the Turkish government decided to declare war on Leopold, to seize the fortresses of Raab (Györ) and Komarom and to assemble an army at Belgrade in May 1683. However, the following year, instead of besieging Raab, the key to the Austrian military frontier, Kara Mustafa, the commander of the Turkish force of over 100,000 decided, without the approval of the sultan, to attack Vienna. After a successful advance, the Turks reached Vienna on 14 July. The siege was closely followed throughout Christendom. In Barcelona, for example, many publications disseminated information on the progress of the war. It is unclear whether their siege would have been crowned with success, though its continuation so late into the campaign season as September was inauspicious, but on 12 September a relieving force defeated the Turks. This force was composed of Poles under Sobieski, Austrian forces under Duke Charles V of Lorraine and troops provided by a number of German rulers led by Max Emmanuel of Bavaria, John George of Saxony and the hereditary prince of Brunswick-Lüneburg, the future George I of Britain.

Despite differences between the allied leaders they were able before the end of the year to make significant gains in Hungary, while for Kara Mustafa the price of defeat was strangulation. These were the beginnings of a conquest that, while not continuous, was to ensure that the victory of 1683 was followed by major territorial changes, unlike the earlier triumph in 1664. Those who urged Leopold to concentrate on the challenge from Louis XIV were overruled. In March 1684 a Holy League of Leopold, Pope Innocent XI, Poland and Venice was created and in 1686 Russia joined the alliance. The creation of a major eastern and central European aggressive alliance was an important achievement which had eluded many earlier opponents of the Turks, such as Tsar Alexis in the 1670s, and further assistance was contributed by German rulers such as Max Emmanuel. The co-operation that had led to the relief of Vienna was sustained, while the Turkish war allowed Leopold to fortify the Habsburg role as the defender of Christendom and the Empire and increased Imperial loyalty in Germany. The conquest of Hungary is some-times presented as marking the creation of a Danubian monarchy and a Habsburg turning away from the Imperial role. In fact it represented and sustained traditional notions of Imperial action and it can be suggested that the general support the Habsburgs received in the Empire in 1685–1740, a marked contrast to the early seventeenth century, reflected not only the decline in religious rivalry and the opposition to Louis XIV, but also the bonding of emperor and empire in the Turkish wars.

The operations of the allied powers were poorly co-ordinated. Using mainly German troops Venice sought to revive her position in the eastern Mediter-ranean. The Morea (the Peloponnese) was captured, as was Athens and several islands in the Aegean. Sobieski invaded Moldavia (eastern Romania). In 1687 and 1689 Russian armies under Prince Golitsyn, the lover and chief minister of Alexis's daughter Sophia (regent 1682–9) invaded the Crimea. The failure of the campaigns helped to ensure the success of the challenge of Alexis's son by his second marriage, Peter (Peter I, 'the Great') to Sophia's authority in 1689. Peter besieged Azov in 1695. A lengthy siege failed, partly because of the ability of the Turks, a major naval power, to reinforce Azov by sea. Peter returned the following year and built a navy on the river Don with the help of which he was able to take Azov. He ordered the construction of a naval base at nearby Taganrog. Peter aimed to establish Russian power on the northern shores of the Black Sea. In 1695 the forts at the mouth of the Dnieper were captured. In 1697 Peter reached an agreement with Leopold and Venice by which they agreed to concert operations against the Turks over the next three years. Leopold and Venice agreed to continue the war until the Turks conceded to Russia the port of Kerch, which controls the passage between the Sea of Azov and the Black Sea. Austria and Russia co-operated in ensuring that the prince of Conti, the French candidate for the Polish throne vacated by the death of Sobieski in 1696, was beaten by Augustus II of Saxony. This prevented the breaching of the anti-Turkish alliance for a protégé of Louis XIV, since 1689 at war with Leopold, could be expected to support the Turks. The most substantial advances were made by Leopold's forces. In September 1686 Buda fell to the besieging forces of Charles of Lorraine and Max Emmanuel of Bavaria, the victory being marked by atrocities, and by *Te Deums* across Europe. 1687 brought a decisive victory at Berg Harsan (Nagyharsany), the deposition of the sultan, and a Hungarian Diet (Parliament) that agreed to make the throne hereditary in the male line of the Habsburg family. 1688 saw the fall of Belgrade.

The collapse of the Turkish position in the Balkans and an Austrian advance into the world of the Orthodox appeared imminent. The Austrians developed links with rebellious elements among the Bulgarians and the Serbs. Negotiations began with the prince of Wallachia, a Turkish client-ruler. The Turks began peace talks at Vienna but the Austrian demands for the complete surrender of Hungary and Transylvania and the dismantling of Ottoman fortresses in Wallachia were unacceptable. In 1689 the Austrians seized Nish and Skopje (in southern Yugoslavia), and that winter reached Bucharest. The Serbian patriarch of Pec was persuaded to take an oath of loyalty to Leopold, who on 6 April 1690 issued an appeal for the support of all Balkan peoples against the Turks and promised liberty under their lawful ruler, himself as king of Hungary.

It is difficult to know what would have happened had the Austrians not felt obliged to direct more attention to the war against Louis. This is not idle speculation as the prospect of a successful war with the Turks while at peace with the rest of Europe was one that was to attract many Austrian, and indeed Russian, leaders over the following century. The late 1680s may have represented the best opportunity for driving the Turks out of all or most of the Balkans until the nineteenth century. The Turkish empire and army were in disorder and faced by a powerful coalition. However, it is by no means clear that the advance of Austrian troops into southern Serbia and the Danubian principalities (Moldavia and Wallachia) indicated the imminent collapse of the Turks. The allied powers confronted formidable logistical problems and the maintenance of large forces south of the lower Danube would have exacerbated these. The resilience of the Turks was arguably even more important. The alacrity with which historians have used the concept of decline to categorize several states in this period, particularly Poland, Spain and the Turkish empire, is unhelpful. The Spanish empire was still the largest in the world in 1700, as in 1800. The Turkish empire took longer to disintegrate than the later western European-based trans-oceanic empires. The oscillating nature of Turkish fortunes at the end of the seventeenth century indicated the importance of the quality of leadership. The chaos that greeted Suleyman II (1687–91), including rebellious janissary troops in the capital and provincial disturbances, was quashed and a new grand vizier from the Köprülü family, Fazil Mustafa (1689–91), helped to restore order to the army and the central government. In 1690 he recaptured Nish and Belgrade and many of the Orthodox Serbs fled north. The following year Fazil and the Turkish hopes of recapturing Hungary were both killed at the major defeat at Zalánkemén, but Austrian chances in both Serbia and the principalities were over. Conflict over the next few years was indecisive and difficult, due to improved fortifications, the depletion of local sources of supply and the problems of fighting in undrained marshy lowlands.

Matters moved to a climax as the result of the accession of the energetic Mustafa II (1695–1703) and the end of the war in Italy in 1696 which enabled Leopold to transfer more troops and his rising general, Eugene of Savoy, to Hungary. At Zenta, in September 1697, the Turks under Mustafa were caught in the vulnerable position of crossing a river and routed with possibly 30,000 casualties. Though the victory was followed by a raid into Bosnia and the sacking of Sarajevo, the lateness of the campaigning season, combined with heavy rains, sickness and logistical problems ensured that there were not significant gains that year. In theory the end of the Nine Years' War with France should have released Austrian resources to resume the conquest of the Balkans, but victories won after several years campaigning were rarely as decisive in creating new opportunities as those, such as Vienna in 1683, gained near the beginning of a war. The retention of Hungary appeared a viable goal, but not the conquest of the Balkans. The shifts in European diplomacy that were likely to follow peace demanded Leopold's attention, especially as the disputed Spanish Succession appeared a more imminent prospect. Peace in western Europe made less effective the French pressure on the Turks to continue the war which, alongside unrealistic demands from both sides, had helped to thwart peace negotiations in 1688–9 and 1692–4. The French ambassador stated that France would resume fighting Austria when Charles II of Spain died but his inability to offer documentary proof of French promises led the Turks to ignore the French overture.

As the war of 1682–98 was the longest Balkan conflict during the period of this study it is instructive to consider the terms of the Treaty of Karlowitz (January 1699), the product of the negotiations of 1698–9 held under Anglo-Dutch mediation. The Turks sought to make peace on the basis of *uti possidetis* (current control) though they sought an Austrian evacuation of Transylvania and its reversion to its earlier autonomous status. The Austrian threat to resume hostilities led the Turks to yield over Transylvania, which went to Austria with all Hungary except the Banat of Temesvár (Timişoara). Poland returned its conquests in Moldavia in return for Kamenets-Podolsk, the capital of Podolia, and the whole of Podolia was ceded to her. Turkish threats to reopen hostilities, Austrian pressure and the fear of isolation led Venice to abandon her gains on the northern shore of the Gulf of Corinth (including Lepanto). The hope that the Morea, which was formally gained at Karlowitz, could serve as the basis of further acquisitions had proved abortive. The Aegean islands of Chios and Icaria captured in 1694 had had to be abandoned the following year in the face of a revival of Turkish naval strength. Peter I had been unwilling to negotiate at Karlowitz and his envoy, instructed to demand Kerch which the Turks would not yield, was obliged to accept a two-year truce rather than a peace settlement.

Karlowitz was a new departure for the Turks for it implied the substitution of political boundaries for open frontiers, and adherence to the concept of the inviolability of the territory of a sovereign state in place of the notion of continuous warfare with the infidel. In place of the usual truces, a peace treaty had been negotiated. Joint border commissions were created to demarcate the frontiers; 'the Ottoman State had along most of its frontier for the first time in its history defined linear boundaries which were differentiated by natural barriers where those existed, and by artificial but visible markers where none existed.'[4] Hungary had not been crucial to the Turkish economy, but its loss diminished Turkish prestige, and thus diplomatic credibility, while enhancing that of the Austrian Habsburgs. The new territories were devastated by war and their integration into the pluralistic structure of the Habsburg territories was to be delayed by rebellion. Nevertheless, the gain of Hungary was important not only because it provided security for the other territories and limited the feasibility of enlisting eastern European powers against the Habsburgs, but also because Hungary was eventually to become a source of wealth and manpower. In the short term it offered a prospect of further conquests. There was no reason to believe that future wars would not bring more gains. Whereas in western Europe the acquisitions of the Austrian Habsburgs were limited by dynastic circumstances, contested by the Bourbons and, to a considerable extent, dependent on the support of other rulers, in the Balkans the constraints were less. As yet Russia did not appear to pose a challenge to the Habsburg claim and hope to act as the liberator of the Balkans.

THE BALTIC, RUSSIA AND THE GREAT NORTHERN WAR

The Baltic in the Late Seventeenth Century

At the beginning of the seventeenth century the Baltic was dominated by three powers. The kings of Denmark also ruled Norway, while their Swedish rivals controlled Finland and Estonia. The most important power on the southern shore was Poland-Lithuania, which controlled Livonia and Courland and had suzerainty over Ducal Prussia (East Prussia). Russia did not have a Baltic coastline. The Baltic was the principal source of 'naval stores', flax, hemp, pitch, tar and timber, for western Europe and a major supplier of copper, grain and iron. Both Denmark and Sweden had intervened in the Thirty Years' War and Sweden was, with France, the guarantor of the Peace of Westphalia. These factors ensured that the western European powers were interested in and intervened in Baltic affairs. In 1679 the threat of French military action forced Frederick William of Brandenburg-Prussia, the Great Elector (1640–88), to hand back to Sweden most of the territory he had seized from her in the conflict that had begun in late 1674. The conflict was part of the larger Dutch War, for Sweden had attacked on the insistence of her paymaster Louis in order to divert German attention from the Rhineland. Like Louis's role in supporting Imre Thököly in 1681–2 and thus attracting Turkish attention to Hungary, this might suggest that central and eastern

---

[4] R. A. Abou-El-Haj, 'The Formal Closure of the Ottoman Frontier in Europe: 1699–1703' *Journal of the American Oriental Society* 89 (1969) p. 470.

European affairs were manipulated by the western European powers. Not only France could be seen as wielding influence. England and the Dutch had major commercial interests in the Baltic, and both powers generally sought to maintain the peace in the Baltic and to prevent either of the two regional maritime powers, Denmark and Sweden, from dominating the sea.

As a result of the 'Northern Hundred Years War', ended with a series of peace treaties in 1660–1, Denmark retained Norway but had to accept the loss to Sweden of the Baltic islands of Gotland and Osel, and of the provinces of Bohuslan, Halland, Blekinge and Skåne (Scania), and of Jamtland in what is now respectively southern and western Sweden. Estonia and Livonia, formerly possessions of the Order of Teutonic Knights, had been won by Sweden in the face of bitter Polish and Russian opposition. A Russo-Polish conflict had left Poland in control of Livonia by the peace of Yam Zapolski of 1582 but Sweden had captured it from her in the 1620s. In 1617 Russia had had to cede the province of Ingria, at the head of the Gulf of Finland, to her. As a result of the Peace of Westphalia, Sweden had emerged from the Thirty Years' War with a number of strategically important gains in the Empire including the former prince-bishoprics of Bremen and Verden, which gave control over the mouths of the Elbe and Weser, the port of Wismar, and western Pomerania, including the port of Stettin.

These treaties reflected a substantial rise in Swedish power and the failure of its competitors in a series of hard-fought wars. However, the Swedish position was a precarious one. Sweden was not the wealthiest or most populous of states and her gains attracted the ambitious attention of other powers. Poland sought Livonia, as did Russia. In 1656 Tsar Alexis had declared war on Sweden and besieged the great Livonian port of Riga, one of the major centres of Baltic trade, without success. Though obliged by the Peace of Kardis of 1661 to accept the Swedish position, Alexis had not abandoned the idea of obtaining a Baltic coastline. The Danes had not forgotten their losses, while the vulnerable Swedish possessions in northern Germany attracted the attention of German rulers, particularly Frederick William of Brandenburg-Prussia who felt that he had been cheated at Westphalia out of his rightful claim to the succession of the whole of Pomerania (where the last duke had died without sons in 1637), and had been forced to accept the poor eastern half of the Duchy.

The Northern War of 1655–60 had seen Sweden bogged down in Poland and confronted by all the other Baltic powers, but although this anticipated the situation during the Great Northern War of 1700–21, there were significant differences. The earlier conflict did not centre on war between Sweden and the other powers. Charles X of Sweden (1654–60) was the principal enemy of Frederick III of Denmark but Alexis was principally concerned with Poland and Frederick William had followed an opportunistic course in order to gain full sovereignty over the Duchy of Prussia instead of holding it as a fief of Poland. In addition, Charles chose to attack Poland in 1655, essentially to make gains, particularly on her Baltic coast, from a Poland that appeared to be collapsing before Alexis's advancing armies. In contrast, in 1700 Charles XII's attack was designed to pre-empt a hostile coalition.

Both the Regency Council that ruled during his early years and Charles XI (1660–97) himself after his majority, wished to preserve the Swedish heritage, rather than to gain new territories. As co-guarantor with France and a prime beneficiary of the Peace of Westphalia, Sweden had clearly an interest and a potential role in preserving the *status quo* but her task was hindered by the expansionist policies of Louis XIV and by her inability to afford large armies without the 'contributions', enforced exactions, that had facilitated her offensive wars earlier in the century. This shortage of funds led to a search for subsidies which compromised the attempt to pursue a policy of neutrality, balance and mediation. Pressure from her French paymaster led to the unsuccessful attack on Brandenburg in 1674.

A minor defeat at Fehrbellin in June 1675 suggested that the skills of Gustavus Adolphus and Charles X had been lost, and it encouraged the Dutch, the Danes and the Empire to declare war. Frederick III took advantage of the unpopularity of the Swedification policy in southern Sweden to try to regain the former Danish provinces. Pomerania was overrun by Brandenburg in 1677, and the Swedish fleet almost totally destroyed by the combined fleets of Denmark and the United Provinces. Fortunately for Charles XI, Poland and Russia were faced by resurgent Turkish power. After French intervention had brought a surprisingly favourable conclusion to the war in 1679, Charles concentrated on domestic changes, seeking to make subsidies unnecessary.

It would be mistaken to present Baltic affairs as simply dominated by the western European powers. Though their intervention could be extremely important as in 1679 or 1689, when Anglo-Dutch intervention forced Denmark to evacuate the territories of the duke of Holstein-Gottorp, a Swedish protégé, and thus ended the threat of a Danish-Swedish war, nevertheless it was not simply because of their role that peace was maintained in the Baltic in 1680–99 and the Swedish empire preserved. Leaving aside the important revival of Swedish strength after the war of 1674–9, it is also worth noting that Sweden's potential enemies had other interests or found it impossible to co-operate. Prusso-Polish relations were handicapped by Sobieski's aim of reclaiming sovereignty over Ducal Prussia, his principal aim before he was distracted by the new Turkish war. Frederick William feared that Charles XI and Sobieski would co-operate to take Ducal Prussia from him. Russo-Polish hostilities had limited the possibility of a powerful anti-Swedish coalition during the Northern War. The Truce of Andrusovo of 1667 opened the possibility of such an alignment, but the two powers were to be more concerned with the Turks. In 1663 Alexis's adviser Afanasy Ordyn-Nashchokin proposed a union with the Poles and a war against the Turks. He suggested that the Poles could serve as a link with the Danubian principalities which could be persuaded to rise against the Turks. Russian attention was directed southwards. In 1673 Alexis pressed for free trading rights at the Swedish Baltic ports of Riga and Reval, but he was not interested in war and in

1677 rejected Danish pressure to attack Sweden and gain a Baltic foothold. Similar advances were rejected in 1682–4 and in 1683 the Russo-Swedish treaties of peace and friendship were confirmed. Far from there being any inevitable drive on the Baltic, Russian relations with Sweden were good throughout the 1680s.

The absence of Russian and Polish support ensured that any plan for concerted action against Sweden would depend on western European support. This was made more likely by the deterioration of relations between Charles XI and Louis XIV from 1679 as Swedish weakness and Charles's determination to uphold the settlements of Westphalia and Nijmegen angered Louis while the expansion of France worried Charles, especially when the German principality of Zweibrücken, to which Charles had the right of succession, was seized by Louis in 1680 as part of the *réunions*. The volatility of European diplomacy was amply illustrated when Sweden, recently France's ally, signed defensive treaties with the Dutch (1681) and Leopold I (1682). In 1683 Frederick William of Brandenburg-Prussia and Christian V of Denmark relied on French assistance when they planned war with Sweden, the partition of her German possessions and a possible reconquest of Skåne. However, Louis, though paymaster of both rulers through subsidy treaties, was unwilling to risk war for the benefit of others. Christian therefore turned his attention to the Danish quarrel with the neighbouring duke of Holstein-Gottorp, declaring his enfeoffed lands in Schleswig forfeit in 1684, and attacked the Imperial Free City of Hamburg in 1686, policies that were opposed by nearby German rulers, especially Brandenburg-Prussia and Brunswick-Lüneburg, and which suggest that Louis XIV was far from uniquely aggressive.

Brandenburg, Danish and, to a limited extent, Swedish troops served against France in the Nine Years' War. The conflict between the western European powers did not spread to the Baltic because no ruler there supported France and Louis's attempt to have a protégé elected king of Poland was unsuccessful. When in 1697 Sweden acted as mediator for the Congress of Ryswick, the settlement of the Nine Years' War, it was an empty honour, but there was little reason to believe that Charles XII (1697–1718), who came to the throne that year, would soon have to fight a major war for the preservation of the Swedish empire. However, it was significant that the Swedish Council decided, without much consultation of the young king, that he should wield the same absolutist powers as his father.

Russia in the Late Seventeenth Century

Russia was far from being an insignificant feature in the European international system prior to the accession of Peter I. Remote and barbarian as it might have appeared from such capitals as Paris and Madrid, Russian strength and intentions had been a matter of considerable concern for the powers of Baltic, central and eastern Europe for over a century. The conquest of the principality of Novgorod between 1465 and 1488 and of Pskov in 1510 had brought Russia to the borders of the Baltic states. In the same period the lands to the east of Poland-Lithuania had been acquired. Poland and Lithuania, united by an Act of Union in 1569, blocked the attempt of Tsar Ivan IV (1533–84, the Terrible) to gain a Baltic coastline. Ivan also claimed that his state, as the 'Third Rome', was the only orthodox state after the fall of Constantinople; as the successor to Russian rulers of the past, he himself was entitled to gather in all the 'Russian lands'. He demanded the return of Kiev, Volhynia and Podolia, 'the patrimony of his forbear St Vladimir' from Catholic Poland. Ivan's defeat at the hands of the Poles was followed by Polish intervention in Russian affairs during the Time of Troubles, the period of protracted disorder and contested rulership that had followed the death of Ivan. Polish and Swedish-backed pretenders in league with Russian aristocrats claimed the throne and one such was crowned in Moscow in 1605. After his death, Sigismund III of Poland (1587–1632) sent an army into Russia which defeated the Russians and occupied Moscow in 1610. The Polish garrison was forced to capitulate in 1612 but the Truce of Dyvilino (1619) left Poland with the powerful fortress of Smolensk, while Sigismund's son, the future Vladislav IV (1632–48), retained his claim to the Russian throne. By the Peace of Stolbovo (1617), Gustavus Adolphus of Sweden returned Novgorod which he had seized during the Time of Troubles and lifted the siege of Pskov, but he retained Karelia and Ivan IV's acquisition of Ingria.

The Swedish challenge had been more marginal than that from Poland and it is not surprising that Poland was the central problem for the first two Tsars of the new Romanov dynasty, Michael (1613–45) and Alexis (1645–76). Having concerted plans with Gustavus Adolphus, Michael declared war in 1632 and besieged Smolensk, but the failure of the siege led to the Eternal Treaty of Polianovka (1634) which left the Poles in possession of the gains made during the Time of Troubles, though Vladislav renounced his claim to the throne. Alexis has never received the attention lavished on his son Peter I, but he prepared the way for many of the domestic reforms of the latter and anticipated his vigorous foreign policy. His attack on Poland in 1654 was ambitious in its scope. His forces captured most of Lithuania in 1655 and in 1656 he persuaded the Poles to agree that he would become their next king. Alexis's success owed something to his reorganization of the Russian army but it also reflected the range of Poland's enemies, which included Sweden and George Rakoczi of Transylvania. The Russian victory in Lithuania was helped by the support received from many Lithuanian magnates opposed to royal authority. In 1654 at Perejaslaw the Cossacks under Bogdan Chmielnicki, who had rebelled against Poland in the winter of 1647–8, brought the Ukraine into Russia's sphere of influence. However, the Polish-Swedish Peace of Oliva (1660) enabled the Poles to concentrate against Russia and their achievements suggest that it is wrong to write off Poland as predestined for defeat by its aristocratic and quasi-federalist political structure. In 1659–61 the Russians suffered serious setbacks in the Ukraine and in January 1664

John Casimir of Poland (1648–68) invaded the eastern Ukraine in alliance with the Crimean Tatars. He was turned back, not by Alexis, but by a rising of Polish nobles under Jerzy Lubomirski, who feared the growth of royal power. As a result the Thirteen Years' War ended in 1667 with the Truce of Andrusovo, which awarded Smolensk to Russia and partitioned the Ukraine, Alexis gaining Kiev and the left bank of the Dnieper. This was a considerable achievement, but in no way the peace hoped for in 1654–6.

The Polish desire to recapture these territories helped to sustain tension and one possible solution, the election of the tsar to the Polish throne, pursued by Alexis again in 1673, failed. The Treaty of Eternal Peace of 1686, by which the terms of Andrusovo were made permanent, was therefore valuable for Russia. The Polish envoy was subsequently accused of having exceeded his instructions, but the Poles, who needed the promised Russian attack on the Tatars, were not in a position to challenge the treaty.

The early years of Russia's new conflict scarcely suggested that she was soon to dominate eastern Europe. Golitsyn's second failure against the Crimea in 1689 was followed by several years of relative inactivity with the consequent danger that Russia would be ignored in the peace negotiations and possibly subsequently exposed to Turkish attack. By 1695, the year of Peter I's first attack on Azov, the port at the mouth of the Don, the war in the Balkans had lasted as long as any previous Balkan conflict that century and Leopold I was clearly in control of Hungary. Peter was indeed to be abandoned by his allies at Karlowitz but his demand of Kerch was unrealistic in light of the widespread use of the principle of *uti possidetis* in the treaty and the limited need of Russian co-operation for Leopold once the Turkish war had ended. Russia accepted a two-year truce but she failed to better her position and in July 1700 a peace was concluded under which she gained Azov, but not Kerch, and had to evacuate her newly erected fortresses on the lower Dnieper.

It is difficult to predict the results of a continuation of the Russo-Turkish war. Peter's epic struggle with Charles XII had tended to divert attention from his great interest in his southern frontier, an interest that was to lead him to invade Moldavia in person in 1711 and to campaign in Transcaucasia and northern Persia in the last years of his reign. The lure of Constantinople (Istanbul) was to be a major theme in eighteenth-century Russian foreign policy, one that owed much to a semi-mystical vision of Russia's role that drew both on the theme of the Third Rome and on the idea of Russia as a Christian crusading power that would free its Orthodox brethren in the Balkans. In the treaty of 1686 the Russians had stipulated freedom of worship for Orthodox Poles.

The end of the Balkan war influenced Peter's diplomatic position. The conflict had determined his relations with other rulers. When in 1697 on his 'Great Embassy' Peter met William III at Utrecht the two monarchs were drawn together for diplomatic reasons. Peter was suspicious of Franco-Turkish links and determined to employ force to block the candidature of a French prince, Conti, for the throne of Poland. This shared interest served as the basis for good relations and led in the summer of 1697 to simultaneous military moves designed to thwart Conti. An Anglo-Dutch squadron prevented the dispatch of a fleet for the Baltic from Dunkirk, while Russian troops moved towards the Polish frontier. This entente ended in 1698 as a result of William's role in facilitating Austro-Turkish negotiations in order to free Austria to confront France in the event of a war over the Spanish Succession. A disenchanted Peter, his crusading mood ended, was forced to adopt new policies. In place of the alliance against Turkey, Peter became a member of an anti-Swedish league, and during the next decade relations with England and Austria became cool, while Franco-Russian contacts became more significant. Both powers found it useful in the mid-1700s to support the Hungarian rebels against Austria. Through his alliance of 1707 with the Hungarian leader Rakoczi, Peter came very close to transforming the two separate European conflicts, the Great Northern War and the Spanish Succession War, into one conflict. Within a decade of Karlowitz Peter was to be seen as an increasingly important and unpredictable figure on the European stage, while the great Northern War became a major struggle that influenced the fate of all the eastern European powers, providing evidence to explode the misguided notion that eighteenth-century conflicts were inconsequential.

The Great Northern War, 1700–21

The major conflict that was eventually to deprive Sweden of most of her overseas empire began with a secret plan intended to achieve just that end. However, the three originators of the plan, Peter I, Augustus II of Saxony-Poland and Frederick IV of Denmark (1699–1730) were not all to be beneficiaries of the war; nor had they envisaged a conflict that would last for over two decades. The scheme for a joint attack on Sweden was not new, but a number of developments at the end of the 1690s appeared to suggest that it might prove successful. The accession of the young Charles XII in 1697 encouraged hopes of Swedish weakness, which were further sustained by over-optimistic reports of discontent among the Livonian nobility arising from Charles XI's policy of resuming crown lands. The end of the Turkish war released Russian forces, while the recent accession of Augustus Elector of Saxony as king of Poland entailed the arrival of a new ambitious element in Baltic diplomacy. Although Russia was ultimately to be the greatest beneficiary of the war, the most active role in negotiating the alliance was taken by Denmark. Danish attempts over the previous quarter-century to reconquer Skåne and to dominate Holstein-Gottorp had suffered from the absence of any power to divert Swedish strength in the eastern Baltic. Danish approaches received a negative response in Moscow in 1697, as Peter was preoccupied with the possibilities arising out of the Turkish war, but Augustus was more receptive. He was essentially uncertain what he would be able to make of Poland, a state where royal authority and power was heavily circumscribed, but his ideas included the growth of Saxon-Polish naval power and trade, both of which would challenge Sweden's dominant commercial position in the eastern Baltic, the source of most of Europe's naval stores. Furthermore, he hoped to gain Livonia and to use it as the basis for establishing a hereditary Saxon dynasty in Poland, rather as John Sobieski had earlier hoped to profit if he could gain Prussia or Moldavia. Augustus reached an agreement with some of the Livonian nobles who promised to raise an army and to accept his overlordship in return for a guarantee of Livonian autonomy and laws. Between March 1698 and January 1700 a number of agreements were reached creating the anti-Swedish coalition. It was agreed that in 1700 Peter, his Turkish war over, would invade Ingria, Augustus Livonia and Frederick first Holstein and then southern Sweden.

The wide-ranging plan was based on the assumption that co-ordinated attacks would divide the Swedish forces and thus ensure a speedy success. It was, however, dependent on the vagaries of military fortune and on the durability of the alliance. Both were swiftly to be proved limited. In early 1700 Augustus invaded Livonia and Frederick IV Holstein-Gottorp, both monarchs accompanying their armies and neither declaring war. The Swedish response was rapid, and critically encouraged by the Treaty of The Hague of 23 January 1700, whereby the Maritime Powers (England and the United Provinces), in return for Swedish guarantees of the Protestant Succession and those features of Ryswick which mattered most to them, promised to intervene against Denmark if she attacked Holstein-Gottorp again. A landing on Zealand threatened Copenhagen and Frederick IV abandoned the war, restoring the duke of Holstein-Gottorp, by the Treaty of Travendal of August. The guarantee of the treaty by English, Dutch and Lüneburg mediators protected Charles's back while he pursued his quarrel with Augustus and Peter beyond the frontiers of the Holy Roman Empire. Swedish forces were then concentrated in the eastern Baltic where the quiescence of most of the Livonian nobility and the strength of Riga's defences had ended the Saxon invasion. Charles XII was therefore able to concentrate on the Russian army under Peter besieging Narva. In November 1700 this force was defeated by a smaller Swedish army that benefited from its greater professionalism and from the favourable direction of a snowstorm.

By the end of 1700 the coalition had therefore failed. Frederick had left the war and Augustus had appealed for the mediation of Louis XIV. Charles did not, however, trust an undefeated Augustus, and his appreciation of the danger that the Saxon-Polish union posed to Sweden led him to devise a plan to replace Augustus by a more pliable ruler. This led to Charles's embroilment for a number of years in the unsteady complexities of Polish politics, and thus to a delay in concentrating his military attention against Peter. This allowed Peter to raise the size and improve the fighting capacity of his army and in 1703 to score successes against the Swedes in the Baltic provinces and found St Petersburg on the Neva estuary. In the same year he signed a new treaty with Augustus by which Peter promised subsidies for the Saxon army in Poland. While Charles was kept busy in Poland, whither Peter sent troops to

Augustus's assistance, the Russians successfully besieged Narva and Dorpat in 1704. Charles used his control of much of Poland to have Augustus dethroned in 1704, and his own protégé Stanislaus Leszczynski crowned king the following year. By 1705 Peter was seeking the mediation of France and the Maritime Powers. However, the war had led to an expansion of goals. By a treaty of November 1705 between Sweden and Poland Charles guaranteed its territorial integrity and promised to help conquer the lands ceded to Russia in 1667 in return for compensation, possibly Courland, thus increasing Swedish control of the eastern Baltic. The treaty also specified measures to increase Swedish control over Poland's Baltic trade. The following year Charles's invasion of Saxony led Augustus to recognize Stanislaus by the Treaty of Altranstadt. However, Peter had made it clear that he was unwilling to give up Ingria and his 'window on the west'. Charles may have been foolish to hope for a military solution against Peter, but a disadvantageous peace with Russia would possibly have encouraged Augustus and Frederick to plot anew, while leaving part of Charles's inheritance in foreign hands and his other eastern Baltic provinces vulnerable. In addition, Peter, facing Cossack risings and growing opposition in the Ukraine, did not appear to be in the strongest position.

The Swedish presence in Saxony over the winter of 1706–7 led Austria and the Maritime Powers to fear that Charles would throw his weight behind France in the War of the Spanish Succession. However, he was more concerned about Peter and in 1708 invaded Russia. Supply problems, the severity of the winter of 1708–9 and the hope that Mazepa, the hetman of the Ukraine, would raise it against Peter led Charles to turn south into the Ukraine. This lent military backing to the dipomatic threat, contained in the Swedo-Polish treaty of 1705, to undo the territorial stability of Russia's western and southern border. The possibility of developing Charles's alliance system to encompass the Crimean Tatars and the Turks was entertained. However, Mazepa's lack of preparation combined with the swiftness and brutality of Peter's military response in the Ukraine and the savageness of the winter of 1708–9 undermined the value of Charles's move south. In early 1709 he won the support of the Zaporozhian Cossacks, but the Don Cossacks, the Tatars and the Turks refused to provide support. The diplomatic and military situation was far from good when on 8 July Charles, hopeful that he would regain the initiative by a major victory, attacked the entrenched Russian army at Poltava. This was not, however, to be a second Narva. The superior Russian force repelled the attack, Charles losing about 10,000 men. The defeat was turned into disaster when most of the withdrawing army surrendered to their Russian pursuers three days later.

Charles succeeded in fleeing to Turkey where he was to stay until 1714. In the meantime the Swedish position around the eastern Baltic collapsed. Augustus, newly allied to Peter, remounted the Polish throne, while another new ally Frederick of Denmark invaded Sweden in November 1709. The loyalty of Skåne and a decisive Swedish victory at Hälsingborg in February

1710 forced Frederick to withdraw his troops. Peter had more success, occupying Courland in late 1709 and successfully besieging Viborg and Riga the following year. In 1711 Russian, Saxon and Danish troops attacked Swedish Pomerania. Charles's only hope appeared to be the Turks who were opposed to the Russian dominance of Poland which appeared to be an obvious consequence of Augustus's reinstatement as a result of Poltava. Thanks in part to the influence of the khan of the Tatars, Turkey declared war in November 1710 and was at war from then until the Peace of the Pruth of July 1711 and then again, as a consequence of Peter's failure to fulfil its terms, for most of the period between December 1711 and June 1713. Peter had sought to avoid war, Turkish neutrality being as important for him in the Great Northern War as it was for the Habsburgs in the War of the Spanish Succession, but he eventually responded by reviving his hopes of the late 1690s. In March 1711 Peter issued appeals for assistance in proclamations to 'the Christian People under Turkish Rule' and to 'the Montenegrin People'. The following month a treaty was signed with Demetrius Cantemir, hospodar of Moldavia, providing for Russian sovereignty over Moldavia, the preservation of Moldavian autonomy, Moldavian assistance against the Turks and the granting of the status of hospadar as a hereditary right to Cantemir's family. As with Augustus in Poland, the desire to make a post hereditary played a major role in international relations.

Peter's planned invasion of the Balkans was, however, to prove a humiliating failure. Though he received Moldavian support, the speedy advance of a large Turkish army dissuaded the hospodar of Wallachia from sending promised support to Peter and he blocked the march of Serbian reinforcements. Outnumbered, short of supplies and surrounded at the river Pruth, Peter was forced in July 1711 to negotiate in a very disadvantageous position. He had expected to have to abandon Livonia and to recognize Leszczynski as king of Poland, but the grand vezier, Baltaji Mehmed, for reasons that are unclear, granted far less stringent terms. Azov was returned to Turkey and Peter promised to interfere no longer in Polish affairs. Though the war had proved a major disappointment for Peter, the peace was equally so for Charles and indeed Baltaji Mehemed's distrust of him and his supporters may well have played a role in his readiness to negotiate. Peter temporarily withdrew most of his forces from Poland but the Swedes were in no position to exploit this. Peter's supporters in the Balkans were abandoned. The Montenegrins held out until 1714, while Cantemir and several thousand Moldavians followed Peter back into Russia. The Turks consolidated their position in the Danubian Principalities and the rule on their behalf of the Phanariots, reasonably reliable Greeks rather than local aristocrats, began in Moldavia in 1711 and Wallachia in 1716.

The restoration of stability to his southern frontier allowed Peter to return his attention to Sweden while leaving Charles in his Turkish exile. With Sweden's eastern Baltic territories securely in Russia's grip, Finland being conquered in 1713–14, attention now turned to her German possessions.

Peter's overwhelming military superiority had ensured that there was no longer any doubt that Russia and not Poland would gain Livonia, but the situation in northern Germany was more complex. The Danes had traditionally sought to expand into the region and they seized the Duchy of Bremen in 1712 and all of Holstein in 1713. The creation of a power vacuum with the collapse of Swedish power encouraged other rulers, hitherto neutral in the war, to intervene, a process facilitated by the end of the Spanish Succession war and the consequent freeing of the forces engaged in that struggle. To pre-empt a Danish invasion George Elector of Hanover occupied Verden in 1712 in collusion with the Swedes. The following year the new king of Prussia, Frederick William I (1713–40) seized Stettin with Russian assistance. In 1715 both rulers declared war on Sweden. George's Electoral declaration of war (there was no declaration as king of Britain) was forced on him by Denmark and Prussia, as only thus would the former vacate Bremen for his forces, and the latter suspend boundary disputes.

However, alongside the broadening of the anti-Swedish coalition, there were already signs of a new configuration in Baltic relations. The precarious and reactive nature of alliance diplomacy was to be demonstrated by the slow disintegration of the coalition and its replacement by an even more precarious one directed this time against Russia. The Swedes had sought to split their rivals suggesting in 1712 a triple alliance with Augustus and Prussia. However, Charles's approaches were hindered by his unwillingness to agree to territorial losses in return for alliances of diplomatic support. Instead he insisted on military support that might help him gain equivalents, comparable territorial acquisitions. The Emperor, Charles VI, had tried to settle the war by means of a congress at Brunswick but Charles XII had refused to co-operate in 1712. Charles's return from Turkey to the Pomeranian fortress of Stralsund in November 1714 was followed by reforms in the Swedish administration but not by military success. Stralsund fell in November 1715, Wismar the following April. However, tension within the alliance was increasing and there was particularly opposition to the growth of Russian power in northern Germany. The collusive surrender of Wismar to the Danes and Hanoverians was effected in order to keep the Russians out. The marriage that spring of Charles-Leopold, duke of Mecklenburg-Schwerin, to Peter's niece Catherine increased concern in neighbouring Hanover and in Denmark. Peter's postponement, possibly in response to Swedish peace-feelers but more likely for military reasons, of a planned invasion of Skåne left a large Russian army in Denmark in late 1716. Rumours flourished about the 'wild undertakings'[5] to which Peter might resort. The Danes opposed the wintering of the Russian army in Denmark, and George of Hanover, since August 1714 George I of Britain, sought Prussian co-operation, without success, to block their wintering in Mecklenburg, while Hamburg feared attack. The Russians wintered in Mecklenburg, the British envoy in Copenhagen writing in December 1716,

[5] BL. Add. 37363 f. 95.

'The Czar makes a very formidable figure in these parts. He has above 35,000 men in Mecklenburg, 30,000 in Poland who are demanding winter quarters in Polish Prussia, a fleet of above twenty ships of the line, and galleys in which he can transport above 50,000 men, and with all, one of the best ports in the Baltic, as he has made it, at Reval. It were to be wished that a peace in these parts might give his Majesty leisure to turn so considerable a force towards his frontiers on the other side, as he so earnestly wishes.'[6]

The divisions in the coalition provided opportunities for Charles, who began separate secret negotiations with George and Peter. However, both rulers wanted recognition of most of their acquisitions and Charles was unwilling to accept such terms while he was preparing a large new army. George I was certainly worried about the possibility of a Russo-Swedish alliance directed against him and he feared that it might lend support to his other opponents, the Jacobites and Philip V of Spain. The British fleet, sent to the Baltic to protect trade against Swedish privateers, was ordered in August 1718 to prevent any joint naval action by Russia and Sweden. Aware of the extent to which policy could alter with a new ruler, Charles's minister Görtz also negotiated with the Jacobites, the supporters of the Stuart family. These negotiations in turn influenced and were influenced by the increasing rift within the anti-Swedish coalition and by the attempts of Peter and George to gain French and Austrian support. 1717–19 witnessed a diplomatic defeat for Peter. George beat him to the alliance of France and in January 1719 Hanover, Charles VI and, as a result of Austrian pressure, Augustus II, signed a Treaty of Vienna aimed against Prussia and Russia. Peter, who in the summer of 1717 had felt obliged to withdraw most of his troops from Mecklenburg and had been persuaded to do so by the French regent Orléans, who had been influenced by his ally George I, now responded by withdrawing from Poland. Carrying out an Imperial legal decree Hanoverian troops expelled the duke from Mecklenburg while Prussia abandoned Peter.

These developments reflected Peter's diplomatic weakness in the face of the hostility aroused by his success, and the difference between the precarious grasp provided by occupying the territories of allies and the firmer hold given by conquest. However, George's success led him to overestimate the extent to which Peter could be persuaded to yield his conquests from Sweden. This was to become serious during the developments that followed the death of Charles XII at the end of 1718. Charles was shot while besieging a Norwegian fortress shortly after he had begun an offensive that was designed to lead to an invasion of Denmark and northern Germany, and to strengthen his hand when negotiating a settlement with Russia. It is unclear what this would have led to in military and diplomatic terms, but the accession first of Charles's younger sister Ulrika Eleonora and then of her husband Frederick I of Hesse-Cassel (1720–51) led to an attempt to regain some of Sweden's losses by diplomacy. With French support George I negotiated treaties in 1719–20 by which Sweden ceded Bremen and Verden to Hanover, Stettin and Pomer-

[6] PRO. SP. 75/36 f. 233.

ania south of the Peene river line to Prussia and her exemption from the Sound dues at the entrance to the Baltic to Denmark which also regained the duke of Holstein-Gottorp's lands in Schleswig, under an Anglo-French guarantee. In return Sweden obtained peace and a guarded promise of British support against Russia. George I sought to create an alliance of Sweden's other former enemies plus France, Austria and Britain in order to impose a Russo-Swedish peace that would return most of Peter's conquests and alleviate northern European fears about Russian power. However, as so often, diplomatic fertility proved unrealistic. Charles VI and Frederick William I proved unwilling to attack Peter, while the financial crises that affected Britain and France, the South Sea Bubble and its Mississippi equivalent, sapped the determination of both powers. Peter refused to be intimidated, while his galleys maintained pressure on the Swedes by raiding their coast. As a result Sweden signed a peace with Russia at Nystad in 1721. Peter kept the bulk of his conquests, Livonia, Estonia and Ingria and, although he returned Finland, he retained the strategic regions of Kexholm and part of Karelia. He promised to respect existing privileges in his acquisitions, and not to intervene in domestic struggles over the Swedish constitution or in the Swedish succession. The first promise was reasonably well observed by Peter and his successors but the other was not. Indeed, the Swedish constitution, which in the so-called Age of Liberty of 1719–72 considerably weakened royal power, a process that was helped by the absence for much of the period of a clear succession, helped to provide Russia, and other powers, with the means to influence Swedish conduct. The Diet and the embryonic political parties could be influenced. The existence of a rival claimant to the throne, Charles Frederick of Holstein-Gottorp, son of Charles XII's eldest sister, who took refuge in Russia after Ulrika Eleonora's victory over him in the succession struggle and was in 1724 betrothed and in 1725 married to Peter's daughter Anna, further increased the possibilities of Russian intervention.

Sweden had not lost all her gains from her age of greatness. Though Wismar and the small remaining section of Pomerania were of limited consequence, she had retained her Danish conquests. Furthermore, the possibility of regaining some of her losses to Russia, either through conquest or by means of a Holstein-Gottorp succession, continued to be entertained. Nevertheless, whatever the future might bring, the situation when Peter died in 1725 was clear. Sweden had been unable to resist Russia and the prospect of collective action had failed to intimidate Peter. In 1720 there was more substance in Frederick William's fears that if he took action Prussia would be attacked than in Polish hopes of obtaining Kiev and Smolensk. Peter was able to cement the new Baltic order by an alliance with Sweden in 1724 aimed against Denmark.

If Sweden was weakened in the international sphere by her constitution and the absence of a clear succession, the same was also true of Poland. Though plans for a partition in the 1720s proved abortive and the territorial integrity of the country was preserved for many years, it was less able to take effective diplomatic and military initiatives. It did not matter that Sweden and

Poland made no peace until 1731 because neither was in a position to fight each other or had anything important to fight about: Livonia was clearly in Russian hands. Though plans for a reordering of eastern Europe in order to reduce Russian power were to play some role in European diplomacy in the period 1725–43, they were recognizably less plausible than in the previous quarter-century. Of the three powers that had competed with Russia for mastery in eastern Europe only Turkey remained strong and had succeeded in outmanoeuvring Peter. It was significant that powers further west, Britain, France and Austria, had had to play a major role in limiting Peter's advance. The weakness of Sweden and Poland was to help to bring Russia and these powers into closer contact.

LOUIS XIV AND HIS RIVALS

Introduction

Recent work has indicated the extent to which Louis XIV's foreign policy neither conformed to any master plan nor consistently centred on one issue. Rather the picture that emerges is a fragmented one. This empirical work is underlined by two conceptual points. First, it is increasingly clear that the reification of early-modern European foreign policy has not been without unfortunate consequences, not least in providing an analytical imperative for historians to clothe events with signs of coherence and consistency. Secondly, the consideration of how decisions were taken calls into question any presentation of a defined policy springing from bureaucratic agencies. The unpredictability of royal methods was combined with a significant inchoate element in the process by which advice was given. It is open to question how far the formal mechanisms for the conduct of diplomacy can be referred to as mature in a bureaucratic institutional sense. The patron/client relationship which flourished among the officials in the foreign office was also found in the diplomatic service, if that is not a misleading term for what was simply another way to serve the king.

Any attempt to fit the analysis of French policy throughout what was an unusually long reign, the longest in French history, onto a procrustean bed thus appears inappropriate. Nevertheless, several themes emerge. It is increasingly realized that Louis's domestic power rested on uncertain foundations, that 'absolutism' required, was indeed the product of, consent and that success was a vital lubricant of obedience. This directs attention to the political benefits gained through the expression and enhancement of monarchical *gloire* by means of a successful foreign policy. Given the habitual tendency to present Louis's policy in an aggressive light, justifiably so in the cases of the Devolution, Dutch and Nine Years' wars, it is worth noting that concern for France's strategic position was a persistent theme. Spain was still a major power and thus the death of Philip IV in 1665 provided Louis with an opportunity to act. Had Philip's successor, Charles II, been a powerful individual, then French fears about Spain might well have been vindicated. Indeed it is interesting to speculate how far the succession of Charles and Louis in each other's countries would have led to dramatically different developments. However, the four-year-old Charles II was mentally and physically weak, his demise anticipated so confidently that Louis and Leopold were to reach a secret partition agreement in 1668 for the partition of the Spanish lands. Charles's accession threw open the question of the Spanish succession, which respresented both an opportunity and a danger for Louis. The former has generally been stressed, naturally in light of Louis's exploit-ation of his position as Philip IV's son-in-law to seize part of the Spanish Netherlands in the War of Devolution (1667–8). The danger was obvious. The very opulence of the Spanish dominions as a field for expansion underlined the danger of their acquisition by another, particularly Philip's other son-in-law, Leopold. It was not necessary to go back to the reign of Charles V, when the Austrian and Spanish Habsburg dominions had been united (1519–56), to appreciate the danger to France of a dynastic union. In the Thirty Years' War Austro-Spanish co-operation, celebrated in Rubens's painting of their joint victory over the Swedes at Nordlingen in 1634, had posed major problems for France, limiting her influence in the Empire and threatening her from the east. Though the French struggle with the Habsburgs is most often presented as a Franco-Spanish duel there was an important Austrian dimen-sion to it, not least in terms of the French sponsorship of Maximilian of Bavaria and of the Swedes. If the Austrian theme receded after 1648 it was still present in Mazarin's successful arrangement in 1658 of a French-sponsored league of German allies, the League of the Rhine.

Thus the Spanish succession focused a long-standing French problem, that of Austro-Spanish co-operation. Indeed the challenge was one obvious continuation between two periods of French foreign policy that are often treated as different, that of Richelieu and Mazarin, and that of Louis's majority, especially from the later 1660s. In one sense the challenge was diminished by the weakness of Spanish leadership and the lack of strong determined action between 1665 and 1717, when Spain, under Louis's grandson Philip V, began again to pose a major problem. This weakness represented a most significant diminution of Habsburg strength and was arguably more helpful to Louis than the diversion of Austrian resources against the Turks. Louis was thus pre-sented with an important window of opportunity, one created by the relative weakness of the Habsburgs. However, the prospect that the situation would be transformed by an Austro-Spanish dynastic union was threatening. The seriousness of it cannot be grasped unless the situation when Spain and Austria were both powerful and active is appreciated. This had occurred in the early 1630s, helping to precipitate full French entry into the Thirty Years' War, and was to be repeated in 1725 in the Austro-Spanish alliance negoti-ated in the First Treaty of Vienna, and in 1731–3 when Britain, Austria and

Spain were united after the Second Treaty. The difficulties that France encountered in those years more than vindicated Louis XIV's concern over the Spanish succession and it is appropriate that many of the diplomats and generals who confronted this challenge in the 1720s and 1730s, such as Cambis, Fénelon and Villars, had been trained under Louis.

If the Spanish succession presented a major challenge, there was no single way in which it could be approached. Nor would it be necessarily appropriate to present it as the sole problem and opportunity confronting Louis. For much of the 1680s the issue was at the front neither of European diplomacy nor of Louis's thoughts. However, if the succession is seen as but one facet of the Habsburg challenge, then a case can be made for regarding that as a central theme of Louis's policy. Western-European diplomacy in the first half of the century has been explained in terms of the struggle between Bourbons and Habsburgs, and there is much to be said for adopting a similar perspective for the period down to 1756, though two major qualifications are that rivalry was not incompatible with periods of co-operation, and that not all powers fitted into the model of a system dominated by this struggle or, if they did, they did so in response to their own interests and without surrendering their capacity for independent action.

Bourbon–Habsburg hostility did not preclude attempts to co-operate, most crucially in discussions about the eventual fate of the Spanish possessions. The failure of schemes to settle the succession without war, was, however, but the most significant instance of the inability to settle disputes without conflict, an inability that was a characteristic feature of Louis's foreign policy. This has traditionally been blamed on Louis. Hostile contemporaries attributed it to his nefarious intentions and his desire for war, and argued that he sought peace only in order to divide his rivals. An unsympathetic English pamphlet of 1689 announced 'to glut his ambition, all times are seasonable and proper; times of peace, of war and truce.'[7] Similar claims were voiced in the United Provinces and the Empire; Louis's steps, such as the *Réunions* and the destruction of the privileges of French Protestants by the Revocation of the Edict of Nantes (1685), serving to develop the themes of Louis as a monarch of machiavellian intentions and a man willing to break agreements with violence. In scholarly circles such arguments have been considered inappropriate for a long time, and in their place has come a more secular interpretation of Louis's shortcomings and his personal responsibility not only for international tension, but also for French failure. This interpretation is compounded of his insensitivity, obsession with *gloire* and failure to comprehend the views of other powers. In place of a machiavellian schemer after universal monarchy has come a ruler who served himself, France and Europe ill by his failings and consequent failures.

This interpretation allows historians to provide a central theme for Louis's policy and yet also offers a focus for detailed studies of particular aspects of

[7] Anon., *The Spirit of France, and the Politick Maxims of Louis XIV* (London, 1689) p. 5.

this policy. These studies can serve to reveal a failure of royal perception and execution, and this failure becomes an apparent key to understanding Louis's policy. The problem with this interpretation is that it is not free from the concept of blame and the difficulties that entails in the context of seventeenth-century international relations. By assuming a perfect model of these relations and an obvious course of action for French policy the theory thus defines a standard of judgement and one by which divergence becomes deviance, the product of failure caused by royal wilfulness or ignorance. Carl Ekberg criticized Louis for having 'difficulty conceptualizing a policy of state interest as a framework for his own actions' and lacking 'a broader policy, rooted in state interest',[8] without probing the difficulties of conceiving and following successfully such a policy. Interpretations that assume an obvious course of action fly in the face of the international situation of the age and the problems and opportunities confronting Louis. Rather than assuming a perfect model of states with well-developed bureaucracies seeking to fulfil obvious and agreed national interests in the context of a 'system' whose workings were understood and where the interests and views of other powers were apparent, it is necessary to question each of these premises. International relations were kaleidoscopic, a natural consequence of the fluidity of politics in the context of competing views on national interests and the interests of other powers and of changing domestic pressures. The whole 'system', if that is not too grand and misleading a term, was shot through with the consequences of dynasticism and factionalism. The imperatives of dynastic aggrandizement and prestige and the vagaries of dynastic chance – births, ailments and death – compromise any attempt to present the international relations of the period in terms of distinct and defined national interests. In this light it is more convincing to portray relations in terms of the overlapping struggle between on the one hand Bourbon and Habsburg, and on the other Louis opposed to Leopold and William of Orange.

Factionalism within government is also crucial in helping to understand the advice that monarchs received. The nature of bureaucratic arrangements exacerbated the consequences of ministerial jockeying for position in the context of a political society and culture, the court, where personal favour and connections were paramount, rivalry endemic, collective responsibility negligible, and the mode of ambition was the humbling of rivals. The extent to which different ministers and factions were associated with particular policies has been long understood and has been refined in detailed studies, most recently those by Paul Sonnino on the origins of the Dutch war. What possibly requires more stressing is the extent to which this advocacy took place within a general vacuum, in that there were no agreed means by which the generally accepted principles of dynastic and national interest (insofar as the two can be distinguished), namely aggrandizement, prestige and security, could be maintained.

[8] C. J. Ekberg, *The Failure of Louis XIV's Dutch War* (Chapel Hill, North Carolina, 1979) p. 182.

French policy was in no way unique in this situation. The same was true of Austria, England, Prussia and most other powers, though there were several, such as Russia under Peter I and Savoy-Piedmont under Victor Amadeus II, where the ministerial debate over policy was effectively stilled by royal decisiveness. The consequences of international volatility were to make it impossible to determine on a fixed policy which would be the best for often imprecise and debated national interests, and modern historical attempts both to do so and to judge Louis by the conclusions are unhelpful. Though the polemic of international debate might be relatively constant policies altered rapidly, and, in such a situation, a grasp of opportunity and a response of opportunism were valuable. Bereft of ideological bonds, most alliances were temporary expedients, reflecting personal assessments of advantage and threat by rulers confronted by a rapidly altering international situation. Major powers might seek to create alliance systems, but they found it difficult to sustain them. As a result it could be profitable to act decisively. Most rulers followed policies of brinkmanship, attempts to obtain benefits or avoid defeats by diplomatic aggression, military preparations and the threat or use of force. Once moves were made it was difficult to retract them, lest that was interpreted, domestically or internationally, as a sign of weakness or failure, and difficult to control their consequences. Equally the pressure for action made it hard to avoid moves that would serve to provoke others or vindicate claims about the malevolence of a state's intentions.

In the light of these considerations it is possible to adopt a less critical attitude to Louis's policies than that which is common. When the charge of insensitivity or even self-deception[9] is made, it is reasonable to point to the perils of hindsight. Louis may have underrated Austrian strength and success in the mid-1680s, but nonetheless the Turkish empire did not collapse after the failure at Vienna, Austrian hopes of conquests in the Balkans proved misplaced and the struggle between the Austrians and Turks was not all one-sided. Indeed the resilience of the Turks after their failure at Vienna in 1683 forms an interesting parallel to that of the Spaniards after the French victory at Rocroi in 1643. In both cases the stress on the military indicator of decline is misplaced. Another failure commonly attributed to Louis is William of Orange's coup in England in 1688. What is not generally appreciated is that first the coup was a close-run thing militarily and secondly that its success embroiled William in a British civil war that was to absorb much of his strength for a number of years, against James II's supporters in Ireland until September 1691 and in Scotland, despite the Scottish parliament's acceptance of the dynastic change of 1689.

The case of Louis's German policy is a more complex one, not least because the large number of rulers and their varied rivalries made it difficult to create a coherent and consistent German policy. Louis has traditionally been accused of pushing his schemes for territorial expansion too hard. This analysis is open

---

[9] R. Place, 'The Self-Deception of the Strong: France on the Eve of the War of the League of Augsburg' *French Historical Studies* 6 (1970).

to a number of qualifications, not least that it is difficult to assess how much expansion is 'enough'. A scholar of Russian expansion a century later noted recently, '"When to stop" can be a very delicate judgement to make, for it implies a clear understanding of the country's goals, resources and structural strength. Few governing elites possess this amount of knowledge or insight'.[10] Leaving aside the problem already referred to, that there may be no obvious goals to understand clearly, this conclusion is a reasonable one when applied to Louis's German policy. It is unreasonable to suggest that up to such a date or such a frontier policy was justified and thereafter folly had been embraced, because there was no consensus over national goals that could or can permit such a judgement. To many Germans any French expansion from the position gained by the Treaty of Westphalia had to be stopped, and that position itself was not immutable, but rather the product of French strength that could be reversed.

Ultimately French hegemony over the lands between the Saône/Marne and Rhine depended on military strength, for the dukes of Lorraine were traditional Habsburg allies and the Empire keenly concerned to prevent the consolidation of the French position in Alsace. In 1688 the French envoy in Vienna reported an alleged plan for a peasant uprising in Franche Comté based on Austrian arms and supported by Austrian troops commanded by the duke of Lorraine. Repeatedly conflict revealed French concern over her eastern frontier, whether Louis's decision in 1673 to abandon his position in the United Provinces in order to guard the frontier or the Marquis de Chamlay's fear in 1689 that Charles V of Lorraine would invade lower Alsace.[11] In light of French successes these fears may appear misplaced, but it is important to realize both France's potential vulnerability and the nature of her enemy's plans. The military difficulties of France in the 1620s and 1630s had been acute and France's allies, Denmark, Sweden, the United Provinces and many of the German states, had let her down on a large number of occasions, refusing to subordinate their own goals to those of France and following what was from the French point of view an erratic or unhelpful military stance.

The argument that French policy under Louis XIV was flawed by a neglect of actual and potential allies is weakened by the French experience of alliances earlier in the century. Unable to rely on her allies, as Louis discovered in the case of Sweden and the United Provinces in 1648 and England in 1674, France was in a vulnerable position, provided that a large number of her enemies could unite. Such a union was difficult to achieve, and the experience of them during the reign revealed the difficulty both of maintaining alliances and of concerting strategy. However, these difficulties did not end the position of vulnerability as France's experience in the Dutch, Nine Years' and Spanish Succession wars made amply clear. The old debate over

[10] G. F. Jewsbury, *The Russian Annexation of Bessarabia: 1774–1828. A Study of Imperial Expansion* (Boulder, Colorado, 1976) p. 2.
[11] AE. CP. Autriche 63 f. 85–6; R. D. Martin, 'The Marquis de Chamlay' (Ph.D., Santa Barbara, 1972) p. 222.

whether Louis's policies were based on a desire for a natural frontier was resolved by Gaston Zeller in favour not of a natural frontier but rather of more variegated defence objectives including 'out-works' across the Rhine. By stressing French vulnerability one can more readily appreciate Zeller's work as well as understand the extent to which defensive considerations could become a source of policy as much as its adjunct. Many of the individually small territorial gains sought by France, particularly in the early 1680s, made sense in strategic terms; to a certain extent the *réunions* policy was the product of France's difficult defensive position during the Dutch war, a conflict that Louis began aggressively but that did not develop as he had wished.

This vulnerability was made more serious by the objectives of France's enemies. In an age when pretensions were retained, the treaties that enshrined French victories were not regarded as final settlements of disputes. The Austrian Habsburgs had reversed a series of earlier limitations through victories in the Thirty Years' War. The temptation to do the same against France was great. Devoid of any unity but their common sovereign, the Austrian lands had to be held together by success, though not necessarily by success through military expansion. Furthermore the major changes in aristocratic landownership in the 1620s, particularly in Bohemia, had created an aristocracy for whom military activities played a major role. At the level of the aristocracy, Austrian society was more militarized than that of France. The willingness to fight was linked with the reform of the Austrian army by Count Raimondo Montecuccoli, Commander in Chief and President of the War Council 1668–80, and the consequence was the difficult position France faced on her German frontier during the Dutch war, though it is worth stressing that Louis began the war and that Leopold was initially hesitant about intervening. It was not solely the Austrians who sought to reverse French gains. The dukes of Lorraine had a long list of demands and it was not surprising that on a number of occasions the duchy was occupied by France, a sure indicator of real or anticipated conflict. The treaties of Vic and Liverdun extorted from Charles IV in 1632 brought French occupation of part of the duchy, followed by the Treaty of Charmes the following year. By 1634 most of it had been occupied and it was to remain so during the war that began officially in 1635. Occupied in 1670–9, and during the Nine Years' and Spanish Succession wars, the duchy remained a problem, made more acute by the links between the dukes and the Austrian Habsburgs. This process, which was to culminate in the marriage in 1736 of the last duke of the family, Francis Stephen to Maria Theresa, led Leopold I's brother-in-law Charles V to become Austrian Commander-in-Chief. There was a series of issues that a powerful duke of Lorraine might press to the prejudice of France. Duke Leopold hoped for the aggrandizement of his states, argued that France's treatment of Lorraine was unjust, claimed that it was in the interest of other states to establish Lorraine as a barrier between France and the Empire and suggested that the duchy should gain the duchies of Charleville and Arches as an indemnity for his claims to the Italian duchy of Montferrat.[12] Louis had no intention of accepting expansion by Lorraine. In the *Mémoires* written by him for the instruction of the Dauphin, Lorraine was seen as a section of the historic patrimony of the French kingdom, which it was a royal duty to regain. In a similar fashion Christian V of Denmark sought to regain the Schleswig lands held in fee by the dukes of Holstein-Gottorp. Louis refused to allow either the discussion of the Lorraine question or the attendance of the representatives of Duke Charles IV at the international peace congress at Cologne in 1673. Leopold's project for creating a bishopric at St Dié that would make Lorraine independent of French episcopal authority was opposed.

On their own Lorraine's grievances were as inconsequential as those of Strasbourg, occupied by Louis in 1681. However, they posed the danger that they might be seized on by other powers as a pretext for action or that the web of dynastic links and imperial constitutional arrangements that bound the German states together might lead to unintended consequences for French actions. To that extent the *réunion* policy was dangerous. French moves on her frontier registered in Berlin, Stockholm, Vienna and Munich as much, if not more, because of specific links with those regions as because of anti-French propaganda. However, before this leads to criticism of Louis it is important to realize that such acts were not the prerogative of France alone. The manipulation of legal claims and judicial institutions and/or the use of force to seize disputed territory were both resorted to by a large number of powers and characterized the essential means by which some disputes, such as that over the Cleves-Jülich inheritance, were conducted. The Dutch proved singularly unwilling to withdraw their garrisons from a large number of nearby towns, including Wesel, occupied in the first half of the century. Their intervention in East Frisia was heavy-handed, while in the opening months of the Spanish Succession war they occupied a number of strategic points along the Ems, Moselle and Lower Rhine. Immediately after the death of William III in 1702, the Dutch seized the Orange counties of Moers and Lingen, in north-west Germany, ostensibly on behalf of a claimant, the prince of Nassau-Dietz, but in reality to prevent the claims of Frederick I of Prussia. Despite protests by Frederick and the Westphalian Circle and a judgement by the Imperial court, the Dutch refused to withdraw. The Prussians argued that the Austrian confiscation of the Silesian duchy of Jägerndorf from a branch of the Hohenzollern family in the 1620s was illegal. Danish conduct towards Holstein-Gottorp, Lübeck and Hamburg was characterized by violence and the threat of violence. William of Orange's English coup in 1688 was devoid of legality and the subsequent fate of the Irish Catholics was as scanty an advertisement for the moral superiority of Louis's opponents as that of the Hungarian Protestants. Rebenac, the French envoy in Madrid, stressed William's vast ambition in discussions with the Spanish government in 1688.[13]

[12] Nancy, Archives de Meurthe-et-Moselle, 3F 29 Nos. 74–9; 30 Nos. 22–4, 26; 32, Nos. 1–4, 12.
[13] AE. CP. Espagne 75 f. 93.

Louis's poor reputation owed something to his failure in the European public relations war that was such a sustained feature of the period. However, it is important not to exaggerate the extent to which European opinion turned against Louis. It was not only the victims of Louis's enemies, such as the Hungarians and Jacobites, who turned to him for help. Throughout the period, not least at the start of the War of the Spanish Succession there were a number of rulers willing to ally with Louis. The ambiguity of the Habsburg reputation helped him in both Italy and the Empire. The movement of Britain into the anti-French camp was the result of violence, the invasion of 1688. Thus the role of contingency emerges in the issue of Louis's reputation as it does in the success of his policies. This emphasizes the difficulty of judging Louis's foreign policy, but such a judgement was and is made inevitable by the strain that Louis's policy placed on France.

Territorially Louis was successful. The revival of Austrian strength which is such an obvious theme for the century from the 1620s did not lead to a reversal of France's gains on her crucial eastern frontier. Dynastically, the Bourbons gained the throne of Spain and were within thirty-five years of Louis's death to add independent principalities at Naples and Parma. Compared to the gains of Austria in Hungary or Russia in the eastern Baltic these advantages might appear minor, but Louis was not operating on Europe's open frontier or in relatively empty lands. The successes of the 1660s, 1672 and the early 1680s helped to re-establish the domestic and international prestige of the French dynasty and government after the difficulties of the previous decades. If this helped to earn a measure of international obloquy, it may also have played a role in explaining why there were no more Frondes.

From the Peace of Nijmegen to the Nine Years' War, 1678–88

The Dutch War (1672–8) was the first of Louis XIV's long conflicts. It changed European attitudes to him because, unlike the war of Devolution, nearly all the leading and second-rank powers of western, northern and central Europe were involved in the conflict. The volume of anti-French propaganda increased markedly, especially in the Empire where the distinction of French and German, rather than Catholic and Protestant was advanced increasingly. The coalition of powers that developed in opposition to France was more extensive than in France's earlier conflicts that century, and on a number of occasions the French were forced onto the defensive. The subsequent treaties of 1678–9, which are collectively known as the Peace of Nijmegen after the Dutch town where the negotiations took place, were a considerable triumph for Louis for two reasons. First they saw considerable territorial gains that enhanced the defensive nature of France's eastern frontier. Territorial exchanges with the Spanish Netherlands in Flanders gave France Condé, Bouchain, Valenciennes and a more defensible frontier. Another exchange brought Maubeuge and a stronger position on the Sambre, one of the possible invasion routes into France. Charlemont strengthened the French position on another route, the Meuse. Bouillon and Longwy fortified the French against the Duchy of Luxemburg, while the Spanish loss of the Franche-Comté improved French links with Alsace. The acquisition of Freiburg in the Black Forest enhanced the French position in the Upper Rhineland.

More significant, however, to France's advantage was the disintegration of the opposing coalition. Skilful French diplomacy and the exhaustion and differing interests of her opponents helped to ensure that there was no single treaty ending the war but a number of settlements, principally with the Dutch, the Spaniards and Leopold I in that order, by which the recalcitrant Emperor, who had hoped to reverse Louis's Westphalian gains in Alsace, was isolated. The collapse of the coalition and the failure to recreate an adequate one was crucial to Louis's success, in the immediate post-war years, in making territorial gains at the expense of most of his neighbours. The overwhelming characteristic of French policy in the post-war period was the use of force and intimidation. For example during the winter of 1678–9 French troops occupied much of the Spanish Netherlands as well as certain fortresses in the territories of Cologne, Liège, Cleves and Jülich in order to collect contributions demanded from Spain for the French army and to exert pressure on the German powers. French might was used to clarify the complex territorial and judicial system of feudal rights, overlordships and contentious sovereign powers that characterized the western portions of the Empire. The manipulation and often fanciful extension of claims to the dependencies of territories ceded to Louis since 1648 led to demands for much of the Spanish Netherlands and of the Empire west of the Rhine and south of the Moselle. Many of these territories were reunited by force in the early 1680s, a period that also saw the acquisition of intimidated Strasbourg in 1681 and the purchase of the major north-Italian fortress of Casale the same year. The weak reaction was orchestrated by William III of Orange, stadtholder (wielder of much executive authority) of the major Dutch provinces since 1672. He was convinced that Louis's power and policies represented a threat to what he discerned as a European system of essentially a territorial status quo guaranteeing the independent existence of the European powers. Between September 1681 and May 1682 William negotiated treaties with Sweden, the Emperor and Spain directed against Louis. The value of this diplomacy was limited by the unwillingness of the powers to fight France, particularly if they were not joined in a powerful coalition. In addition, skilful French diplomacy and intrigue, facilitated by the use of bribery, helped to weaken potential rivals, provoking the fall of the English Danby ministry and the dissolution of Parliament in early 1679. The subsequent Exclusion Crisis made England an unattractive ally, but Louis responded to Charles II's treaty with Spain in 1680 by signing a treaty with him in March 1681 under which Charles agreed not to call another Parliament in return for French subsidies. In the United Provinces there was hostility towards William among the anti-Orangist oligarchic Regent governments of the towns of the province of Holland, especially Amsterdam, which was exploited by the French envoy D'Avaux in order to

hinder William's schemes for assistance to the endangered Spanish Netherlands. France was the chief market for Dutch goods and the French manipulated their tariffs in order to influence Dutch opinion. Nevertheless, in 1682
the prospect of Dutch military attack led Louis to raise the siege of Luxemburg,
the major Spanish military base from which eastern France was threatened.

Success encouraged Louis to persevere with his territorial claims. In the
winter of 1682–3 he determined to stage a significant demonstration of
military might the following summer in order to intimidate the Spanish
Netherlands. In the autumn of 1683 French troops were sent into Spanish
Flanders, ordered to live off the land, and when the Spanish governor general,
the Marquis de Grana, forbade contributions to the French reprisals were
begun. In October 1683 Grana levied contributions on some French territory,
leading Louis to order the burning of fifty Spanish villages for every French
village devastated.[14] It is not surprising that Spain declared war on France on
1 December 1683 but, at this stage, French provocation was not enough to
have created an effective anti-French coalition. Leopold was committed to the
Turkish war, many of the German princes were similarly committed or in
receipt of French subsidies, while William's attempt to augment his army was
thwarted by French-supported pressure from Amsterdam.

The fall of Luxemburg led Spain to settle in 1684. However the new
diplomatic order represented by the Truce of Regensburg (Ratisbon) was in
some respects far less satisfactory than that of Nijmegen. The powers that
opposed French gains were yet again divided but Louis's success in negotiating with his rivals separately had brought him a twenty-year truce leaving
him in possession of Luxemburg, Strasbourg and his *réunion* gains but no
definitive peace ceding them to France. Though the opinion was expressed in
France that an opportunity to conquer the entire Spanish Netherlands had
been lost, Louis had to consider the danger of provoking Leopold to settle with
the Turks, as he had done in 1664, and the effects of his policies on the Spanish
government. Louis hoped to be able to turn the terms of the truce into a peace
but his position was placed under increasing strain during the next few years.
Moves against the French Protestants, the Huguenots, culminating in the
abrogation of what little remained of their privileges as originally conferred by
the Edict of Nantes (1598) by the Revocation of the edict in 1685, dissipated
support for France in Protestant Europe, especially the United Provinces and
the Empire, without producing commensurate gains in Catholic Europe,
where Leopold appeared a more convincing champion. The opposition of
much, though not all (Denmark being a conspicuous exception) of Protestant
Europe to Louis was to play a major role in the success of William of Orange's
invasion of England in 1688. The Catholic James II of England (1685–8) was
seen as a French protégé, although in fact he was determined to take an
independent line in international affairs. In 1688 the States General supported William's invasion, while the willingness of the new elector of

[14] R. D. Martin, *The Marquis de Chamlay* (PhD Santa Barbara, 1972) pp. 146–55.

Brandenburg, Frederick III (from 1701 King Frederick I of Prussia), and of the rulers of Hesse-Cassel, Brunswick-Celle, Brunswick-Wolfenbüttel, Saxony and Württemberg to provide troops helped to provide the Dutch with a measure of security against a French attack and to cover the Rhineland against an uncontested French invasion. The Glorious Revolution was, however, not to be the first move in a war of religion. Although in England William was to seek to present his cause as that of Protestantism, in Europe he sought to create an alliance of Catholic and Protestant powers opposed to Louis. Conversely James II was unwilling to associate himself too closely with Louis, for both domestic and international reasons, but sought to win the support of the Catholic powers, the Pope, Leopold and Spain. James was concerned to keep the peace in western Europe because he feared correctly that increased tension would drive these powers to ally with William and thus to connive at or sympathize with action he might take against England.

James's task was made more difficult by his not possessing any leverage over Louis and by continued concern over the views of France. In 1686 many of the princes of the Empire, including Leopold, created the League of Augsburg to which Spain and Sweden adhered, a union designed to guarantee the public security of the Empire and the agreements of Westphalia, Nijmegen and Regensburg. Military quotas were stipulated. Though in theory not aimed at any particular ruler there was no doubt that the purpose of the League was to prevent France from disturbing the war against the Turks. That the League was formed under Imperial sponsorship constituted an obvious contrast to Mazarin's sponsorship of the League of the Rhine less than thirty years earlier. The League of Augsburg complemented the anti-French defensive alliance signed by Leopold and Frederick William of Brandenburg in 1686, and was one of the important diplomatic rebuffs Louis suffered from 1685 onwards. In May 1685 Max Emmanuel of Bavaria married Leopold's daughter Maria Antonia, a real Habsburg success, and that September the birth of a second son to Leopold, the Archduke Charles, further strengthened the Emperor's position. Tension was increased by uncertainty as to Louis's intentions over two contentious issues. In 1685 the succession of a new ruler to the Electorate of the Palatinate in the Rhineland led Louis to advance claims on behalf of his Palatine sister-in-law. The apparently imminent death of another Rhenish elector, the archbishop of Cologne, led Louis to seek the succession of a sympathetic prelate. In addition, Louis appeared to be unwilling to respect the provisions of the Truce of Regensburg. His construction of new fortifications in the Empire at a number of strategic points, including Trarbach on the Moselle and Landau led to protests and a sense that Louis was unwilling to confine himself notwithstanding specific assurances.

The unwillingness of Innocent XI to support the French candidate for Cologne, William Egon von Fürstenberg, when the elector died in June 1688, led Louis, possibly affected by a failure of nerve, to decide that a demonstration of military power was required in order to underline his determination and strength and the vulnerability of the Rhineland. Innocent's stance was seen as the product of anti-French spite, because no other cause seemed plausible, and in order to punish this the papal enclave of Avignon in southern France was occupied. The principal French military effort was devoted to the Rhineland where a large army under the ostensible command of Louis's heir, the dauphin, besieged the fortress of Philippsburg on 27 September. Louis claimed that his moves were designed to settle all occasions of dispute and to establish the peace of the Empire but he also made it clear that he was determined not to abandon his protégé Fürstenberg. However, he was to be proved wrong in his expectation that the electors who understood their 'true interests' would not support Leopold[15] and in his expectation that his attack would lead to a short and successful conflict. However, arguably more serious in both the short and the long term were the consequences of 1688 in Britain.

The Nine Years' War, 1688–1697

France invaded the Empire in 1688 claiming that the League of Augsburg was an aggressive coalition aimed against her, and Louis gave an ultimatum of three months within which Leopold and the Empire were to convert the Truce of Regensburg into a treaty and to accept Fürstenberg in Cologne. In return, his manifesto offered the restitution of Freiburg and the abandonment of territorial claims to the Palatinate in exchange for a cash settlement to be reached by arbitration. Possibly this offer was no more feasible than the attempts made earlier that year to settle the Cologne dispute by negotiation or the hints dropped by the French envoy in London to his Austrian counterpart, once William of Orange had successfully invaded. The suggestion then was of a Catholic alliance of the Bourbons, the Habsburgs and the Stuarts, coupled with the return to the Empire of Freiburg and Strasbourg. However unsuccessful, these suggestions are worth noting because they demonstrate that to contemporaries the idea of a lengthy conflict between France and a coalition organized around an axis of Leopold and William was far from inevitable. Similar suggestions of a Catholic League were advanced by French envoys elsewhere and the Austrian envoy in London thought that they might be an opening to prevent a war that would otherwise stop the Austrian advance in the Balkans. In early 1689 Louis held out tempting offers to Leopold, including a hint that Lorraine would be returned to the duke if an alliance could be negotiated, and this at a time when the Turks had broken off peace negotiations by insisting on the return of Transylvania and a string of fortresses in Hungary.

War with Louis entailed for Leopold, therefore, a struggle on two fronts, as well as support for William's coup in England. Leopold had been profoundly unhappy about the invasion, concerned about the consequences for British Catholics and disinclined to support any dynastic revolution. He approved the invasion, but only as a means of bringing James to a sounder mind. Leopold

---

[15] AE. CP. Autriche 63 f. 216–17.

had no time for the claims that James's baby, the future James III, was an imposter introduced in a warming-pan and he did not approve of William's declaration questioning the birth. On 13 November 1688 the Austrian Council decided that no explicit consent or opposition to the invasion would be voiced and Leopold noted that it was important not to consent in case William sought to influence the British succession. When it became clear that William did intend to become king Leopold had a severe crisis of conscience, but he silenced his concern because of the need to confront France, whither James had fled, and because of his interest in the Spanish succession. In 1688 and again in the Grand Alliance of 1689 William promised to uphold Habsburg claims to the entire Spanish succession. It was possible that Charles II of Spain would die at any moment and indeed his wife died in 1689.

For Leopold, therefore, the fate of Britain was bound up in the wider Habsburg–Bourbon struggle. By supporting, however unwillingly, William's coup he won support for Habsburg claims while weakening France in the person of its ally James. In March 1689 French troops accompanied James when he landed in Ireland. In June 1690 the victory of the French fleet over the English and Dutch off Beachy Head gave France temporary command of the Channel. The French were unable to exploit this but the Anglo-Dutch victories at Barfleur-La Hogue in 1692, though they brought supremacy at sea, were similarly difficult to follow up. In England it was hoped that naval success would force Louis XIV to an acceptable peace settlement, or at least compensate for military reverses in the Spanish Netherlands but this was not to be. Attacks were planned on the French coast in 1693 and 1694 but in 1693 the troops did not disembark and in 1694 the landing near Brest was unsuccessful. Louis XIV was able to rely on his militia and concentrate his army on the conflict along his frontiers.

Initially French forces advanced into the Empire seizing Mannheim and Heidelberg and bullying the margrave of Baden-Durlach into accepting a French garrison in Pforzheim. However, William's success in inspiring German opposition to Louis bore fruit. On 15 October 1688 Ernest Augustus of Hanover, John George of Saxony, Frederick of Brandenburg and Charles of Hesse-Cassel concluded a treaty of alliance for the defence of the Middle Rhine. Their forces stiffened the Rhenish electors, whose weak defences had encouraged French action and intervention for several decades. Hessian troops in the elector of Trier's town of Coblenz kept the French out and on 14 November John George marched into Frankfurt. Partly in order to intimidate the German princes and partly to secure defensive positions the French devastated a large area of south-western Germany in 1689, destroying all fortified towns. In the Palatinate, which was seriously affected, the response was guerilla warfare, attacks on French communications and troops and a brutal struggle. The destruction helped to inflame German feelings and it did not prevent a deterioration in the French position, Mainz being lost in September 1689.

In the meantime the scope and purposes of the struggle had widened. In

November 1688 Louis declared war against the United Provinces. The following May William, as king of England, declared war on Louis, while in April Louis declared war on Spain, which had refused to promise to be neutral. On 12 May 1689 Leopold and the Dutch made an alliance with the declared aims of returning France to the frontiers stipulated by the treaties of Westphalia and the Pyrenees and of returning Charles of Lorraine to his duchy. As king of England, William acceded to this Grand Alliance later in the year. Aside from the promise over the Spanish succession, the treaty provided for joint peace negotiations and the continuation of the alliance after the war. In May 1689 an Austro-Bavarian treaty brought Bavaria into the war. Max Emmanuel's wife, the Archduchess Maria Antonia, the only child of Leopold's Spanish wife, reaffirmed that renunciation of her rights to the Austrian and Spanish inheritances made in her marriage contract of 1685 with the specific exception of the Spanish Netherlands. In effect Leopold had agreed to secure this area for Max Emmanuel and in 1691 Austrian pressure brought him appointment as Lieutenant Governor and Captain General of the Spanish Netherlands, despite Spanish fears that he wanted to annex it. In 1690 Victor Amadeus II of Savoy-Piedmont, fed up with French tutelage and eager to dislodge the French from Pinerolo and Casale, joined the alliance. The formation of such a large alliance to the north, east and south of France represented a significant defeat for Louis and ensured that the conflict would be wide-ranging. It also offered Louis the prospect of dividing the allies and thus wrecking the alliance. Although military operations were far flung, ranging from Hudson's Bay to Pondicherry in India, the important fighting was restricted to western Europe. Trans-oceanic operations could affect the flow of wealth to Europe but, in general, the crucial movements, such as the Spanish plate fleets, were not affected. Individual bases, such as Pondicherry which fell to the Dutch in 1693, were seized but amphibious operations were far from easy and often unsuccessful. English attempts to take the major French Caribbean bases of Guadeloupe (1691) and Martinique (1693) failed. The most decisive operations were those in Britain. William's supporters were successful in Scotland, despite a defeat at Killiecrankie in 1689, while that year James overran most of Ireland except for Protestant Ulster. His attempt to besiege Londonderry was unsuccessful and in 1690 William beat James at the battle of the Boyne. The French continued to send troops and supplies to Ireland but in 1691 the last Stuart strongholds, Galway and Limerick, fell. The Treaty of Limerick (1691) offered the Irish a general indemnity and a return to the conditions of Charles II's reign and, although Protestant Irish pressure ensured that much of it was not honoured, it was followed by the agreed voluntary exile of most of the Catholic gentry. William was fortunate that Ireland and Scotland did not pose a long-term military problem comparable with that faced by the Habsburgs from their Hungarian opponents.

Nevertheless, the diversion of so much of the Anglo-Dutch military effort to Ireland until 1691 and the revival of Turkish energy against the Habsburgs in 1690 created a window of opportunity for Louis. However, the French invasion of the Spanish Netherlands in 1690 only produced an indecisive victory at Fleurus. In 1691 the transfer of German troops to Hungary and northern Italy left the initiative with the French but, though they captured Mons, a major victory eluded them. The decisive nature of the war in Britain ended immediate hopes for the Stuarts, while its indecisive character elsewhere, coupled with serious financial strains for all the powers, encouraged peace-feelers. In February 1692, responding to pressure for peace, Charles II informed Pope Innocent XII that he was opposed to peace until Louis, who he claimed was the greatest violator of treaties ever, had his power reduced. However, that September William acknowledged that he had given up hopes of achieving the full aims of the Grand Alliance. Negotiations between Louis and Leopold began that year and lasted until 1696. Concerned about the position of the Stuarts, Leopold hoped that James II's son could be accepted as the heir to William and Mary if, as seemed likely, they had no sons. He also wanted the promise of complete toleration for William's Catholic subjects and toyed with the idea of an Anglo-Dutch-French alliance conquering part of North Africa for the benefit of James. Negotiations between Louis and William began in 1693 but William refused to make his succession a subject of negotiation so they failed. Mutual suspicion between William and Leopold could not be assuaged by their renewal of the Grand Alliance.

William survived Jacobite plots and the French failed to achieve decisive victories, despite the successes of their forces in the Spanish Netherlands at Steenkerk (1692) and Neerwinden (1693), a stalemate which encouraged Louis to continue his efforts. French prestige was shaken when Namur fell in 1695 to a besieging force commanded by William and Max Emmanuel. The following year the Grand Alliance was broken by a unilateral peace between Louis and Victor Amadeus of Savoy-Piedmont. The war had not gone well for him and, after his serious defeat at Marsaglia (1693), it was clear that France would only leave Pinerolo and Casale as the result of negotiations. Louis agreed to do so as part of the Treaty of Turin (1696), a peace that forced Austria and Spain to accept a neutralization of Italy later that year. That allowed France to increase her forces in Catalonia and to successfully besiege Barcelona in 1697. This defeat led to a dramatic change in the Spanish position. In late 1696 Spanish ministers argued that the minimum acceptable terms were the frontiers established by the Peace of Aix-la-Chapelle in 1668 while the ideal terms were the re-establishment of the frontiers of the Peace of Pyrenees. However, the fall of Barcelona led Charles II to order his envoys to settle at once. Negotiations between William and the French had already reached the stage of a peace congress, opened in May 1697 at William's palace of Ryswick near The Hague. Several causes combined to produce a settlement: growing war-weariness in England, the United Provinces and France, Louis's concern to improve his diplomatic position before the death of Charles II, and William's concern about the stability of the Grand Alliance and hope that peace talks with Louis might produce a basis for subsequent negotiations. All the powers signed on 20 September 1697, apart from Leopold. With the

Spanish succession in mind, he wished to preserve the anti-French coalition and to continue the war, largely fought by others, in order to weaken France. In addition, he did not want to recognize French gains from the Empire. However, it was no longer credible to think of driving France from Alsace and Leopold, still at war with the Turks and deserted by his western European allies, had to accept the peace on 30 October.

Louis evacuated Catalonia, returned fortresses seized from Spain during the *réunion* period, including Luxemburg, abandoned Philippsburg, Breisach, Freiburg, Kehl and her *réunion* gains east of the Moselle, but had his acquisition of Alsace, including Strasbourg, recognized. Lorraine was restored to the duke though on terms which left it vulnerable to French occupation. Louis yielded in both the Cologne and the Palatine disputes. France recognized William's position in Britain, though Louis refused to expel James as William desired. The Dutch gained a favourable commercial treaty with France. The peace was a blow for Louis because of his recognition of William and his territorial losses. The return of fortresses for which Louis had schemed and his subjects died did not, however, make France appreciably more vulnerable to attack, as Vauban's fortification programme had provided Louis with a large number of modern fortresses. Instead, the returned fortresses limited Louis's ability to intervene in neighbouring areas. Sir John Lowther wrote in September 1697

> Strasbourg it is true they keep, but that is sufficiently balanced by the equivalent . . . parting with Luxemburg, which secures the electors upon the Rhine, whose greatest fear was that these two should have been both in the same hand. To tell you how all stocks, bank bills etc are improved is unnecessary, nor that this is from any present advantage we propose, but from the prospect that it will be lasting, since we see no likelihood that the French can ever break again to so much advantage as they might have now done, had they been in a condition to do it.[16]

Contemporary judgement of the peace was made difficult by uncertainty as to its consequences. If it meant the permanence of the Grand Alliance was assumed it could be seen as bad for Louis. However, it was clear that no such assumption could be made. All the rulers were conscious that a number of dramatic changes were imminent. The Spanish succession was now at the top of the diplomatic agenda, and the probability of peace in the Balkans suggested that Leopold would adopt an aggressive position. Baltic affairs were becoming more volatile and there was uncertainty about the strength of William's position in England and about English policy after his death. Count Tallard, the French envoy accredited to William after the peace, was convinced of English weakness, particularly financial exhaustion.[17] Far from closing the door to French expansion, Ryswick appeared to create a more favourable opportunity for French expansion, not least because by not

[16] Lowther to Lord Lonsdale, 16 Sept. 1697, New Haven, Beinecke Library, Osborn Files.
[17] AE. CP. Ang. 174 f. 105–6, 115–16.

settling the vexed question of the Spanish succession it made the settlement tentative and incomplete. It was in order to attempt to solve this problem that Louis and William sought over the next two years to create a new diplomatic order in western Europe, one based on co-operation and expressed in an agreed partition of the Spanish dominions.

The Partition Treaties, 1698–1700

The importance of dynastic considerations was amply demonstrated by the extensive diplomacy that the Spanish succession aroused. The dominions of the king of Spain were the largest dynastic prize in western Europe to have ever come up. Aside from the Spanish Netherlands and the largest, most populous and wealthiest European trans-oceanic empire they included all of southern Italy (the Kingdom of Naples), Lombardy (the Duchy of Milan), Sicily and Sardinia. There were three principal claimants. The marriage of Philip III of Spain's daughters to Louis XIII and the Emperor Ferdinand III and of their sons, Louis XIV and Leopold I, to Philip IV's daughters produced substantial interests on the part of the Bourbons and the Austrian Habsburgs. Both the princesses who married into the Bourbon dynasty specifically renounced their rights of succession for themselves and their heirs, but it was by no means clear how acceptable this was to Spanish custom and law. When Louis XIV married Maria Theresa in 1660 her renunciation was regarded even then as a matter of form only, in order to allay mistrust internationally. Leopold's claim was better because his mother, Philip III's younger daughter, had not made any renunciation. However, Leopold's sons, Joseph and Charles, were the sons not of his first, Spanish wife but of his third wife Eleanor of Neuburg. By his first marriage Leopold had only had a daughter, Maria Antonia, and her Bavarian marriage had produced a son, Joseph Ferdinand.

The inheritance rules of the period were a combination of positive law, traditions and the testaments of rulers. National conventions were often ambiguous and they frequently clashed with those of other countries. Legal claims played a major role in the diplomacy of 1698–1700, influencing the willingness of rulers to compromise, for all monarchs had to consider their responsibilities to their dynasties. However, such considerations did not influence those rulers who had no dynastic claim to the succession and either wished to make gains for themselves or feared the consequences of acquisitions by others. In addition, the experience of the recent war suggested that compromise was a likely consequence of any conflict and that pretensions, however strongly held, had to be moderated. It was against this background that Louis approached William in early 1698 to discuss the succession. He had correctly identified Leopold as likely to be his most obdurate opponent and had appreciated that the crucial point of tension in the Grand Alliance had been the relationship between the Emperor and the Maritime Powers. Though Leopold had been willing to negotiate a partition treaty of the Spanish inheritance in 1668, success in the Balkans had brought an increased measure of determination. The French envoy, Tallard, told William that a failure to settle the succession would result in each ruler taking steps as soon as Charles II died and that it would then be too late to negotiate.[18]

In April 1698 Tallard proposed that the bulk of the Spanish empire, including Spain, should go to a French prince. He argued that such a monarch would quickly adopt the views of his new kingdom at the expense of France and claimed that France would have no authority or cabal in Madrid able to influence his conduct. Tallard alleged that this would not be true of Leopold's younger son Charles, that Joseph Ferdinand's rights were limited and that the acquisition of the Spanish Netherlands by Max Emmanuel should end Anglo-Dutch fears of France. William was willing to consider a partition though he pointed out that it was audacious to determine matters which he and Louis could not control.[19] It rapidly became clear that the future of the Spanish possessions in Italy was a particular problem and that one possible solution was the use of equivalents. William feared that the gain of Naples and Sicily would allow the Bourbons to dominate Mediterranean trade. Tallard therefore suggested that France propose the acquisition of Lorraine, in return for the cession of Sicily to the duke of Lorraine. The Milanese was a particular problem. A part of the Empire, held in fee by Spain, it was the acquisition Leopold was keenest on, crucial to the strategic domination of northern Italy and a very wealthy area. William supported the idea of granting it to Archduke Charles while Tallard suggested that it should be given to Victor Amadeus II, who had some claims on the Spanish succession, in order to balance Habsburg power in the peninsula and prevent Austrian designs on other Italian princes. In an important departure from the principle that only claimants on the succession should make gains the French considered the possibility of offering England Sardinia or Spain's North African ports. William asked for Minorca, Ceuta and Oran. He also expressed interest in the trade of the Spanish empire and suggested that Havana be granted to England and the United Provinces jointly, an idea that was rejected by Louis. William was very concerned about the possibility of French territorial gains. In 1698, by agreement with Spain, Dutch troops had been moved into the leading fortresses of the Spanish Netherlands towards France, including Luxemburg, Mons, Ath and Courtrai, in order to create a stronger 'barrier' against any future French advance. William stressed to Tallard the vulnerability of the area and, rejecting suggestions that France needed Luxemburg for her security, he argued that it dominated Jülich and Cologne, menaced the Lower Rhine and could serve as the base for a French advance on Nijmegen. The French rejected William's suggestion that the Barrier be enlarged by French cessions while William criticized the idea that France gain the Navarre region of northern Spain, arguing that it would allow France to dominate Spain.

While the negotiations served to define the views of William and Louis,

[18] AE. CP. Ang. 175 f. 30.
[19] AE. CP. Ang. 174 f. 139–47.

they also served Louis's ends by separating William from his former allies, for neither Leopold nor Spain was involved in the discussions. William was aware of the problem, pointing out to Tallard in May 1698 that if he supported a partition, 'he could no longer count on past alliances, that there would no longer be any question of Austrian support and that he would only be able to count on a French alliance.'[20] At the same time William's options were limited, as he did not want to commit himself to Leopold, while the concentration of French forces near the Spanish frontier in 1698 made it clear that Louis's views had to be considered. An Austrian attempt to renew the agreement of 1689 was declined by William. Instead on 11 October 1698 he signed what was to become the First Partition Treaty with France. William's objectives of preventing too great an accretion of Bourbon strength and of allocating the Milanese to Charles were both achieved. Spain, her trans-oceanic possessions, the Spanish Netherlands and Sardinia were allocated to Joseph Ferdinand, Naples, Sicily, the *presidii* (Tuscan coastal forts) and the Basque province of Guipuzcoa to Louis's heir, the Dauphin Louis. The treaty provided that the signatories should impose it by force if any power refused to comply. William agreed to Louis's proposal to postpone the official notification of the treaty to Leopold until January 1699, by which month, it was assumed, Charles would be dead. Max Emmanuel accepted the provisions of the treaty, but Spanish opposition to the idea of partition led Charles II to make a will on 14 November 1698 leaving the entire inheritance to Joseph Ferdinand.

The likely consequences of this were still unclear when, after a short illness that gave rise to rumours of Austrian poisoning, Joseph Ferdinand died on 6 February 1699. Due to the difficulties affecting the negotiators this contingency had not been provided for. As there was no other suitable third party (Louis rejected William's suggestion of Pedro II of Portugal), Louis and William had in their negotiations for the Second Partition Treaty only to consider the distribution of territory among the Habsburgs and Bourbons. The treaty was not concluded until 25 March 1700. The delay reflected the problems created for William by the destruction of the solution of awarding contentious areas to a third party. The French stressed the danger of awarding too much to the Habsburgs, and pressed for Navarre. As before, the fate of the Milanese was a difficult issue, and William emphasized the need to produce a solution that could be offered to Leopold, who, however, refused to accede. The second treaty offered far more to the Habsburg claimant than the first though, as before, this was Charles who was not, unlike the dauphin, the direct heir to his father's territories. Spain, her trans-oceanic empire and the Spanish Netherlands were allocated to Charles. The dauphin received the same portion as in the first treaty and was to receive Lorraine while its duke was allocated the Milanese. The duke agreed in June 1700. For the benefit of William's closest adviser Tallard had compared Lorraine to a suburb or a small

[20] AE. CP. Ang. 175 f. 32.

chateau in the midst of a landlord's estates, and had argued that its acquisition would be a convenience for Louis rather than an appreciable increase in strength.[21] However, there was no doubt that this exchange, like the projected swap of Naples and Sicily for Savoy-Piedmont, would have represented a considerable strategic gain.

Neither Leopold nor the Spaniards accepted the new treaty. The prospect of Austrian military action in Italy helped to encourage the French to begin military preparations while, in order to increase the strength of the partition pact, France sought the alliance of Victor Amadeus, an essential support in any conflict in northern Italy. In August 1700 the Spanish envoy pressed Louis to abandon the idea of partition, claiming that Charles II would live for a long time, only to meet with the reply that all were mortal and that Louis's only aim was to bring peace to Europe. In Spain the idea that the monarchy could be preserved from partition only by France gained ground and was actively sponsored by Cardinal Portocarrero, the archbishop of Toledo. The pious Charles, who disliked the partition, was pressed hard by clerical supporters of a French candidate. On 2 October he signed a will leaving everything to the Dauphin's second son, Philip Duke of Anjou, on condition that the crowns of France and Spain never be united in one person. If this was not accepted by the Bourbons, the whole empire was to be offered to Archduke Charles. Charles added the suggestion that Philip marry an Austrian archduchess in order to ease tension. On 1 November he died, and on 16 November Louis presented Philip to his court as king of Spain. Explaining this decision, the French argued that it should please Europe more than the partition treaty because by accepting the will France gained no territory. Their envoy in The Hague pointed out to the States General in December 1700 that by accepting it France had ended English and Dutch fears that her acquisition of Naples and Sicily would harm their Mediterranean trade. Louis was aware that Leopold would appreciate neither the will nor French acceptance of it, but had he declined it and the inheritance been offered to Charles Louis knew that the Austrians were not already bound to accept the partition treaty and he had no confidence that England and the United Provinces would oblige them to do so.

The Outbreak of the War of the Spanish Succession, 1700–2

Philip V, acclaimed throughout the Spanish empire, reached Madrid on 18 February 1701. He was recognized by England in April and the United Provinces in February, and the prospect of an Anglo-Dutch-French triple alliance was discussed in diplomatic circles. The process by which relations deteriorated between France and her possible allies has been thoroughly studied but it was not itself responsible for the war. It was rather Austrian and French military preparations and initiatives that brought conflict near and

[21] AE. CP. Ang. 180 f. 37.

eventually led, on 19 June 1701, to the first shots being exchanged as the French sought to block an Austrian invasion of the Milanese, which Leopold claimed as an escheated fief of the Empire. France was in a far stronger diplomatic position than she had been during the recent Nine Years' War. The Ryswick negotiations and the partition treaties had clearly ended the Grand Alliance and this encouraged second-rank powers, such as Portugal, to regard France as a possible ally. In March 1701 Max Emmanuel of Bavaria made an alliance treaty with Louis by which the French agreed to pay him to maintain 10,000 troops. His brother, the archbishop-elector whose election to Cologne Louis had sought to prevent in 1688, signed a similar treaty that spring. It was clear that other countries were preparing for war, irrespective of the actions of the Maritime Powers, and indeed their attitude was not crucial to these manoeuvres for the key area of dispute was Spanish Italy, which Leopold did not intend to renounce. Having accepted Charles's will Louis was in no position to negotiate: Philip had been accepted on the basis that there would not be any Spanish territorial losses. Leopold was prepared, in light of the will, to accept a partition but he was determined to gain Spanish Italy and on 18 November 1700, the night he heard of Charles's death, he ordered his ministers to plan the seizure of Milan. Three days later Prince Eugene was appointed to command a force that was designed to undertake this task the following year.

It was the advance of this force, which set off in February 1701, that led to the beginning of hostilities. These moves helped to set the pace of negotiations between Leopold and the Maritime Powers. The English Secretary of War. William Blathwayt, then with his patron William III in the United Provinces, wrote in July 1701.

> We are impatient to hear of some success the Imperial army may obtain in Italy for I take such a step to be very necessary to determine us for though all our negotiations at The Hague will be carried on jointly with the Emperor yet the coming so suddenly to a breach with France without some such incident or other new provocation is not very probable.[22]

French action was already considered provocative in both England and the United Provinces. The replacement of the Dutch garrisons in the Barrier fortresses by French forces in February 1701 seemed to demonstrate the continued subservience of Philip to Louis and led to Dutch protests. The following month French troops were moved towards the Dutch frontier. The Dutch urged that many of the major fortresses should be occupied by Anglo-Dutch forces in order to lessen French influence in the Spanish Netherlands. Nothing came of the suggestion which might have alleviated Anglo-Dutch concern about concessions to France elsewhere in the Spanish empire. French merchants had been granted better conditions in Spain and the French Guinea Company was given for ten years the *Asiento* contract to transport slaves from West Africa to Spanish America, a lucrative opening

[22] Blathwayt to George Stepney, 21 July 1701, New Haven, Beinecke, Osborn Shelves, Blathwayt Box 21.

into the protected trade of the Spanish empire. In January 1701 French warships were given permission to enter Spanish American ports and that March they were given permission to sell goods there. This was to be the basis of extensive and unregulated sales of French goods. These developments encouraged alarmist rumours. For example one British Under-Secretary wrote in April 1701, 'The French are getting together a great fleet of ships and gallies in the mouth of the Streights [of Gibraltar], with intention, it may be supposed, to stop the passage into the Mediterranean, and to make us pay for it, in good time.'[23] A popular anti-French agitation combined with growing fears of French intentions to shift parliamentary attention from opposing William's men and measures while ignoring, to William's mind, the fate of Europe, to resolving to support the king in his growing conviction that Louis's acceptance of the will had to be resisted. Initially, parliamentary moves were restricted to an expression of support for the Dutch on 2 April 1701 but by June William had benefited from growing support for 'the common cause' to the extent of a new willingness to fund and support an active interventionist policy in continental affairs.

The French responded not by conciliatory offers, which would have handicapped Philip, but by military and diplomatic preparations for war and that, in turn, made it more likely. By the beginning of August the English ambassador in Paris was expressing the view that his continued stay could serve no useful purpose. Instead William was negotiating with Leopold and on 7 September 1701 the Grand Alliance of The Hague brought Austria and the Maritime Powers together to support a partition of the Spanish inherit-ance which was to award Spanish Italy to Leopold, create a barrier for the Dutch in the Spanish Netherlands and allow England and the Dutch to retain their conquests in the Spanish Indies. At this time the objectives of the Grand Alliance did not include dethroning Philip, much to Vienna's frustrated anger. Nine days later, before Louis knew of the treaty, James II died at his palace near Paris. The English ambassador thought wrongly that Louis would deny royal honours to the new pretender for some time, but instead he was recognized as James III. Though Louis's measure might be considered im-prudent in light of the hostile response in England where it helped to end doubts about his intentions, he already saw William as a rival, and hoped that the step would win papal support which could be very important both in Italy and in the war already beginning between the Catholic powers. In theory the Treaty of the Grand Alliance was not an offensive alliance. It stipulated an attempt to achieve its ends by negotiation with France. However, Louis's move threatened to add to his conflict with Leopold, a revival of the British War of Succession. His attempt to ensure recognition of James III from his allies, such as Portugal, was unwelcome in England where in January 1702 Parliament suggested an article in any treaties made by William 'that no peace shall be made with France, until His Majesty, and the

[23] BL. Add. 7074 f. 12.

nation, shall have reparation for the great indignity offered by the French king.'

Though William did not respond by declaring war, preferring to build up the anti-French alliance so that it could protect the United Provinces, the last months of peace were not spent in negotiation with Louis. Instead, in November 1701 William pressed the Austrians to send troops to the Rhine rather than to Italy or Hungary. Though William died on 8/19 March 1702, before any declaration of war, measures such as the French and Spanish prohibition of the import of British manufactures the previous autumn helped to further embitter relations.

Louis's attempt to exploit William's death by opening negotiations with the Dutch was unsuccessful and on 15 May Austria and the Maritime Powers simultaneously declared war.

THE WAR OF THE SPANISH SUCCESSION, 1702–14

The war was a complex struggle involving a variety of interests. For Austria, France and Spain dynastic considerations were predominant. For England, which was constitutionally united with Scotland in 1707, the Protestant succession was involved, for the United Provinces the prevention of Bourbon control of the Spanish Netherlands, and for both colonial and commercial considerations, especially West Indian trade. The issues at stake became more serious in the years after war began as the result of commitments to allies. The support of most of the German princes was won by the Grand Alliance without excessive commitments, though at the cost of heavy subsidies. Elector Frederick III of Brandenburg was gained by Leopold's promise to recognize his new title of 'King in Prussia'. However, Pedro II of Portugal was only won from his Bourbon allies in 1703 by the promise of territorial gains in Spain, and of the candidature of Archduke Charles for the Spanish throne, both as a guarantee of support from the Allies and because he would be a less threatening neighbour than a Bourbon. Victor Amadeus II similarly deserted the Bourbons in 1703 in return for subsidies and part of the Milanese. The opportunities that the conflict appeared to offer minor powers were illustrated by Max Emmanuel. His demands indicate the extent to which both territorial divisions were not seen as fixed and the international system was seen as full of opportunity. As the elector of Saxony had recently become king of Poland, the elector of Brandenburg king in Prussia and the duke of Brunswick-Lüneburg become in 1692 elector of Hanover and in 1701 had his place in the English succession recognized, it was not surprising that Max Emmanuel sought to turn the rivalry of the major rulers to his own advantage, and in 1701–4 negotiated with both sides. In the summer of 1702 the Austrian envoy offered territorial concessions in the Empire and the possibility of an exchange of Bavaria for Naples and Sicily. Max, who had been in the Habsburg camp from 1681 to 1697, demanded in reply royal status for Bavaria, the cession of the Habsburg possessions of Tyrol and the Burgau, subsidies, the marriage of a daughter of Leopold's heir Joseph, who had no sons, to his own heir, and the possible exchange of Bavaria and Naples and Sicily at his own option. Leopold was willing to offer money rather than Habsburg territories, but in November 1702 Max demanded, in return for an offensive alliance, subsidies, the Milanese, the Burgau, and the Spanish Netherlands, either to keep or to exchange for the Lower Palatinate. He also used the opportunity to try to pursue the feud of the Bavarian Wittelsbachs with the Palatine Wittelsbachs, demanding Neuburg which was one of the possessions of Leopold's brother-in-law, John William, Elector Palatine. He had already signed an offensive alliance with France in June 1702 by which he received subsidies and the promise of the Lower Palatinate or Spanish Gelderland. That summer Max obliged Louis to persuade Philip V to rescind his elder brother's patent as vicar general of the Spanish Netherlands and to award it to him. Concerned about the response in Spain, Philip promised Max Gelderland and the hereditary governorship of the Spanish Netherlands, but insisted on secrecy.[24] Max's ambitions extended to neighbouring independent territories. In April 1702 he defined his goal as the Imperial Free Cities of Augsburg, Nuremberg, Regensburg, Rothenburg and Ulm, and in September he began hostilities in southern Germany with an unprovoked seizure of Ulm. Max's continued talks with Leopold and the French need for German allies in the face of Leopold's success in winning allies in the Empire led to a new treaty in November 1702 in which Max gained the promise of the Palatinate and of full sovereignty over the Spanish Netherlands, with the exception of frontier fortresses reserved for France. By 1703, therefore, the objectives of both alliances had increased greatly. France was committed to creating a German power that could rival the Habsburgs, while her opponents were now fighting to keep the Bourbons out of the entire Spanish inheritance. These commitments helped to make compromise difficult in the tentative and active negotiations that continued during more of the war. When in February 1704 Prussia attempted to detach Bavaria from France, Max demanded the Milanese, a broad corridor to it through the Tyrol and his conquests in Swabia and Neuburg. Wide-ranging commitments also ensured that peace came through exhaustion and the unilateral action of one of the members of the Grand Alliance, thus precipitating the collapse of the alliance.

Wartime diplomacy was both greatly affected by strategic considerations and intertwined with the fortunes of war. Initially these were mixed and, despite the Grand Alliance's success in overrunning Brunswick-Wolfenbüttel and the Electorate of Cologne (1702–3), the junction of French and Bavarian

---

[24] Paris, Bibliothèque Nationale, nouvelles acquisitions françaises 486 f. 78, 89.

troops in southern Germany (1703) threatened the collapse of an Austria that was gravely weakened by a Hungarian rebellion. The arrival of Anglo-Dutch troops from the Low Countries under the duke of Marlborough the following summer helped to rescue the situation and on 13 August 1704 Marlborough and Eugene defeated the Franco-Bavarian army at Blenheim on the Danube, proof that decisive military verdicts were possible in the warfare of the period. This was followed by the retreat of the French from southern Germany and the overrunning of Bavaria. French strategy became mostly a matter of frontier-defence, a course of action that made it difficult to gain allies. Responding to pressure from John William of the Palatinate, Leopold's successor, Joseph I (1705–11), and the Imperial electors placed the electors of Bavaria and Cologne under the imperial ban in 1706, depriving them of their rights and privileges. Fearing princely opposition, Joseph abandoned hopes of annexing Bavaria, though John William was invested with the Bavarian territory of the Upper Palatinate in 1708.

The conquest of Bavaria made the conflict more intractable. Max refused to renounce the idea of regaining the acquisitions he had made since 1702, and Louis believed that his honour was involved. In November 1704 a Franco-Bavarian treaty committed Louis to continue the war until Bavaria was retaken, made a kingdom and embellished with much of Swabia, conditions Louis pressed in negotiations with the Dutch in 1706. In contrast John William sought to retain his gains and to add the governorship of the Spanish Netherlands. Thus, Max's earlier Bourbon-supported determination to dramatically alter the territorial configuration of much of Europe was now matched.

The Bourbons were also driven from Italy. The French force besieging Turin was defeated by Eugene and Victor Amadeus in 1706 and the French evacuated Italy. Naples was seized by the Austrians the following year. Thanks to Marlborough's victories at Ramillies (1706) and Oudenarde (1708) the French were driven from the Spanish Netherlands. However, the Grand Alliance had less success in conquering Spain and invading France. The attempt to establish Archduke Charles as Charles III failed, despite English naval power, support from the provinces of Catalonia and Valencia, and the intervention of English, German and Portuguese troops. Madrid was captured briefly in 1706 and 1710, but Castile, the key central area of Spain, remained loyal to Philip and his cause was increasingly identified with national independence despite his military dependence on French troops, who decisively defeated the Allies at Almanza (1707) and Brihuega (1710).

By the time that major attacks were launched on France, exhaustion was beginning to affect the Grand Alliance. Marlborough's plan to invade Lorraine up the Moselle in 1705 had to be abandoned due to a lack of German support. The Austrian invasions of Alsace in 1706 and Franche-Comté in 1709 and the combined Anglo-Austrian attack on Toulon in 1707 were unsuccessful. Marlborough's desire to follow up Oudenarde by a march on Paris was thwarted by Dutch caution and he had to settle for the successful sieges of Lille

(1708) and Tournai (1709). In defending France Louis had reason to be grateful both for his earlier acquisitions and for Vauban's fortifications. All the powers were affected by financial problems and by the savage winter of 1708–9.

PEACE NEGOTIATIONS, 1705–1714

Initially Louis's overtures had been largely designed to divide the Grand Alliance by winning over the Dutch, a course that Dutch determination to maintain their English alliance defeated. In 1705 he proposed a partition of the Spanish inheritance awarding Naples and Sicily to Charles and a Barrier to the Dutch in a Spanish Netherlands that was to become an independent republic. English insistence on the allocation of Spain to Charles led to the failure of the negotiations but after Ramillies Louis tried again, proposing that Spain and the Indies go to Charles, Spanish Italy to Philip and the Spanish Netherlands to the Dutch. These proposals came to nothing not least because Joseph I, while willing to make concessions on behalf of his brother Charles, was determined to acquire the Milanese for Austria, in accordance with a secret agreement Charles had been obliged to make in 1703. The English were unprepared to accept the possible commercial consequences of a Bourbon acquisition of Naples and Sicily. Nevertheless, the basis of the eventual settlement of 1713–14 was already present: a new partition treaty accompanied by a Dutch barrier and French recognition of the Protestant succession in England. Military developments, Oudenarde and Lille, made Louis more eager to settle but they also left less room for manoeuvre. The likelihood that the Austrians would agree to concessions in Spanish Italy was lessened by their conquests there. In 1708 British naval power helped Charles conquer Sardinia and Minorca and Charles promised Britain both Minorca and the *Asiento*. In negotiations in 1709 Louis abandoned his demands for an establishment for Philip, agreed to restore Lille and all he had taken in Alsace since 1648 including Strasbourg, met English wishes about their succession and agreed that 'James III' should leave France. The sticking point was that Louis could not guarantee that Philip would accept any settlement, and was unwilling to promise to help depose him. Distrust of Louis played a major role in the formulation of this humiliating demand which was cited by Louis, in his appeals to the French public and his correspondence with Philip, as the reason why he rejected the preliminaries. Eugene attributed the decision to the provisions concerning Alsace, and it might be suggested that the refusal to leave Philip any compensation for what Louis saw as his right to the Spanish inheritance was decisive.

The eventual peace terms were not as bad as Louis had been willing to consider in 1709. In part this reflected military developments. Charles was unsuccessful in Spain and Marlborough's pyrrhic victory at Malplaquet

(1709) was followed by only slow progress in capturing French fortresses. Fresh negotiations at Geertruidenberg in early 1710 collapsed on the Dutch insistence that Louis expel Philip before peace could be considered, but political changes in Britain, where the Whigs were replaced in 1710 by a Tory ministry that was prepared to compromise on its allies' demands in unilateral negotiations with France made the terms offered in 1709 and early 1710 appear redundant. Dutch and Austrian demands were certainly more of a hindrance to peace than their British counterparts, for insularity ensured that Britain did not need to consider the strengthening of territorial frontiers. Instead she essentially sought, aside from the recognition of the Protestant succession, territorial gains in relatively uncontroversial regions: North America and isolated bases in the Mediterranean. In contrast, the Austrians sought a strong German barrier against France, demanding, for example, in September 1709 the three bishoprics of Metz, Toul and Verdun, which the French had acquired in 1552, and the restoration of Lorraine's 1624 frontier with France. A meeting of the representatives of the Imperial circles demanded as a condition of any peace settlement a barrier that would include Strasbourg, Landau, Metz, Toul and Verdun. In October 1709, in response to Dutch pressure, the English Whig ministry had signed the Treaty of the Barrier by which they agreed that the Dutch were to make gains in French Flanders and to be allowed to garrison thirteen fortresses in the Spanish Netherlands which were to enjoy full autonomy from the government in Brussels.

Given such demands, it is understandable that the Tory ministry felt that it could proceed more successfully, and gain more satisfactory terms for Britain if it negotiated alone, a clear breach of the terms of the Grand Alliance. In December 1710, following the defeat at Brihuega, English willingness to leave Philip in possession of Spain and the Indies was signalled. This was made more politically acceptable by the death of Joseph I on 17 April 1711. When Joseph's brother Charles died, also without a son, in 1740 his possessions passed to his elder daughter as a result of a special arrangement, the Pragmatic Sanction. No such arrangement existed in 1711 to prevent Charles succeeding his brother while maintaining his own pretensions to the Spanish empire. That represented, however, a strengthening of Austrian power that none of her allies sought, and this helped to ensure that the British initiative in beginning negotiations was followed by many powers. Most of the terms were settled in Anglo-French discussions in 1711 which served as the basis for the negotiations held at Utrecht in 1712–13. Affairs were complicated in February–March 1712 when Philip's elder brother, the Duke of Burgundy, and the latter's eldest son, the Duke of Brittany, both died, while Burgundy's other son, the infant duke of Anjou, nearly died. This brought Philip very close to Louis's succession and revived fears of French influence in Spain. A dynastic union of France and Spain was as unwelcome as one of Austria and Spain. In June 1712 Henry St John, Viscount Bolingbroke, effectively the British foreign minister, warned his French counterpart, Torcy, that the need to prevent such a union was essential for Britain and that Queen Anne considered that she would be responsible to her subjects, her allies and the future for her conduct in this respect.[25] The French insisted that agreements could not contradict their fundamental laws and that any renunciation by Philip of his claim to the French succession would be of no value, because France was a patrimony that the monarch received not from his predecessor or the people but in accordance with the law, which only God could change. It was stressed that as soon as one monarch died another succeeded, without his own personal choice or the consent of anyone being an issue.[26] Torcy rejected the idea that any renunciation could be ratified by the Estates General or by the provincial Estates.

French insistence on Philip's right to succeed in France gave rise to discussions about the cession of Spain to another, possibly his cousin, the duke of Orléans, or Victor Amadeus II in exchange for the latter's territories. Philip, however, made it clear that the only acceptable solution was, in the event of his nephew's death, his inheritance of France and his abdication then of Spain to his son. Dynastic considerations were not the only issues under negotiation. Indeed it is too easy to present the terms of the Peace of Utrecht as though they inevitably arose from the Anglo-French negotiations. In fact it proved difficult to settle many issues and the proposals advanced in 1711–13 indicate the unpredictable nature of the eventual settlement. The Barrier and the settlements for Max Emmanuel and Victor Amadeus proved especially contentious. Notions of honour and compensation were more important than any attempt to create a balance of power on a logical basis. Italy proved a rich field for proposals and new kingdoms. In 1711 the French proposed that Victor Amadeus be given the Milanese and made king of Lombardy; instead he was to receive Sicily as a kingdom. In the same year they suggested that, in addition to the return of his dominions, Max Emmanuel should gain much of the Spanish Netherlands and in 1712, having pressed for him to receive Sicily or the Netherlands, they persuaded Bolingbroke to agree that he receive Sardinia and royal status. Torcy thought the idea plausible, despite the distance and the absence of links between Bavaria and Sardinia, because there was no diplomatic reason why they were incompatible. The gain of Bavaria and the Spanish Netherlands by Austria in return for Max acquiring Naples was also discussed in 1711.

Alongside the creation of kingdoms, the diplomats had to discuss frontiers. These discussions witnessed a mixture of strategic considerations and traditional bases for territorial claims. Resisting Dutch demands that the Barrier include part of French Flanders the French pressed for the return to them of Lille, Tournai, Aire and a number of other places. They argued that these places would close the French frontier without threatening their neighbours and claimed that Tournai was part of the ancient domain of the kingdom but, although they regained Lille, Valenciennes, Maubeuge and other forts

[25] AE. CP. Ang. sup. 4 f. 156.
[26] PRO 78/154 f. 284–5.

promised to the Dutch by the Barrier Treaty of 1709, the French did not regain Tournai. Victor Amadeus's demands for an extended Alpine barrier were rejected by the French as leaving the Dauphiné vulnerable and, in a modern touch, Torcy urged Bolingbroke to consult a map. He also refused to accept the claim to Monaco, both because it was essential for the security of Provence and because it was important to protect the interests of the duke of Monaco. Torcy also protested against the loss of any 'ancient domaine of the Crown' to Victor Amadeus, leading to Bolingbroke's sceptical observations, 'yet this point of honour is to be got over, and this domaine is to be parted with, provided the valley of Barcelonnette be given in exchange.'[27]

By early 1713 the Anglo-French negotiators had produced terms that would satisfy Victor Amadeus, the United Provinces, Portugal and Prussia, and on 11 April their plenipotentiaries signed the peace treaties. The Emperor, Charles VI, was willing to abandon his claims to Spain, where he still held Barcelona and Majorca, but insisted on the exclusion of Max Emmanuel from Bavaria. Britain gained the recognition of the Protestant succession, the value of which was increased by Anne's ill-health, Nova Scotia, Newfoundland, St Kitts and the return to Hudson's Bay. An Anglo-Spanish peace treaty, signed at Utrecht on 13 July, ceded to Britain Gibraltar, which she had captured in 1704, Minorca, the *Asiento* and the right to send an annual 'permission ship' to the West Indies to trade with the hitherto closed Spanish territories. Britain and France agreed that Charles VI was to receive the Spanish Netherlands and Spanish Italy bar Sicily which was to go to Victor Amadeus along with a settlement of his Alpine frontier that was less generous than he had sought but was more geographically consistent than the old frontier. The Dutch gained a Barrier and the French privateering base of Dunkirk was to lose its fortifications. Philip V renounced his claims to the French succession, while the disposal of the less contentious Orange succession brought Louis XIV the enclave of Orange in southern France, and Frederick I of Prussia a scattering of small territories that bore little relation to his existing possessions. His claim to Neuchâtel, an enclave between France and Switzerland, was also recognized, an apt demonstration of the importance of dynastic pretensions in the peace settlement. Britain and France agreed on mutual territorial restitutions in Iberia between Spain and Portugal, though the two powers did not sign an agreement, the last of the Utrecht treaties, until February 1715.

In the meantime a short burst of fighting had brought Charles and the Empire into the peace. The Imperial Diet at Regensburg declared in July 1713 that the French proposals would 'tarnish the glory of the German nation', but, outnumbered by the French and without promised supplies and funds from the exhausted Empire and the *Erblande* (Austrian hereditary lands), Eugene was forced to accept the loss of Freiburg and Landau and to press Charles for peace. Charles had hoped to attack Victor Amadeus in order to gain Sicily but

[27] PRO 78/154 f. 358–9; Bolingbroke to Shrewsbury, 17 Feb. 1713, New York, Montague Collection vol. 10.

instead he had to order Eugene to negotiate the Treaty of Rastatt. Desiring peace and fearful that a Hanoverian succession in Britain might lead to the revitalization of the Grand Alliance, Louis accepted terms that were favourable for Charles. Instead of pressing his demands for the eviction of Austria from Italy and for a kingdom for Max Emmanuel, Louis accepted the simple restitution of the electors of Bavaria and Cologne and the acquisition of the Spanish Netherlands and all of Spanish Italy, bar Sicily and the cessions to Victor Amadeus, as well as the Duchy of Mantua by Charles. The German settlement was based on the Peace of Ryswick, with France retaining Strasbourg and Alsace, but not any possessions on the right bank of the Rhine. Charles was obliged to sacrifice the ambitions of John William of the Palatinate.

The terms agreed at Rastatt on 6 March 1714 served as the basis for the congress for the signing of peace between the Empire and France which met later that year and produced the Treaty of Baden, signed on 7 September 1714. A host of rulers complained about the settlement, including those of Bavaria, Cologne, Lorraine, Spain and several Italian princes concerned about the extent to which the Austrians were using their power in the peninsula to determine territorial and judicial disputes to their satisfaction. However, with the obvious exception of Victor Amadeus who benefited from British sponsorship of an apparently useful protégé, the expansionist views of the minor rulers were generally neglected in the settlements of 1713–14. Louis had predicted correctly in 1712 that little attention would be paid to the views of Duke Leopold of Lorraine[28] and, indeed, a common theme of the negotiations of the period was their dominance by the major powers. The growth in the size of armed forces in the second half of the seventeenth century, the true 'military revolution' of the century, in so far as there was one, and the wars of the period 1683–1721 had increased the distinction between major and minor powers and had witnessed the failure both of several second-rank rulers, such as Max Emmanuel, to achieve greater power, and of several regions that possessed a strong sense of identity to retain or gain independence. Moldavia, Wallachia, Scotland and the Ukraine had all seen their autonomy lessened. Hungary had not achieved independence during its 1703–11 uprising though it had distracted substantial Austrian forces from the war with Louis, to his pleasure and Anglo-Dutch fury. Philip V successfully besieged Barcelona with French troops in 1714 and Catalan privileges were dramatically limited. The new order was symbolized by the construction of a new citadel in the Catalan capital. Rebel causes were abandoned, including the Jacobites, for whose benefit the French had sent an invasion fleet to Scottish waters in 1708 and the Camisards, Protestants in southern France, who had rebelled during 1702–11 and received some, though very little, British help.

---

[28] AE. CP. Lorraine 81 f. 95.

Philip did not sign any treaty with Charles and his marriage in 1714 to Elizabeth Farnese, niece of the childless duke of Parma, a duchy Vienna claimed as an Imperial fief, indicated that he was still interested in Italy. In 1715 his forces captured Majorca from Charles's supporters and the possibility that he would seek to disrupt the Utrecht settlement in Italy appeared strong. Similarly there was believed to be a danger that the accession of George I in Britain (1714) and the disgracing of Anne's Tory ministers, would lead to a rekindling of Anglo-French tension and the revival of French support for the Jacobites.

The settlements of 1713–14 left a host of differences. Some, such as Austrian resistance to the demand by Cardinal Rohan, bishop of Strasbourg, that his German possessions entitled him to representation at the Imperial Diet, were hardly threatening but rather indications of the extent to which local territorial and judicial disputes could become diplomatic issues because of the absence of any monopolization of sovereign powers by coherent states with clear frontiers. Others were more serious and the wars fought in western Europe between 1717 and 1748 suggest that it is misleading to regard the settlements as having created a new international order. Indeed some of the major themes of the period, especially Franco-Spanish differences in 1717–29 and French sponsorship of anti-Austrian German princes, particularly the Wittelsbachs, indicate that it is misleading to exaggerate the changes created by the War of the Spanish Succession and the subsequent peace. It has been suggested that they marked the end of French hegemony in western Europe but the existence of this hegemony can be queried, particularly in light of the willingness of so many rulers to defy Louis in 1688. It was rather that French hegemony had been feared though even then many Austrian ministers had been more concerned by Turkey and Hungary while the Scandinavian and north German rulers were more interested in Baltic affairs. The predominance of one dynasty had been feared in 1700 and this was, arguably, a more realistic anxiety than earlier fears of French hegemony. However, claims that Philip would not follow the French lead were to be fully vindicated after the war ended, and it is easy to appreciate why many German and Italian princes were more concerned about Austrian than Bourbon power and intentions in the first three decades of the century. Their perspective was a valid one, was to be shared by the Maritime Powers in the 1720s and should be placed alongside their earlier concern about the Bourbons.

II

1714–1763

EUROPE AND THE NON-EUROPEAN WORLD IN THE EIGHTEENTH CENTURY

To devote much space to colonies and trans-oceanic conflict in any work on eighteenth-century Europe might be held to reveal a western European bias. It was the case, however, that expansion outside Europe was of significance, politically, economically and culturally, not only for the maritime powers, or for those countries, including in particular Russia, that were to some extent frontier states. The diplomatic interrelationship of states ensured that conflict or peace outside Europe could affect other European powers. Peter the Great's campaigns against Persia in the early 1720s helped to keep the peace in the Baltic; the Spanish expeditionary force of 1732 attacked Oran in North Africa and not, as had been feared, the island of Sardinia or Austrian Italy. The outbreak of Anglo-French hostilities in North America in 1754 helped to precipitate the Diplomatic Revolution by leading the British to step up diplomatic efforts to prevent an attack on Hanover. The financial strain caused by intervening in the War of American Independence was largely responsible for France's weak position in European diplomacy in 1787–9. The economic benefits of extra-European possessions and trade could also be extremely significant in international relations. They brought profits and, though not always, improved the fiscal strength of governments. This enabled a number of powers, principally Britain, France, Spain and the United Provinces, to pay subsidies to other European states, which could be of considerable importance in affecting peacetime diplomacy and the durability and strength of alliances in wartime. These subsidies, being paid in cash, provided a crucial basis for the raising of loans. In 1703–13 Anglo-Dutch subsidies represented approximately an addition of 25 per cent to the Savoyard budget. Spain paid Charles Albert of Bavaria nearly 2 million livres annually in order to support his challenge to Maria Theresa in the War of the Austrian Succession. During the same conflict French government expenditure, which had already reached 300 million livres in 1742, rose to an annual figure of 350 million (£16 million) in 1744. This exceeded British expenditure by a third, while Austrian expenditure reached a peak of £3 million in 1745. Both Britain and France spent £1-2million annually in subsidies to other powers during the war. The recipients of British subsidies included Austria, Hanover, Hesse-Cassel, Sardinia and Russia, and of French Bavaria, Sweden and the Spanish prince Don Philip, while those of the United Provinces went to Austria and Saxony. In the early 1750s the British paid subsidies to Bavaria and Saxony and, during the Seven Years' War, paid for Hanoverian and Hessian troops and for the equivalent of 19 per cent of Frederick the Great's war costs. In 1757–62 France paid Austria the equivalent of £450,000 annually, while Austria paid Russia a smaller sum.

The general movement of money between governments in the form of subsidies was thus one from west to east, from maritime to continental Europe. There were naturally exceptions to this pattern. The Turks were ready to subsidize powers opposed to Russia, particularly Sweden, and an Austro-Turkish agreement of 1771, aimed against Russian penetration of the Balkans, led to a small subsidy to Austria. Nevertheless, the overwhelming impression is of a movement from maritime to continental Europe, one that would have been more marked if all the sums promised had been paid and stronger if more than merely a fraction of all the subsidies sought had been granted. The movement of money was not simply due to the commercial strength of the maritime states. Western Europe was more populous, wealthy and agriculturally developed than any comparably sized region between the Elbe, the Aegean and the Urals. However, the ability to move funds internationally reflected in part the commercial strength and sophistication of societies that were able to raise large sums of cash; and this owed something to their trans-oceanic commerce.

If the wider world was of political, economic and cultural significance for Europe, the extent of its impact varied. Much clearly was outside the perception of most of the population. If silver was in short supply, not everyone could relate this to the need to finance the negative balance of trade with the Orient that led, for example, to average annual bullion exports thither from Amsterdam of 3 million florins in 1721–6. Economically the impact was obviously greatest on areas making goods for distant markets or consuming products from them. Politically it was the frontier and particularly the major maritime powers that were most affected. However, this varied considerably. Though it was to be pregnant with future consequences, expansion into Siberia and central Asia had only a limited effect on Russia, especially as Peter the Great's successors continued his direction of Russian attention and intentions towards the west and south. Territorially Russia expanded. The cession of the Amur valley to China by the treaty of Nerchinsk (1689) was not reversed until 1858, but gains were made on Russia's southern frontier and more settlements established in Siberia. Omsk was founded in 1716 and Petropavlovsk on the Kamchatka peninsula, a region slowly acquired during the century, in 1740. Native peoples, such as the Chukchi in north-eastern Siberia, were slowly brought under control. The New Siberian Islands in the Arctic were discovered towards the end of the century. But Russian penetration of central Asia remained limited. The Kazakh nomads to the east of the Caspian were nominally vassals, but the area was not fully dominated militarily until the 1850s. The Khanates of Bukhara, Khiva and Kokand were not to be conquered until the second half of the nineteenth century. While central Asia represented a formidable military problem, Alaska posed serious logistical difficulties. A project for a Russian colony in California had been discussed in the 1730s, but it was to be Alaskan fur that brought the Russians further east. In 1724 Peter the Great ordered the Dane Vitus Bering to discover a serviceable sea route from Siberia to North America, and, sailing from Kamchatka in 1728, Bering enlarged public knowledge of an earlier discovery of the strait separating Asia from America that now bears his name. In 1741 Bering and Chirikov explored the Alaskan coast and subsequently a Russian company was formed which established fur-trading stations along the coast and on the nearby islands. This led to the nearly complete extermination of the sea-otter, Steller's sea-cows and of the native Aleutian population. Similar extermination of native populations and wildlife had marked other episodes of European expansion. The dodo, a bird found on the islands of Mauritius and Réunion, became extinct in 1681 as a result of being killed for food and the eating of its eggs by pigs introduced by the Europeans. As the sea-otter became scarcer, the Russians moved south along the west coast of North America, leading Spain, which laid claim to the area, to make forestalling moves in the late 1780s.

Russia may have missed an opportunity to become a major Pacific power in the eighteenth century, though there were formidable obstacles to such an ambition. Siberia operated as a greater barrier than major oceans such as the Atlantic. The distances were formidable, the climate ferocious and the rivers flowed north–south and were ice-bound for months on end, as was the coast. Demographically Siberia was only a minor part of Russia, and the return of the granary of the Amur valley restricted its development possibilities. Immigration was limited and, including the native peoples, the population was only about 600,000 by the end of the century. If war with China was not a realistic possibility for rulers busy with Sweden, Poland and Turkey, nevertheless relatively little effort was devoted to Pacific and North American exploration. Propinquity was no substitute for profit and glory. Furs were not as valuable as gold, and it was understandable that the government took the practical step of leaving most of the exploitation of the area to local initiative and to a trading company.

The Russian attitude was mirrored to a certain extent by that of Denmark. The inhospitability of its possessions of Greenland and Iceland and their limited value except for whale fishing, led Danish kings to devote their energies to gains in Holstein and Danish merchants to seek profits in the Canton trade. However, the Danes were not solely guided by profit. Danish missionaries spread Protestantism in India and Greenland, while Christian VI financed an expedition to explore the interior of Egypt in 1737–8. Other powers proved slow to seize opportunities overseas. This arose from a feeling that colonies were less useful and valuable than trading stations, as well as from the cost of overseas exploration and settlement, the resistance of native peoples and the absence in many areas of push and pull factors in terms of emigration and resources that could be profitably exploited. The combination of insufficient demand and limited opportunity was responsible both for the restricted nature of European conquest and settlement overseas, compared to the following century, and the unequal distribution of what did occur.

The resistance of already established powers, either native peoples or successful conquerors, was of considerable significance. The Portuguese empire was particularly affected by this. The discovery of gold in Brazil, first in Minas Gerais and subsequently in the Cuiaba, Goias and Mato Grosso regions, led to a major movement of population into the interior, both from the rest of Brazil and from Portugal itself. In contrast the rest of the overseas empire was both short of settlers and faced with more serious opposition. In 1693–5 the attempt by the Portuguese to expand their influence in south-east Africa was defeated by the Bantus. In 1698 their leading base in east Africa, Mombasa, fell to the Omani Arabs, who, possessing muskets and artillery, posed a military threat far greater than that of the Amerindian tribes of Brazil. Retaken in 1728, Mombasa and the attendant suzerainty over the Swahili islands and states of east Africa were lost again in 1729. Goa on the western coast of India was an exposed settlement with very few Portuguese settlers. In alliance with the British of Bombay, the Goan forces were unable in 1721 to capture the principal base of the Angria family, formidable corsairs who challenged the Portuguese naval position in Indian waters as did the well-gunned Omani warships. In 1737–40 Goa was involved in a disastrous war with the Maratha confederation. Portuguese lands north of Bombay were lost and Goa only escaped occupation by paying a large indemnity. The Portuguese were not the only power to encounter serious resistance. The Spaniards met with significant resistance from the Indians of Chile. Louis XIV's intervention in Siam (Thailand) had been unsuccessful, and both the British and the French were defeated when they sought to benefit from the Burmese civil war in the 1750s. In 1741 the Bey of Tunis seized the offshore island of Tabarca which the French had purchased from the Lomellino family, defeated a French counterattack and sacked the French Africa Company's base at Cap Negre. A major problem confronting the European powers was the vitality and aggressive expansionism of many overseas states. It was not always a case of European powers competing to exploit the weakness of overseas states; it is clear that these were often divided, that some were powerful and that the divisions among both European and non-European powers could produce alliances between them. Tongking (Vietnam) conquered Cochin China, Burma and Arakan, though it failed to gain Siam, and China launched abortive invasions of Burma and Tongking. The Afghans intervened in both Persia and India. In the latter, struggles between the local princes played a far larger role than European activity in the first half of the century, and the Anglo-French conflict in mid-century southern India was waged substantially as auxiliaries to local princes.

Native resistance to political control could be matched by limited interest in establishing settlements. Though the Dutch explorer, Abel Tasman, had discovered Fiji, New Zealand, Tasmania and Tonga in the mid seventeenth century, the Dutch East India Company was not interested in establishing the value of these discoveries. Spanish settlement of northern New Spain was limited and slow. Military governments were established in Texas (1718), Sinaloa (1734), New Santander (1746) and California (1767). Los Angeles was not settled until 1769, interest in the coast further north in the 1780s was largely a response to fears of British and Russian activity, and, by the end of the century, the population of California was much less than 10,000. On the other hand expansion in some areas was considerable. North America provided an example both of the expansion of British trading bases, in the Hudson's Bay region, and of the settlement of large numbers, in the thirteen colonies on the Atlantic seaboard, the latter growing in the face of opposition by the Indians and by other European powers, in this case France and Spain. The Hudson's Bay Company, set up in 1670 and granted monopoly rights to fur-trading in northern Canada, ran its affairs like most companies enjoying an exclusive trade with little government supervision and only limited support. Its history illustrates the influence of war on European overseas activity. Sporadic hostilities with the French in 1683–1713 led to no dividend being paid in 1690–1718. In the 1690s no regular English troops were sent to help and only in 1696–7 did naval vessels reinforce the Company's ships. Awarded to Britain at the Peace of Utrecht, the Company's bases competed with those of French Canada. Until about 1730 competition was noticeable only at the bottom of the Bay, but in the 1730s and 1740s the French expanded from the Great Lakes past the Lake of the Woods (Fort St Charles, 1732) and Lake Winnipeg (Fort Maurepas, 1734) and on to the Saskatchewan river (Fort La Jonquière, 1751). The line of French posts lay across the canoe routes to Hudson's Bay. They were clearly aimed at the British. In 1743 the President of the French Council of Marine, the ministry that ran French colonies, ordered his Canadian subordinates to prevent the British from using Hudson's Bay as a base for establishing posts on the Great Lakes, cutting the communications between the French colonies of Canada and Louisiana and possibly finding a route to the Pacific. In response to this and to domestic criticism, the British company adopted a more energetic attitude to exploration and expansion after 1750 and began constructing posts away from the Bay in the 1770s, beginning with Cumberland House in 1774.

Territorially the western hemisphere witnessed major changes in this century, both among the European powers and between them and the native peoples, but these were largely in North America. In central and south America Spanish control remained paramount with the principal exception of

Brazil. The Dutch colonized Surinam as a plantation economy. In North America the Indians near the European colonies were increasingly brought under their control, leading to a series of bitter conflicts, but the major territorial shifts were between the European powers, even if the territories ceded, such as Louisiana transferred by France to Spain in 1763, were only partially controlled.

In the eastern hemisphere territorial changes between the European powers were less marked. When France was defeated by Britain in the struggle for influence in India in mid-century, this did not entail the transfer of large areas of territory. Similarly in west Africa gains such as that of Senegal, taken from the French by Britain in 1758 and returned in 1783, were essentially those of coastal slaving stations. There was little attempt to penetrate into the interior because of the climate, the dominance of trade by the coastal stations and the strength of the Ashanti and of the kings of Dahomey. Guadja Trudo of Dahomey used powder and shot in 1727 to conquer the major slaving port of Whydah, where Brazilian tobacco was exchanged for slaves of Sudanese origin to the profit of the Dutch. Territorial claims were often no guide to real power. The French annexation of Madagascar in 1768 had little impact. The island was not controlled from the posts of Fort Dauphin and Ile Ste Marie, though the French had staked a claim to a possible base on the route to the Orient. The hesitation of European powers to expand territorially was fully seen in the latter region, where policy was controlled, in the case of the British and Dutch, not by royal officials but by trading companies. Though the Dutch had bases in Sumatra, Borneo and the Celebes, Java was the only major island on which they were a territorial power. This power was in opposition to the wishes of the Directors in Amsterdam, but in response to the massive expansion in the cultivation of coffee after the plant was introduced to the local chiefs by the Dutch in 1707. Javan peasants under the control of local chiefs served the same function as negro slaves in the western hemisphere. The spread of Dutch control was gradual and entailed conflict, both with some of the local chiefs and with the Chinese population, over 10,000 of whom were slaughtered in 1740. Chinese economic influence in the Philippines also led to tension and moves towards expulsion of the Chinese were made in 1709, 1747, 1755, 1763 and 1769. In 1763, 6,000 Chinese were reputedly massacred for participating in an anti-Spanish Filipino conspiracy. In India Britain became a territorial power in mid-century. The perception of Britain's role and capacity changed dramatically in the 1760s and 1770s, with the servants of the East India Company, whose private army had risen from 3,000 in 1748 to 69,000 in 1763, thinking of the conquest of China. Bengal, Bihar and Orissa were brought under British control after the victories of Plassey (1757) and Buxar (1764). The Northern Circars were added in the late 1760s, Benares and Ghazipur in 1775. Whereas France had challenged Britain in India in the mid-century conflicts, her impact was more limited in the War of American Independence, despite the vigour of Suffren's naval campaigns. Britain's principal rivals were native,

Hyder Ali and Tipu, rulers of Mysore, and the serious difficulties she encountered with them in the 1780s and 1790s revealed the problems of intervening in local disputes. By March 1784 the East India Company's debts in India had risen to about £8 million, colonial conflict proving, like its European counterpart, a major fiscal strain. Following the defeat and death of Tipu in 1799 when Seringapatam was stormed, Britain became the major territorial power in southern India.

The balance sheet of European expansion therefore reveals significant gains, particularly once the hesitation about territorial expansion in many circles is grasped. However, in 1800 most of the world's population had never seen a European, and penetration of Africa, Asia and Australia was limited. Japan, with its population of about 30 million, was isolated, unwilling to trade with Europeans except through a small artificial island in Nagasaki harbour. In much of the eastern hemisphere the major conflicts did not involve Europeans. In 1739 Nadir Shah, who had seized power in Persia, destroyed the Mughal army of maybe 200,000, seized Delhi and massacred the inhabitants, while in Africa the expansion of Islamic proselytism led to a series of major holy wars in the 1790s. European powers were the only ones able to operate around the world, but the benefits of maritime power were often only commercial and their impact on the land empires episodic.

THE INTERNATIONAL SYSTEM
1714–55

The decades after 1714 have not received as much attention as the period 1680–1714 or the second half of the century. They have appeared to be relatively inconsequential, with the conspicuous exception of Frederick II (the Great) of Prussia's attack upon Maria Theresa in 1740. Certainly the diplomacy and wars of the 1720s and 1730s have appeared to be less important and more limited than their counterparts in 1680–1714 or such later episodes as the Seven Years' War and the First Partition of Poland. In so far as the period 1740–55 has appeared worthy of mention it has largely been as preparation for the so-called Diplomatic Revolution, the Franco-Austrian *entente* of 1756. To a considerable extent this situation has been matched in scholarly studies of the monarchs of the period. The Russian rulers of 1725–62 have never enjoyed the attention lavished on Peter the Great and Catherine the Great. The Emperor Charles VI (1711–40) and Frederick William I of Prussia (1713–40) have received insufficient attention compared to their successors and much Mediterranean history in this period is obscure. Ferdinand VI of Spain (1746–59) is scarcely a familiar figure and the same is true of Charles Emmanuel III of Sardinia (1730–73), as the rulers of Savoy-

Piedmont were known after 1720. Partly as a result the diplomatic history of the period has both been relatively neglected and presented in familiar terms, the Anglo-French alliance of 1716–31, the recovery of France in the 1730s, the Prussian attack on Austria and the background to the Diplomatic Revolution. Convenience, the need to present an orderly account of complete events and a sense that international relations had changed in the period 1680–1714 have combined to ensure that Europe after 1714 has been seen as essentially one political system with the concomitant that it is realistic to write of an overall European-wide balance of power.

Contemporaries certainly argued that events were interconnected and that once a conflict broke out it was difficult to prevent it spreading to the whole of Europe. The image of a flame spreading was used, for example by the Dutch statesman Goslinga in 1715 and the French first minister Fleury in 1727. The idea that a European system existed was expressed by, among others Frederick II in 1748. The same year he suggested that Britain and France were the powers that determined what happened in Europe. In 1723 his father, Frederick William I, had claimed 'that there was no doubt that if France and George I united, we could affect all the affairs of Europe.'[1]

The role of Britain and France in the Baltic crisis of 1748–50, both helping to restrain their respective allies Russia and Austria, and Sweden and Prussia, seemed to bear out Frederick's comment. The interrelationships of affairs were demonstrated by the concern of western European powers to encourage or inhibit the march of Russian troops into central Europe in 1730, 1735 and 1748. The direct military intervention by France in the War of the Polish Succession (1733–5), their mediation of a Balkan peace in 1739 and their encouragement of Sweden to attack Russia in 1741 suggest that powerful countries did indeed seek a continent-wide reach for their diplomacy and their alliances.

However, the idea that international relations were in some fashion predictable and limited in their scope because of the operation of the balance of power, the principle of collective security and the supposed absence of serious issues at stake is misleading. Major efforts were made to overthrow dynasties, the Habsburgs in the Austrian Succession War (1740–8) and the Hanoverians in the French-supported Jacobite invasion attempts of 1744 and 1745–6. Substantial territorial changes were effected through warfare, particularly the establishment of two of Philip V's sons by his second marriage in Italy in 1734–48. The Turks recaptured the Peleponnese and lost, and then regained, Serbia and Little Wallachia. Others were blocked through warfare, for example Philip's attempt to regain much of Spanish Italy in 1717–20. Dynastic changes that would have created such territorial groupings as Russia–Sweden and Russia–Prussia were actively considered. New entities were considered. In 1737 Tsarina Anna made her lover Biron duke of Courland. When she died in 1740 he became regent for the infant Ivan VI but

[1] AE. CP. Prusse 73 f. 51.

he was speedily disgraced both because his domestic position aroused envy and because he had planned enlisting Swedish help to create a state of Courland, Livonia and Estonia, which was to be placed under Swedish suzerainty. The creation of direct land bridges between Saxony and Poland, and Brandenburg and East Prussia was discussed as were other changes at the expense of Poland.

The extent to which Europe was increasingly one system is open to qualification. Britain and France had intervened in both Baltic and Balkan diplomacy prior to 1714. Russian policy had affected the course of the Thirty Years' War; Louis XIV had sought to place a protégé on the Polish throne in 1696. The principal changes helping to integrate European affairs arose from the actions of eastern, not western, European powers. Contrary to the customary argument that Austria had become a Danubian monarchy as a result of her successes in the war of 1682–97, she made no Balkan gains between 1718 and 1878 with the exception of Dalmatia from Venice (1797 –1805, 1815–) and the small and barren territory of Bukovina from the Turks (1775). Far from pursuing in the Balkans the theme of conquest, Austria was generally more concerned about Russian advances, while in the period 1699–1740 she was more interested in Italy. Her acquisitions from the Spanish inheritance helped to make her a western European power that had inherited from Spain the task of confronting the Bourbons in Italy and the Low Countries, adding it to the already existing conflict for influence in the Empire and for a secure Imperial barrier in the Rhineland. Austria's new role was matched by that of Russia. Her defeat of Swedish and Polish aspirations, her territorial gains from both and the domestic weakness of both powers helped to destroy their role as buffers between Russia and the other European states. The new Russian diplomatic and military range was amply demonstrated in the 1710s and it ensured that resistance to her pretensions and power would have to involve other states. The weakness of Sweden and Poland helped, for example, to increase Prussian concern about Russia and thus ensured that powers that wished to benefit from Prussia or prevent Prussian action had to consider Russian views.

However, these relationships should not be exaggerated. Though power blocs were created by for example the Anglo-French alliance of 1716 and the Austro-Russian pact a decade later, there was a marked willingness to consider self-interest. Alliances were generally weak even if long-lasting and powers that were forced to rely on them were swiftly disabused as Austria was in the War of the Polish Succession and France in that of the Austrian Succession. Europe could act as a system when, in some circumstances, powers felt it necessary and were able to influence distant allies but, in general, the striking feature is the extent to which such influence was not only episodic but also ineffective unless it reflected shared views.

War Against Islam, 1714–39

Having defeated the Russian challenge in 1711, the Turks next sought to regain from Venice the Peloponnese, the most resented of the losses at Karlowitz. In 1714 they declared war and in the following year they overran the Peloponnese, the Venetian garrisons of which enjoyed scant support from the predominantly Orthodox population. The Venetians turned for help to the Austrians but, aside from mutual hostility arising from Venetian opposition to Austrian dominance in Italy, the Austrians were more concerned about possible trouble with Spain. Furthermore, a Turkish embassy assured the Austrians in May 1715 that the Turks had no wish to attack Austria. Austrian attitudes changed when the death of Louis XIV on 1 September 1715 freed them from the fear of united Bourbon action and when Turkish success led to the prospect of an invasion of Venetian Dalmatia that might endanger the Austrian position in Croatia. Unlike in 1682, the Austrians were confident of a short and successful war and willing to fight without a major ally. In April 1716 the Turks were presented with an ultimatum demanding the return of their conquests from Venice and, on their failure to comply, Austria declared war in May. The Turkish army was crushed at Petrovaradin and the Grand Vizier killed, and Temesvar, the last major Turkish fortress north of the Danube, was captured. Having ignored Turkish attempts for an armistice, the following year (1717) Eugene besieged Belgrade and in August defeated the Turkish relief army and captured the city. This spectacular success seemed to justify hopes of major conquests and to inspire new ones, including replacing the Turks in Moldavia and Wallachia, a move that would have closed the Balkans to Russia. However, there was little of the crusading spirit in Austrian ministerial circles. In 1716 appeals for liberation from Macedonia and Montenegro had been slighted. Eugene was more concerned to consolidate the Austrian frontier and dissuade the Turks from the idea of reconquering Hungary. Furthermore, the successful Spanish invasion of Sardinia awakened fears that the rest of Austrian Italy would be attacked. Turkish proposals for negotiations were therefore heeded. Austrian pressure for a peace that would give them all of Serbia and the Bosnian fortresses was defeated by the Turkish insistence on *uti possidetis*, a principle that was also extended to Venice. As a result the peace of Passarowitz of July 1718 gave Austria the Banat of Temesvar, Little (western) Wallachia and northern Serbia. The Venetians lost the Peloponnese but their successful defence of Corfu in 1717 maintained their position in the Adriatic. The Venetian-Turkish frontier was thus stabilized for the rest of the century. The Turks were to control Greece but not the Adriatic. Similarly though the Austro-Turkish war of 1737–9 was to alter the frontier, the essentials of the Austro-Turkish settlement were now clear. The Habsburgs were to rule the Hungarian plains but not the Balkan mountains. The crucial area of tension on the frontier between Christendom and Islam was not to be the Adriatic or the Balkans but the northern shores of the Black Sea.

If Austro-Turkish relations were relatively easy from 1718 the same was not true of Russo-Turkish relations. This was due not to any revival of Peter's hopes of Balkan conquest but to the clashing interests of the two powers in Persia (Iran).

Persia was scarcely part of Europe but, in so far as there was a European international system, it was affected by the unpredictable and fast-changing developments in the 'sub-system' of Persia, Turkey and Russia. The volatility of eighteenth-century international relations and the major issues that could be at stake were amply illustrated by events in Persia. Whereas the Spanish empire had become the target of competing powers because of dynastic factors and the Great Northern War arose through an alliance to despoil Sweden, Russo-Turkish competition over Persia was a consequence of a collapse of power provoked by another outside force, an Afghan invasion. In 1722 Peter I advanced into the region to see what he could gain and to block the Turks from the Caspian. Darband and Resht were occupied in 1722, Baku in 1723 and in September 1723 Shah Tahmasp was persuaded to yield the provinces along the southern and western shores of the Caspian. The Russians promised to aid Tahmasp in pacifying Persia and defeating the Afghans. The shah however, did not ratify the treaty, while Russian gains were in a traditional area of Turkish interest and the Turks advanced to benefit from Persian weakness. In June 1724 the Turks accepted, by the Treaty of Constantinople, Peter's proposal for a partition. Peter recognized Turkish occupation of Georgia and a number of Persian provinces, which the Turks had had to renounce in 1639, while the Turks accepted the Russian gains from their 1723 treaty. Both agreed that if the shah refused to accept the terms, they could seize their allocated territories by force. Due to his failure to accept those allocated to the Turks, they attacked Persia in 1724–5. Initial Turkish successes which worried the Russians were followed, after a period of instability in Persia, by the emergence of a capable military leader, Tamas Kuli Khan (later known as Nadir Shah) and a Persian revival. By the Treaty of Rescht of 1729 the Russians promised to withdraw from some of their conquests and they were threatened with the loss of the rest unless they provided assistance against the Turks. Unwilling to fight the Persians and disillusioned by the cost of retaining their unhealthy Caspian provinces, the Russians signed another Treaty of Resht in 1732 by which they agreed to evacuate most of Peter's gains.

However, the crucial struggle was not that involving the Russians, but the Turko-Persian war. In 1730 Tamas captured Hamadan, in 1732 the Turks lost Tabriz and in 1733 their army was defeated at Baghdad. The Russian goal of keeping the Turks from the Caspian was achieved by Tamas. The Turkish commitment, and their defeats, made fears of Turkish attack in, for example, Italy and Malta in 1723 unfounded, plans by European diplomats to turn the Turks against Austria and/or Russia impracticable. The British and French worked to this end in the late 1720s and the French sought to engage Turkish attention in the cause of Louis XV's father-in-law, Stanislaus Leszczynski, as the next king of Poland. Persian affairs, however, prevented any Turkish commitment either before the outbreak of the War of the Polish Succession in 1733 or during the war itself which was begun by a Russian invasion of Poland. A Turkish complaint in April 1733 about apparent Russian intentions towards Poland was forwarded to St Petersburg by the Russian envoy, Nepluiev, with the assurance that the Turks were in no position to intervene. When in August 1733 the Turks reminded Nepluiev of Peter I's promise not to intervene militarily in Poland, he reported that their willingness to act would depend on peace with Persia. However, Tamas Kuli Khan, after whom an English racehorse was named, rejected all Turkish peace proposals. European diplomats generally presented Turkish policy as arising from Byzantine court intrigues, Villeneuve, the French envoy, writing in 1735, 'it is difficult to base a solid system on Turkish intentions; changes are too frequent there and government maxims are not followed consistently enough for there to be any certainty'.[2]

Such comments were the common response of diplomats throughout Europe faced by the difficulties of assessing court policies and intrigues. Villeneuve suffered because he hoped to benefit from Turkish concern about Poland when the Turks were engaged against Persia and seeking to influence events in Poland but only by diplomatic means. In 1734 a special Russian envoy encouraged Persia to reject all Turkish peace proposals and the Russians provided the Persians with siege engineers. War did break out between Russia and Turkey but it was over the unsettled frontier in the Caucasus rather than Poland and it began not in 1733, when it would have helped Stanislaus, but in 1735. Neither power planned for a major conflict and both had responded in 1733–4 to what were regarded as provocative actions by the other without fighting. Far from following a 'forward' policy of aggression towards its Islamic neighbours, the Russians, by the treaty of Gence of March 1735, had returned Baku and Derbent to Persia and recognized Persian suzerainty over the Daghestan region of the eastern Caucasus. The Turks responded by ordering the Crimean Tatars to assert the Turkish claim to Daghestan, a move that would take them through Kabardia, an area claimed by Russia, and that would repeat a step which had led to clashes in 1733. The Russians, unwilling to accept the Turkish claim to Daghestan and convinced that the Turks would not support the Tatars militarily, believed it necessary to help the Persians in order to prevent them settling with the Turks and either uniting against Russia or allowing the Turks to re-establish themselves on the Caspian.

Thus, far from there being any confident Russian plan for a long-term war to drive the Turks from Europe, consideration of the Russian situation in 1735 reveals anxiety over the views of others, uncertainty over Russia's response and the defensive mentality that had led to a refusal to provide assistance for Vakhtang VI of Georgia in his struggle with the Turks in 1724–5, and to the

[2] Bibliothèque Nationale, Nouvelles Acquisitions Françaises, 6834 f. 58.

withdrawal from Persia. A lack of Russian preparation ensured that the attempt to seize Azov in order to block the Tatars from expanding into Kabardia was unsuccessful in 1735. The following year the Russians seized Azov and attacked the Crimea but these were insufficient to persuade Tamas Kuli-Khan, who made himself shah in 1736, to continue his war with the Turks or to refuse a peace with them unless it included the Russians, as he had originally wished. The Turks refused to yield the latter point but their willingness to offer terms reflecting the Persian military advantage led to the Treaty of Erzeum of 28 September 1736. The Russians therefore found that the favourable position they had enjoyed in 1724–35, under which they had essentially benefited from the conflict between Turkey and Persia while not having to commit themselves heavily, had disintegrated. Nadir Shah devoted 1737–9 to war with the Afghans and an invasion of India, conquering Kandahar, Ghazni, Kabul, Peshawar and crossing the Indus in 1738 and defeating the Mogul army at Karnal in February 1739 before seizing Delhi. Thus the Turkish-Persian peace was maintained sufficiently long to enable the Turks to devote the bulk of their resources to resisting Russia and Austria.

Deprived of Persian assistance, the Russians devoted greater attention to ensuring that Austria, their ally since 1726, entered the war. In 1730 they had reached an agreement that if the Turks declared war on one of the allies, the other would consider itself at war. Though exhausted by the War of the Polish Succession (1733–5), the Austrians feared the loss of their only surviving major ally. In January 1734 the Austrians rejected suggestions of joint action against the Turks but felt it necessary to promise assistance if necessary. In February 1736 they urged the Russians not to begin any war until the peace with France was ratified and Poland stabilized. Russia, however, declared war on Turkey on 12 April 1736 and fought the first campaign alone. In October the Austrians promised to honour their alliance commitments in what they hoped would be a short war. Venice and Augustus III of Poland refused to provide assistance and the first Austrian campaign achieved little. Meanwhile, to the concern of the Austrians, Russian ambitions had expanded. Veshniakov, their envoy in Constantinople, had suggested an invasion of Moldavia and Wallachia and an advance as far as Adrianople. In unsuccessful negotiations at Nemirov in 1737 the Russians demanded the annexation of the Crimea and the Kuban, free trade for the Russians throughout the Turkish empire and the bringing of Moldavia and Wallachia under Russian protection. The terms were rejected by the Turks and the Austrians. They were anyway too optimistic. Though the Russians under General Münnich took Ochakov on the Bug in 1737, logistical problems hindered both this campaign and the 1738 attempt to invade Moldavia and Wallachia. In 1739 they were more successful capturing the Moldavian capital of Jassy, but the Austrians had followed their unsuccessful campaign of 1738 with a disastrous one in 1739. French mediation ended the conflict by the Treaty of Belgrade, Austria ceding to Turkey besieged Belgrade, Little Wallachia and northern Serbia. Russia gained some of the southern steppe and was allowed to retain an unfortified

Azov, while the Russian merchants were given freedom of trade in the Turkish empire. However, she still lacked a coastline on the Black Sea and was not permitted merchantmen or warships on it. Though Münnich opposed the terms, they were accepted by Russia at the end of 1739 and unresolved articles and border demarcations were resolved by May 1741.

Turkey was not to fight Russia and Austria again until 1768 and 1788 respectively. Opponents of Austria and Russia attempted on a number of occasions, but without success, to inspire a Turkish attack on them, the British diplomat, Joseph Yorke writing in 1753, 'If France and Prussia could draw the Turk upon the two empresses, that would change the scene, but Mahomet seems to be too good a Christian just at present, to give into those unjust and ambitious projects.'[3] Four years earlier the crown princess of Sweden, urging her brother Frederick II to form a league to balance that of Austria, listed Turkey as one of the potential members, alongside Prussia, Sweden, France, Spain, Sardinia, Denmark and Saxony. The mid-century, therefore, represented a clear break from the period that lasted from the early 1680s until 1739. However, rather than assuming that it represented a turning away from a long-term ambition to conquer lands from the Turks, it is more accurate to note the short-term causes of the individual conflicts, the responses to particular opportunities and fears that they represented. Although it was attractive for contemporaries to construct the image of a system whose nature and workings would be measured and predicted, often mechanically, and which was characterized by long-term, because 'natural', goals, it is apparent that the rulers and ministers of even the major powers felt themselves forced to respond to a number of challenges within the context of domestic and international problems that could not be predicted. An assessment of the wars against the Turks suggest that it is essential to consider Persia as part of the 'system'. When in the early 1740s Austria turned to meet the challenges arising from the succession of Maria Theresa and Russia to confront a Swedish attack and a contested succession, the Turks had to face the revival of their conflict with Persia which lasted until 1748, including a major siege of Mosul in 1743. The attempts of the Swedish envoy to turn the Turks against Russia rather than Persia were unsuccessful. Any account of European international relations in the period would necessarily depend on the perspective adopted but the striking feature of accounts of the mid-century is how they generally omit the role of Persia and neglect the importance of Balkan peace.

Poland and the Baltic 1721–55

In the last years of his reign Peter I consolidated his powerful position in the Baltic and eastern Europe. The collapse of the plan of 1720–1 for a grand coalition aimed to drive him from the Baltic did not prevent other anti-Russian initiatives, such as the Treaty of Charlottenburg between George I

[3] BL. Add. 35363 f. 324.

and Frederick William I in 1723, but it made it unlikely that a united anti-Russian front could be created among the other north and east European powers and this gave Peter opportunities for diplomatic initiatives. In February 1724 the Russo-Swedish Treaty of Stockholm provided a defensive alliance but also an agreement for common action to return Schleswig to the duke of Holstein. This helped to drive the two Scandinavian powers apart and Scandinavian unity was to form as unrealistic a goal as the hopes of common action by the native-ruled Italian powers. However, though the hopes of united anti-Russian action had proved deceptive and though Russia militarily dominated its neighbours, she was not to be free of anxiety on their count during the quarter century after the death of Peter in 1725. Concern about the possibility that an unfriendly king of Poland would articulate anti-Russian tendencies in her borderlands, especially the Ukraine, led to intervention in the Polish crown election in 1733 helping to cause the War of the Polish Succession. Attempts to prevent hostile Swedish moves by manipulating Swedish politics were unsuccessful and in 1741 Sweden attacked Russia, which was fortunately for her no longer at war with Turkey. The Russian victory was followed by the adoption of the same method that had been used for Poland, sponsorship of a monarch who would, it was hoped, act as a protégé. In Poland Russian money and troops had helped Augustus III of Saxony to succeed his father. In Sweden the favoured candidate was a member of the house of Holstein-Gottorp, Adolf Frederick, though he rapidly proved a disappointment to his sponsor the Tsarina Elizabeth.

It would, however, be misleading to present the history of the region in terms of a struggle to enhance or restrict Russian power. That would suggest a unity and consistency of purpose that was lacking, not least in Russia. Indeed one of the most interesting features of the period is the extent to which policy was debated in Russia, Sweden and Poland, though the domestic constitutional, political and institutional nature of the debates varied greatly. Within Russia there were a number of overlapping struggles: that of westernizers, concerned to protect the legacy of Peter I, against Old Russ; disputes between those who thought attention should be concentrated in particular geographical directions; quarrels over the succession that reflected the absence of a clear succession law and the failure of any ruler until Catherine II to leave a son to succeed; and bitter ministerial disputes. These disputes were both the despair of foreign envoys seeking favourable action on the part of Russia and an opportunity for others to seek to influence Russian politics and policies. The British envoy complained about the advice Elizabeth was receiving in 1744, 'There are those about her that tell her, that the affairs of Europe do not in the least relate to her. The Russian nobility, nation and clergy really think so, that they are too powerful to be attacked in their own dominions, and that it is a matter quite indifferent to this Empire what passes in the rest of Europe'.[4] However, though to outsiders Russian politics and policy often

[4] *Shornik Imperatorskago Russkago Istorickeskago Obschestva* 102 (St Petersburg, 1898) pp. 108–9.

appeared foolish and too easily manipulated, Russian rulers and ministers generally had a better appreciation of their varied territorial commitments than diplomats who tended to see Russian commitments in a narrower focus. Russian policy was more cautious than many hoped or feared. This was not simply due to the replacement of Peter by more hesitant and domestically weaker successors. Peter himself had been less bold than his image: in the 1710s he had not invaded Skåne or resisted militarily the attempts to make him withdraw from Mecklenburg and Poland. His naval demonstrations against Denmark on behalf of Charles Frederick of Holstein-Gottorp in the early 1720s went no further. This was equally true of his widow and successor Catherine I (1725–7). In 1726 a request from the duke of Mecklenburg for the assistance of Russian troops was rejected. Catherine firmly supported Holstein claims to Schleswig but was thwarted by an absence of Swedish support, Danish firmness and a British naval demonstration in the Baltic. This was a failure of brinkmanship and intimidation, as there is little evidence of serious military preparations for war.

However, this Baltic dispute helped to affect other negotiations involving Russia. The collapse of the anti-Russian plan of 1720–1 had been followed by such negotiations as other powers sought to derive some benefit from Russia's rise. These became more serious as a consequence of the diplomatic revolution of 1725, the Austro-Spanish Alliance of Vienna, and the response, the Anglo-French-Prussian Alliance of Hanover of that year. Though French unwillingness to guarantee Russia's Baltic and Turkish border was very important, a major restriction on French attempts to improve relations from the early 1720s was her alliance with George I, who had had no diplomatic relations with Russia since 1719. George's commitment to Danish control of Schleswig served in the mid-1720s to articulate anti-Russian action rather as his earlier commitment to the return of Sweden's Baltic provinces had done. If concern about Russia's Baltic objectives helped to embitter Anglo-Russian relations, the Russians in 1725–6 were more concerned about Turkish pressure on Persia and the possibility of war with Turkey, a prospect that made an alliance with Austria necessary. By the treaty of 1726 Russia was guaranteed Austrian support in the event of a Turkish attack.

Russian support was valuable to Austria as it helped to gain the alliance of Prussia and Saxony. In January 1730, Charles VI requested the dispatch of 30,000 Russian troops and, though they were not sent, hopes and concern about them led foreign commentators to follow carefully the political disputes that followed the death of Peter II (1727–30) and the accession of Tsarina Anna (1730–40). The Swedes revived their hopes of a reconquest of the Baltic provinces but Anna was able to impose strong government and the alliance with Austria was reaffirmed. This helped to lead Frederick William I of Prussia to reject British diplomatic approaches. Thus, the Russo-Austrian-Prussian bloc created in 1726 and based on the Russo-Austrian alliance lasted. It helped to bring stability to eastern Europe and to limit the influence of western

European powers. Though Frederick William was not always happy with the policies of Russia and Austria, and was to be particularly offended by their support for a Saxon succession in Poland, he did not oppose the alliance. In contrast, his son, Frederick II's, defiance of it, his attempts to dissolve or counteract it and the responses of Austria and Russia were the fundamental causes of instability in eastern Europe from 1740.

The unwillingness of any of the powers to push their disputes to the point of hostilities in the late 1720s and the strength of the Austrian-Russian alliance ensured that proposals for action that would weaken the allies, such as Anglo-French supported moves by Sweden or Turkey, were not pressed. 1722–31 was also a decade of peace in Europe because Austria-Russia did not use their military superiority for aggressive purposes. Indeed when Frederick William planned an attack on Hanover in late 1729 he was discouraged by the refusal of his allies to provide assistance. Russian strength and the absence of any Russian territorial pretensions kept the peace in the Baltic, not any system of collective security. Russian unwillingness to accept any limitation of her power within her sphere of interest was demonstrated in 1726 when force was used to reverse the election of Maurice of Saxe, one of Augustus II's numerous illegitimate progeny, as duke of Courland. However, a willingness to compromise elsewhere was revealed in the negotiations with Christian VI of Denmark that led to the Treaty of Copenhagen of May 1732. This guaranteed the European possessions of the two states and provided for Danish compensation for the Holstein claims to Schleswig, settling for the while the Holstein issue. This ended the tension between the two powers and helped to leave both Russia and Denmark as powers concerned to preserve the *status quo* in the Baltic, thus isolating Sweden.

The Treaty of Copenhagen was a prominent example of the strengthening of the Austro-Russian bloc that occurred in 1731–2. In 1731 Austria gained the alliance of Britain and Spain without losing that of any power. Improved Anglo-Russian relations followed the Anglo-Austrian treaty of 1731. French diplomacy sought to challenge the new arrangements, but the only apparent threat to the Russian position in eastern Europe was the Polish succession. In 1730 the Austrians accepted a Russian proposal for joint action on the basis of the exclusion of Stanislaus and support of the future Augustus III only if he was willing to accept conditions. They subsequently suggested a Portuguese prince but in 1733, when Augustus died, pressed Russia to support the Saxon candidate. The Russian General Münnich, who supported better Franco-Russian relations, explained to the French envoy, Magnan, that Stanislaus was an unacceptable candidate because of his French and Swedish connections. In their discussions with Magnan, Russian ministers stressed Stanislaus's treaty with Charles XII for the reconquest of former Polish territories. For these men there was no compartmentalization of history, based on notions such as the Rise of Russia, or on chronological divisions such as the Baltic after the Great Northern War. Instead Russian views were made clear by the draft treaty offered to Augustus in the summer of 1733 which included a reciprocal guarantee of possessions, a renewal of all Polish-Russian treaties, and a promise that Augustus would not alter the Polish constitution.

However, the Polish Convocation Diet of May 1733 voted to exclude all foreign princes from the Election Diet. On 29 June the Russian Council decided to use force to prevent Stanislaus's election. They had still not fixed on an alternative candidate but their determination to prevent any strengthening of the bases for a possible future coalition of France, Sweden, Poland and Turkey was clear. In mid July the Russian forces were ordered to invade on 8–12 August, before the Election Diet, and an agreement was reached with Augustus. Stanislaus was elected in Warsaw before the arrival of Russian forces but, capturing the city, they had Augustus elected king on 5 October. The Russian step aroused outrage elsewhere, being seen as a clear infringement of Polish liberties. Count Gustaf Bonde, a Swedish Councillor of State, told the French envoy that 'if the Russians succeed in Poland, the same danger will menace Sweden all too closely, and that he would not give five pence to live under their form of government and to have their liberty'.[5] However, outrage elsewhere was no more helpful to the Poles than it was to be at the time of the First Partition. Though the Swedes discussed sending troops to Poland a proposal to accept French subsidies to this end was rejected. The Poles proved unable to challenge the Russians successfully in the field and a small French force sent to relieve besieged Danzig in 1734 was easily defeated. The Russians were able to send troops to the assistance of Austria in 1735 and the provision in the peace treaty that Augustus should be recognized as king of Poland caused no surprise. The peace was accompanied by no Russian territorial acquisitions for the Russians appreciated that that would compromise their effective protectorate over Poland and was in no way necessary for any Russian goals.

From the mid 1730s Poland did not present a serious problem for Russia for several decades. Instead Sweden and Prussia attracted concern and the combination of the two at the end of the 1740s challenged Russian dominance of the Baltic. In 1735 this dominance had appeared clear. Denmark acknowledged Russia's right to the Baltic provinces by the Treaty of Copenhagen (1732), the War of the Polish Succession installed a Russian protégé in Poland, thus ensuring continued control over Courland, and in 1735 the Russo-Swedish treaty of 1724 was renewed, with the exception of the Holstein article, for a further twelve years. As a result the French refused to ratify a subsidy convention with Sweden that had been negotiated earlier that year.

However, this apparently pro-Russian step of the ministry of Count Horn in Sweden helped to lead to his fall at the Diet of 1738 when his rivals, increasingly known as the party of the Hats after the French *Tricorne* which its younger members wore, used anti-Russian sentiment to achieve domestic power. A French subsidy treaty of December 1738 precluded Sweden from concluding any other alliance without first notifying France and led to

[5] AE. CP. Suède 172. f. 223.

Russian fears of a French-financed Swedish naval build-up. In 1739 a French squadron appeared in the Baltic and the Russians were aware of Swedish attempts to obtain Polish help in the event of war. The Swedes hoped that the Turks would make the return of the Baltic provinces a goal. Conflict was delayed by the Russian willingness to ratify the Treaty of Belgrade, and thus end their war with Turkey, and by French attempts to maintain the peace but that did not prevent the Hats from envisaging a war that would bring major territorial changes. In 1739 it was hoped that the dispatch of troops to Finland would persuade the Russians to yield Viborg, Ingria and St Petersburg. In 1741 it was hoped that war would bring the return of all the Baltic provinces and the gain of the territory between Lake Ladoga and the White Sea. Political tension within Russia following the death of Anna in 1740 helped to encourage the Swedes to attack in 1741. Peter I's daughter Elizabeth promised concessions in return for Swedish support for her plans for a coup. The French, hoping to prevent Russia from helping Austria, then attacked by Frederick II, encouraged the attack. The discovery that the opposition grouping known as the Caps – after the epithet 'Night-caps' applied to them by critics who accused them of inertia – had suggested a Russian occupation of Swedish-ruled Finland for their domestic ends, helped to lead to a declaration of war in July 1741. The invading Swedes issued a manifesto in support of Elizabeth who in November carried out a coup against the infant Ivan VI.

Negotiations in which she refused the cession of any territory were followed in 1742 by a Russian manifesto urging the Finns to establish an independent state to serve as a buffer between Russia and Sweden, a successful Russian invasion of Finland and the capitulation of the Swedish army, at the end of one of the most decisive campaigns of the century.

In 1741 the Russian ambassador in Stockholm had advised that Russia would never be secure until she annexed Finland and attained her 'natural frontier' on the Gulf of Bothnia but, as with Poland, territorial gains were not the prime objective in the negotiations that led to the Treaty of Åbo of August 1743. Instead the Swedish succession was the central issue of Baltic diplomacy in the years from 1743. In the treaty Finland was returned to Sweden with the exception of Karelia which created a stronger defensive shield around St Petersburg, and the Nystad clause giving Russia the right to prevent changes in Sweden's constitution was dropped. Frederick I of Sweden had no legitimate children and Elizabeth saw this as an opportunity and a danger. Christian VI of Denmark hoped to secure the election of his eldest son in order to restore the Union of Kalmar, the Swedo-Danish dynastic union of 1397 –1523. There was support for this within Sweden and in March 1743 the Danish crown prince was elected by the peasant estate. Christian VI promised Danish help in the reconquest of Finland. The upper Estates, however, held back, the nobles fearing an alliance of the peasantry and strong monarchy on the Danish model. Elizabeth, as a condition of the lenient peace, insisted that the Swedes elect as successor Adolf Frederick, cousin and heir of her nephew and adopted heir Charles Peter of Holstein-Gottorp, the future Peter III. The prospect of Holsteiners in Russia and Sweden, and Adolph Frederick's refusal to give up any claims on Schleswig-Holstein that he might inherit, led Christian VI to prepare an invasion of Sweden in 1743. He was dissuaded when it became clear that he would receive no foreign support and when the Russians, in response to Swedish appeals, sent 12,000 troops in the autumn of 1743. These remained in Sweden until the following summer and in 1745 she signed a new defensive alliance with Russia.

Her success in Sweden encouraged Elizabeth to support plans for an offensive alliance against Frederick II of Prussia, but her position was swiftly eroded by Adolf Frederick's refusal to act as a protégé, a course that was encouraged by his 1744 marriage to the dynamic sister of Frederick and her sponsorship of the Hats. Russian pressure on Adolf Frederick and their attempt in 1746 to secure the overthrow of the Hats were unsuccessful and in 1747, despite Russian protests, defensive alliances were concluded with France and Prussia. Prusso-Swedish co-operation against Russia had been a French goal since the mid-1730s. The Russian Chancellor Bestuzhev accordingly laid plans in 1748 for a war to overthrow the Hats, depose Adolf Frederick and possibly establish Finland as an autonomous duchy. In 1749 the Russians revived the Nystad clause relating to the Swedish constitution. Danish, Austrian and, in particular, British unwillingness to support Russian action, which in light of French and Prussian backing for Sweden would cause a major war, led the Russians in August 1749 to decide not to act. Russian attempts to win the support of Denmark, successful in 1746–8, were blocked when in 1749 French good offices secured a settlement of the Holstein-Gottorp issue by which Adolf Frederick agreed to renounce his claim and to accept an exchange of the territories for Oldenburg and Delmenhorst, Danish possessions in north-western Germany. The betrothal of Adolphus's son Gustavus and a Danish princess followed in 1751. The Hats abandoned any idea of supporting constitutional changes on the succession of Adolf Frederick and Russia was given assurances to that effect in 1749. As a result Adolf Frederick succeeded peacefully in 1751 and Elizabeth turned her attention to Frederick II.

Baltic affairs in the decades after Nystad have not received much attention in general works on eighteenth-century international relations. They were clearly less central than in the late 1710s and less far-reaching in their consequences than in the late 1700s, but it would be a mistake to assume that they were inconsequential, predictable or controlled by non-Baltic powers. Instead they reflected the uneasy relationship of local and distant influences that characterized all of European diplomacy and indicated the continued importance of dynastic factors and the unwillingness to accept the settlements of 1713–21 that was to help lead Sweden to attack Prussia in the Seven Years' War.

The Italian Question 1714–52

There was no war between any of the signatories of the peace treaties ending the Great Northern War for 20 years. In contrast hostilities broke out in Italy in 1717, with the Spanish invasion of Sardinia, only four years after the Peace of Utrecht. There was war in Italy in 1717–20, 1733–5 and 1741–8, and tension for the remainder of the period down to 1748. This was essentially due to the fact that whereas in the Baltic the power that was dissatisfied with the *status quo* was Sweden, in the case of Italy both Austria and Spain were dissatisfied and the satisfied powers were the weak, small Italian states, such as Venice, that had nothing to gain from change. The prizes offered by the anticipated extinction of local dynasties, the Medici grand dukes of Tuscany and the Farnese dukes of Parma, which ended in the male line in 1731 and 1737 respectively, exacerbated the dispute between the major powers for Philip V sponsored the claims of Don Carlos born in January 1716, his eldest son by his second marriage to Elizabeth Farnese, while Charles VI sought to exercise jurisdiction over both territories as imperial fiefs. The conflicts and diplomacy of the period were to result in the transfer of control over more than half of Italy, mostly with no attention to the wishes of local rulers or inhabitants. Italian rulers did seek through diplomatic means to advance and defend their interests but they were generally unsuccessful. Cosimo III of Tuscany sought support in 1710 for the eventual re-establishment of republican government before deciding to support the succession of his daughter after that of his childless sons. In 1713 the latter was decreed and recognized by the Senate of Florence and the Council of Two Hundred but Cosimo was to have less success in achieving international guarantees for his daughter than Charles VI, who rejected Cosimo's claim in 1714. Charles's daughter Maria Theresa was to find these guarantees of limited value but Charles, unlike Cosimo, did not have to face the allocation of his territories to others being decided during his lifetime. In 1716 Cosimo chose the Este family of Modena as the successors to his daughter, hoping for a union of the territories. If Cosimo's wishes were ignored, so also were those of other Italian rulers. Charles VI refused to recognize Victor Amadeus II as king of Sicily, in the treaty of Rastatt refused to guarantee the integrity of his possessions, and in 1716 sent troops into Novi in the Republic of Genoa in furtherance of a border dispute. The effect of changes of ruler on the local population can be queried and most did not respond. In the case of Naples most opinion was loyal to Spain until the death of Charles II and accepted the succession of Philip V, though there was an abortive coup in favour of the Austrians in 1701. There was no opposition to the Austrian conquest of 1707. The old Spanish loyalists had some adjusting to do in relation to the coup attempt of 1701, but managed this quite successfully and there was no major change of regime or personnel. Pragmatism was matched by a consistent wish to secure as much autonomy as possible for the Kingdom of Naples and its elite under whoever came to be king. Full independence was not anticipated and its advent in 1734 was unexpected; the point was to avoid complete, direct subordination to an oppressive monarch.

This was not, however, the objective for independent Italian rulers but their limited room for manoeuvre was indicated by the enforced exchange of Sicily for poorer Sardinia that Victor Amadeus was obliged to accept in November 1718. This satisfied Charles VI's wish to reunite Sicily to the Kingdom of Naples and thus rule all of Spain's former Italian territories. Meaningful resistance came not from Victor Amadeus but from more powerful rulers concerned to keep Charles out of Sicily. Victor Amadeus owed the island to the support of France and, in particular, Britain. A British naval squadron took him there in late 1713, just as another was to escort Don Carlos to Tuscany in 1731. However, George I did not continue the anti-Austrian policies of Anne's Tory ministers while after the death of Louis XIV, Victor Amadeus complained bitterly about the French failure to restrain Austria in Italy. The fate of Sicily swiftly became bound up with Carlos's claims to the Medici and Farnese successions. In the autumn of 1716 James Stanhope, effectively the British foreign minister, devised a scheme of equivalents that was designed to bring peace to Italy and to remedy a major fault of the Utrecht settlement, the failure to satisfy Philip V. Sicily and Sardinia were to be exchanged to the benefit of Charles, while Carlos was to have the reversion of Tuscany and Parma. Philip's claim to an acceptable settlement was increased by his successful invasion of Sardinia in 1717. Anglo-French attempts to mediate won Charles's acceptance of Stanhope's scheme in April 1718 but Philip rejected it and his chief minister, the Parmesan Giulio Alberoni, demanded immediate occupation of the principal Parmesan and Tuscan fortresses by Spanish garrisons as security for Carlos's succession, and also the cession of Sardinia to Spain. Cosimo, who opposed any restriction of his sovereignty, helped to obtain the Austrian rejection of the Spanish garrisons. Victor Amadeus similarly disliked the scheme. The impossibility of creating a powerful league of Italian rulers ensured that he, like Cosimo, had to seek outside help. Alberoni tried to tempt Victor Amadeus to attack the Milanese, but he preferred to seek Austrian support for exchanges, either Sardinia and part of the Milanese or Parma and Tuscany in return for yielding Sicily, or Naples and Sardinia in return for Savoy-Piedmont. Typical of the zeal for rearranging territories, a zeal that was to lead in 1719 to an Austrian plan to divide Parma and Tuscany between the dukes of Modena and Lorraine, Victor Amadeus's proposals reflected the difficulties of small powers. He is best remembered for his remark that Italy was like an artichoke to be eaten leaf by leaf, but his position was far more precarious that this might suggest.

Victor Amadeus's diplomacy was rendered redundant by the unexpected Spanish invasion of Sicily on 1 July 1718, the failure of most Sicilians to support the king and the rapid conquest of most of the island. Spanish fortunes were affected not by Victor Amadeus but by the actions of other powers determined to ensure that changes to the Utrecht settlement took place only with their consent. The British fleet, whose preparation had failed to dissuade the Spaniards from invading, destroyed most of the Spanish fleet off Cape Passaro on 11 August. Meanwhile on 2 August Charles VI had signed a treaty with Britain and France, a treaty mistakenly known as the Quadruple Alliance because the United Provinces did not adhere as anticipated. The treaty provided for an alliance between the powers, a settlement between Charles and Philip in line with the provisions of Utrecht, the exchange of Sicily and Sardinia, and Carlos's reversion to Parma and Tuscany to be guaranteed by Swiss garrisons. Philip refused to accept the terms and sought to effect by means of a plot managed by his ambassador in Paris, the Cellamare conspiracy, the replacement of the pro-British regent, the duke of Orléans, by more sympathetic courtiers led by the duke of Maine. The conspiracy, broken in December 1718, in fact helped to win French domestic support for the declaration of war on Spain, published on 9 January 1719. Britain had declared war the previous month.

The war went badly for Spain. A poorly supplied Austrian force failed to drive the isolated Spaniards from Sicily but their position was weakened by British naval mastery. A French invasion of north-western Spain under James II's illegitimate son the duke of Berwick revealed that Spain could not defend her frontier provinces and the major Spanish attempt to invade Britain on behalf of the Jacobites was defeated by a storm off Cape Finisterre. A smaller force was defeated in Scotland. The British and French appreciated that any lasting settlement would have to satisfy Philip but in November 1719 they agreed with Charles VI to bar Carlos's expectations unless Philip acceded to the Quadruple Alliance within three months. The Duke of Parma persuaded his daughter Elizabeth to have Alberoni dismissed in December 1719, and, after the accession of Victor Amadeus to the Quadruple Alliance on 19 January, Philip acceded on 17 February 1720. This was followed by the development of a Franco-Spanish alignment that led to a convention signed at Madrid on 27 March 1721. This defensive alliance of mutual guarantee stipulated support for the treaties of Utrecht and London (the Quadruple Alliance), promised Franco-Spanish support for the duke of Parma and French backing for Spanish pretensions to Gibraltar and invited Great Britain to accede, which she did by the Triple Alliance of Madrid of 13 June 1721, though without offering a firm promise to return Gibraltar. The alliance was cemented dynastically by the betrothal of Louis XV to Philip's daughter Maria Anna, born in 1718, and by the marriage in January 1722 of Philip's heir Louis to one of Orléans's daughters, a scheme that was less daring than the proposed marriage of Orleans's son to Peter I's daughter, the future Tsarina Elizabeth, and his succession to the Polish throne. Spain hoped to use the new diplomatic alignment to isolate Austria at the peace congress that had been summoned at Cambrai to settle outstanding differences and, in particular, to ensure the substitution of Spanish for Swiss garrisons. Charles VI, in no hurry to make concessions, hoped that delay would divide the new allies. Charles did not concede until December 1723 the letters expectative of eventual investiture of Don Carlos, or his heir, for Tuscany and Parma, which Philip had insisted should be a prerequisite of the opening of the congress. The congress opened the following April but it was stalemated by the Spanish demand for Spanish garrisons and the Austrian request for a guarantee of the Pragmatic Sanction. Charles's attempt to substitute Duke Leopold of Lorraine for Carlos as the eventual successor in Tuscany did not aid matters.

Anglo-French mediation had failed Spain at Cambrai and both powers rejected Spanish proposals for the coercion of Tuscany to establish Carlos's position. As a result, in November 1724, the former Dutch diplomat Jan Willem, Baron van Ripperda, was instructed to go on a secret mission to Vienna to propose the marriage of Carlos and his brother Philip to Charles VI's daughters, which would establish a Bourbon-Farnese claim to the Habsburg inheritance. This improbable scheme, typical of the adventurous dynastic diplomacy of the period that was generally unsuccessful but introduced a powerful element of unpredictability, was helped by Austrian isolation and by a breach in Franco-Spanish relations. After Orléans's death in 1723 the duke of Bourbon had become the chief French minister and in order to weaken the position of his rival and Louis XV's heir, the new duke of Orléans, he sought a speedy marriage for Louis, a policy that ill-health on the king's part lent weight to. Maria Anna was therefore sent back to her parents in March 1725 and Louis married Maria Leszcynski that August. Although France stood by its promises as to Tuscany and Parma for Carlos, Spain broke off diplomatic relations and recalled her plenipotentiaries from Cambrai, the congress dissolving in May 1725. On 30 April Ripperda concluded treaties of peace and defensive alliance at Vienna with Charles VI's ministers, a commercial treaty following on 1 May. The Austrians took advantage of the situation to destroy the Madrid alignment while committing themselves to little. Carlos was granted the reversion of Tuscany and Parma but denied the security of garrisons. He and his brother gained the prospect of Habsburg marriages, while Spain guaranteed the Pragmatic Sanction and granted special privileges to the Ostend Company, a trans-oceanic trading company founded in 1722 that threatened Anglo-Dutch trade to the East Indies.

The treaties and the new alignment created a lot of unease in Britain and France. Bourbon's ministry was concerned about the prospect of Austrian support for Philip V's claim to succeed Louis XV and the British were worried by rumoured secret articles in support of the Jacobite Pretender, fears that were unfounded in so far as the actual Austro-Spanish agreements were concerned. Both powers feared that the challenge to their diplomatic influence represented by the new treaties could force them into making concessions in the myriad of disputes in which they were involved. On 3 September 1725 Britain, France and Prussia signed the Treaty of Hanover guaranteeing each other's territories and rights inside and outside Europe. Austria and Spain responded with a secret treaty of marriage and offensive alliance, signed at Vienna on 5 November 1725. This stipulated a double marriage between Carlos and Philip, and two of Charles's daughters, though stating that the crowns and territories of France, Spain and the Habsburg family would remain forever separate. Philip V promised to provide subsidies to Charles, who agreed to assist in the return of Gibraltar and Minorca to Spain.

Charles, however, did not want war, dynastic union with Spain or the establishment of Carlos in Italy. He concentrated on building up a powerful alliance, gaining the support of Russia and Prussia in 1726 and offered Cosimo III's successor John Gaston a private guarantee of grand-ducal sovereignty. 1725–7 witnessed major military mobilizations. Britain dispatched three large fleets, one to the Baltic to persuade Denmark and Sweden successfully that an accession to the Hanover alliance would not leave them vulnerable to Russia, one to the West Indies to blockade the Spanish treasure fleet and thereby prevent Spain from being able to provide Austria with subsidies, and one to Spanish waters to menace attack and prevent a blockade of Gibraltar. The Spaniards fired the first shots when they began an unsuccessful siege of Gibraltar in February 1727. George I, anxious about Hanoverian vulnerability to Prussian and Austrian attack, persuaded France to move forces towards the Rhine. Throughout the period of tension negotiations had continued between some of the powers of the two alliances. Cardinal Fleury, Louis XV's former tutor, who became his chief minister in 1726, was determined to avoid war and he attempted to restrain the more aggressive British ministry, leading to some British doubts about the degree of his commitment to the alliance. Aware that Austria was less interested in conflict than Spain, Fleury used an ultimatum to persuade Charles to settle. On 31 May 1727 the Preliminaries of Paris, the terms for a pacification of Europe, reaffirming the treaty of the Quadruple Alliance and suspending the trade of the Ostend Company, were signed by the representatives of Britain, France, the United Provinces and Austria. Spain sought to defy the new agreement but lack of Austrian support, the failure to woo France from her British alliance and Philip's ill-health led Spain to settle by the Convention of the Pardo of 6 March 1728. This postponed contentious issues to a congress that opened at Soissons in June 1728 but that proved as unable to settle issues and consequently as much a cause of a new diplomatic alignment as Cambrai had been. The Austrian rejection of Spanish pressure for Carlos's marriage in early 1729 led Spain to settle with Britain and France on condition that they supported Spanish garrisons. It might seem surprising that this apparently relatively minor issue was so important in the diplomacy of the period but for Spain, which had little confidence in international guarantees, they were the only secure basis for Carlos's succession, while for the rest of Europe they were seen not so much as a minor infraction of the Quadruple Alliance, but as a possible means by which Spain might destroy the existing Italian system and launch herself on a career of Italian conquest. The Treaty of Seville of 9 November 1729 settled most outstanding differences between Britain, France and Spain and committed them to accept the Spanish garrisons. The unfounded rumours that secret clauses stipulated the return of Gibraltar, Minorca, Naples and Sicily to Spain were typical of the world of distrust and rumour within which diplomats operated.

Charles refused to be intimidated and as neither the Fleury nor Walpole ministries really wanted to fight, the Seville alliance quickly collapsed into recriminations. An Austrian attempt to link negotiations of the admission of the Spanish garrisons to a guarantee of the Pragmatic Sanction was countered by an Anglo-French insistence that only Charles's Italian dominions could be guaranteed, which Charles rejected. In August 1730 Fleury stated that the Pragmatic would 'disoblige the princes of Italy and the Empire and subject them to a perpetual bondage to the Imperial court', while his foreign minister Chauvelin made it clear to the British and Dutch envoys that he supported the expulsion of the Austrians from Italy. As the French urged the need to plan for a general war in 1731 it was clear that the Anglo-French alliance had become, by the summer of 1730 under the stimulus of Spanish demands, the basis of a possible recasting of the European system tied to the abasement of Austria, which was to become a matter of planning and action, rather than speculation. However, in August the British envoys in Paris noted that 'it never was His Majesty's intention to new model the possessions of Europe, and to make a new distribution of dominions and territories for pleasing the queen of Spain.' Nevertheless, the British did not wish to lose the Spanish alliance and, as a result, when they opened secret unilateral negotiations with the Austrians they insisted on the Spanish garrisons. In the Second Treaty of Vienna of 16 March 1731, Austria, Britain and the United Provinces mutually guaranteed each other's territories and rights and the last two guaranteed the Pragmatic Sanction on condition that the archduchesses should not marry Bourbon or Prussian Princes. As security for Carlos's succession to Parma and Tuscany, 6,000 Spanish troops were to be admitted immediately. Reports of a secret agreement to compel France and Spain to guarantee the Pragmatic Sanction were false.

The British hoped to reconcile France and Spain to the new treaty, creating a new international order based on the Pragmatic Sanction to complement the new Italian order based on the Spanish garrisons. The understandable French refusal destroyed the Anglo-French alliance but the Spaniards rejected French approaches while the Austrians' dismissal of a Spanish attempt to negotiate an alliance excluding Britain and including an archduchess for Carlos was followed by an Anglo-Austrian-Spanish agreement, signed at Vienna on 22 July, recognizing Spain's acceptance of the Second Treaty of Vienna. Three days later, at Florence, Spanish and Tuscan representatives signed a treaty recognizing Carlos as the heir to Tuscany. An Anglo-Spanish fleet convoyed the Spanish troops to Livorno (Leghorn) in October and Carlos, similarly escorted, landed there on 27 December 1731. As the Duke of Parma had died on 20 January 1731 and the pregnancy of his widow, on which Europe's diplomats waited, had been shown to be false, Carlos became the new duke.

France was obviously opposed to the new European order based on the

Anglo-Austrian-Spanish alliance and sought, with some success, to stir up opposition in the Empire. However, even with her German allies, Saxony and Bavaria, she was not in a position to begin a war. Her willingness to attack Austria in 1733 and the extent of her success in the War of the Polish Succession (1733–5) arose from the disintegration of the alliance and the eagerness of Spain to attack Austria. The Bourbon effort was aided by the alliance of Victor Amadeus's heir Charles Emmanuel III. Austrian difficulties stemmed in large part from Italy where British diplomacy had failed to solve differences with Charles Emmanuel over the overlordship of the frontier region of the Langhes and differences with Spain over Carlos's vassalage and the size of the Spanish forces. These issues were serious irritants in a society where rank and recognition were crucial indicators of status and power but it is also clear that Philip and his wife were looking for an opportunity to return Italy to the Spanish sphere of influence. In addition, however critical some commentators might be of their condition and however much their pay might be in arrears, the Spanish armed forces were large while the vigour of Spanish policy had been amply displayed in 1732 when an expedition, having aroused fears of invasion in Austrian Italy, the island of Sardinia and Britain, seized Oran in North Africa.

Spain was too powerful, her ruler too volatile, to be regarded as a client state or a power following predictable policies. It was inappropriate to direct at her threats similar to those that Prince Eugene aimed at Charles Emmanuel III in 1732 when he warned that he shouldn't 'follow the dangerous maxims of his father, which, though may have succeeded hitherto, will . . . one day or other end in the ruin of his family. Since if the court of Turin believes they shall be always skillful enough to take an advantageous party of aggrandizing themselves little by little, according to every exigency, without adhering to one system, or being tied down to any obligation of friendship or engagement, the first power that will be able to do it, whether that of Austria or that of the House of Bourbon will swallow them up.'[6]

A war with Austria might have appeared the obvious policy for Spain once the crisis in Poland made a French attack on Austria likely in 1733 but the Spaniards were willing to consider the revival of the scheme for a marriage between an archduchess and Carlos even as they considered French approaches. The French did not manage to tie the Spaniards in the Treaty of the Escorial, later known as the First Family Compact, until 7 November 1733, after the French declaration of war of 10 October and the beginning of operations by French and Sardinian troops. The Treaty of Turin, signed with Charles Emmanuel on 26 September, provided that Carlos should have Naples and Sicily, Charles Emmanuel the Milanese.

French and Sardinian forces easily conquered the Milanese that winter and in the following summer Carlos conquered Naples, the city falling on 10 May and the Austrian forces being defeated at Bitonto on 25 May in one of the

[6] Robinson to Harrington, 16 September 1732, PRO. SP. 80/90.

most decisive campaigns of the century. Austrian pressure on Britain to send naval assistance in accordance with the Second Treaty of Vienna was evaded with the argument that Charles's role in the Polish dispute was not blameless, though that had little bearing on Spanish operations. On 15 May Carlos published a decree of Philip V ceding his rights in Naples and Sicily to Carlos, who in consequence proclaimed himself king of Naples and appointed his younger brother Philip as heir to Tuscany. Though Charles Emmanuel was already governing the Milanese under the Treaty of Turin, and sought Mantua, still held for Charles VI, Philip V wanted both and his wife thought that Parma, Tuscany, Naples and Sicily should be the inheritance of her sons. To a certain extent such demands were negotiating counters but they also indicated the bold wish to reallocate territories that characterized much of the diplomacy of this period. The wide-ranging schemes of 1741–2 after the death of Charles VI to partition his territories were prefigured in 1733–5 by discussions about the fate of his Italian possessions. In the Anglo-French-Dutch negotiations held at The Hague in the winter in 1734–5 the French pressed for the granting of the Milanese to Charles Emmanuel and of Naples and Sicily to Carlos.

That Charles VI finally obtained better terms in the Preliminary Articles of 3 October 1735 that served as the basis of the Third Treaty of Vienna of 18 November 1738 owed little to his forces. Their attempt to reconquer northern Italy was defeated at Parma on 29 June and Guastalla on 19 September 1734, and in 1735 they were reduced to the defence of Mantua, in which they were aided by serious Sardinian-Spanish differences. However, French determination to beat their allies to a separate peace was aided by their willingness to compromise over Italy. Compromise and equivalents were an integral feature of the treaties of the period but that of 1738 depended on Sardinian weakness and the Spanish inability to continue fighting on her own that led her troops to retreat before the Austrian advance in late 1735 after France and Sardinia had suspended operations. The peace left Carlos with Naples, Sicily and the *presidii* but, in exchange Parma went to Charles and the Tuscan reversion to Duke Francis of Lorraine in return for the acquisition of Lorraine by Stanislaus. As in the Partition Treaties, Italy was required to provide the equivalents and the equalling-out that compensated for gains elsewhere. With the death of John Gaston in July 1737 Francis, who had married Maria Theresa in February 1736, succeeded to Tuscany. Charles Emmanuel had to return the Milanese but his gains included some of it, not least the area around Novara, increasing the vulnerability of what remained with Charles.

Peace did not survive Charles's death and again Spain, seeking to reverse the losses of 1738, played a major role in disrupting it. She supported French attempts to co-ordinate anti-Austrian actions in the Empire signing a subsidy treaty with Charles Albert of Bavaria, the Treaty of Nymphenburg, on 28 May and a treaty with Saxony on 20 September 1741. In Italy in contrast to the previous war Bourbon action was hindered by British naval action, the threat of bombardment forcing Carlos on 18 August 1742 to declare his neutrality in one of the most striking displays of naval effectiveness that century, and by Charles Emmanuel's hesitant decision to gain concessions in the Milanese by alliance with Austria and Britain, rather than opposition to them. Initially he had sided with the anti-Austrian alliance but British pressure on Maria Theresa obtained the promise of Piacenza and part of the Milanese for him by the Treaty of Worms of September 1743. A month later the Second Family Compact committed France to help conquer Milan, Parma and Piacenza for the benefit of Don Philip. Spanish forces occupied Charles Emmanuel's Duchy of Savoy in 1743, holding it for the rest of the war, but Bourbon attempts to storm his Alpine defences failed. The Italian war was far from static. Winning the alliance of Genoa in April 1745, the Bourbons defeated Charles Emmanuel at Bassignano in September, captured Asti, Casale and Milan before the end of the year and signed a secret armistice with Sardinia in February 1746. Keen to expel the Austrians from Italy, the French foreign minister D'Argenson proposed that Charles Emmanuel become king of Lombardy and leader of an Italian federation. D'Argenson's argument that the Italian rulers sought liberty against the excessive and tyrannical power of Austria and that the Bourbons should exploit this was countered by Philip V with the claim that the league was impossible or would take many years to negotiate, that it would depend on Bourbon armed support, that any league required a number of near equal powers which Sardinian power prevented, that Charles Emmanuel would not maintain the projected 'Republic of Sovereigns' but would seek to despoil it, and that he would despoil, not help, Don Philip.[7] The project was rendered academic by Charles Emmanuel's decision to rejoin the Austrians which led in March 1746 to the recapture of Asti, Casale and Milan and to the Austro-Sardinian victory at Piacenza on 16 June 1746, another of the century's decisive battles, The Austro-Sardinian invasion of Provence at the end of the year was a failure. The Austrians did not drive Carlos from Naples as they had hoped and after they had been expelled from captured Genoa by a popular revolt in December 1746 they failed to regain the city. The war and the subsequent peace left the Bourbons dominant in southern Italy and the Habsburgs in the north, though Maria Theresa had to yield Parma and Piacenza to Louis XV's son-in-law Don Philip while Charles Emmanuel gained more of the Milanese.

Unlike the Baltic where the Peace of Aix-la-Chapelle was followed by a serious crisis, Italian politics became relatively quiescent, the British envoy in Turin writing in July 1749, 'everything in these parts is in a perfect state of tranquillity, and indeed almost of lethargy.'[8] However, as in the Empire where the election of Maria Theresa's son as king of the Romans, heir to the Imperial title, was sought, an attempt was made to settle possible future disputes. In the first 'diplomatic revolution' of the 1750s, a treaty of defensive alliance based on Aix-la-Chapelle, was signed between Austria, Sardinia and

[7] AE. CP. Espagne 488 f. 65, 139–41.
[8] PRO. SP. 92/58 f. 150.

Spain. The preliminary articles, signed at Madrid on 14 April 1752 contained reciprocal guarantees for the territorial integrity of Tuscany, Milan, Naples, Sicily, Parma and Sardinia. In the definitive treaty, signed at Aranjeuz on 14 June 1752 Austria, Sardinia and Spain guaranteed each other's Italian possessions, the Emperor, Maria Theresa's husband Francis I, in turn guaranteeing all their possessions as grand duke of Tuscany.

This settlement ended the Italian Question and ensured that Italy was mostly peaceful until the early 1790s. Spain and Austria, their Italian interests secured, were able to turn their attention from Italy, Austria to conflict with Prussia, a partitioning role in Poland and, in the 1780s, renewed conflict with Turkey, Spain to oceanic struggles with Britain. The Italian settlement both helped to ease the path for and was in turn consolidated by the Diplomatic Revolution, the Franco-Austrian alliance of 1756. The treaties of 1752 made it clear that France did not need to oppose Austria in order to win Spanish support, while the alliance of 1756 removed French interest in undermining the Austrian position in Italy. Sardinia's expansionist aspirations were effectively muzzled by the new territorial stability in Italy. France was unwilling to lend support to schemes for gaining territory from the Milanese, no power would support Sardinia in her plans to acquire sections of the Ligurian littoral from Genoa, the pursuit of which in the case of the port of Finale in the 1740s revealed the weakness of the idea that Charles Emmanuel might act as an impartial leader of an Italian league. To a certain extent Italian stability represented a success for the partitioning habit in eighteenth-century international relations. Prior to 1748 partition schemes had been ineffective, because the three major powers capable of intervening effectively in Italian affairs, Austria, France and Spain, had never united to accept any territorial settlement. After 1748 Austria and France turned their attention to the Empire where it proved impossible to devise an acceptable partition between an Austrian and a Prussian sphere of influence. A crucial element in the mid-century change in Italian affairs was dynastic. Philip V's successor Ferdinand VI (1746–59) had little sympathy for his half-brothers, and the Farnese drive to fulfil dynastic claims was both satisfied by the terms of Aix-la-Chapelle and extinguished with the replacement of the meteoric and opportunistic Philip V and Elizabeth Farnese by the more cautious Ferdinand. Ferdinand had no children and his successor, Don Carlos, now Charles III of Spain (1759–88), was no longer primarily interested in Italian questions. The interrelationships of dynastic and geopolitical considerations are difficult to assess but contemporaries had little doubt that the crucial element producing instability in Italy and therefore affecting the diplomacy of all the powers who had interests there in the three decades after Utrecht were the rulers of Spain.

France, the Empire and Britain, 1714–55

The central relationship in western Europe was that between France and Austria. Generally it was one of rivalry and hostility but that did not preclude periods of co-operation, as in 1718–20 and 1736–9, and suggestions that relations might improve. Militarily western Europe was dominated by the armies of the two powers and the most protracted clashes were the wars between them, the Wars of the Polish and Austrian Successions in 1733–5 and 1741–8 respectively. However, though their relationship was the dominant one in the diplomatic and military spheres it was affected by independent initiatives by other powers, particularly Britain, Spain and the leading German powers.

Uneasy Peace 1714–31

Austria, Britain and France all had in common an uncertain dynastic position. Louis XV, who succeeded his great-grandfather in 1715, was born in 1710. He did not marry until 1725 or have a son until 1729 and it was not until the late 1750s that the succession to the throne was firmly assured in his line. The claims of his uncle, Philip V, to the succession placed the regent, the duke of Orléans, who controlled France from 1715 until his death in 1723, in a precarious position and encouraged him to look abroad for allies who could counteract the Spanish threat to intervene if Louis died. Philip doubted the validity of the Utrecht renunciation of his claims to the French throne, which placed Orléans, Louis XIV's nephew, next in line. When in October 1728 Louis XV contracted smallpox, Philip prepared for the seizure of power in France and rumours spread of a possible civil war between his supporters and those of the duke of Orléans, the son of the former Regent. Louis recovered swiftly but the vulnerability of the situation is suggested by the political crisis that affected Russia in early 1730 when the childless Peter II died of smallpox.

The challenge of Jacobitism posed a major problem for successive British governments. It was suggested at the time that the threat of Jacobitism was deliberately exaggerated to discredit the principal opposition group, the Tories, and it had been suggested recently that they were largely free from Jacobitism. Such a view would have found little support from George I (1714–27) and George II (1727–60), both of whom believed that, although individual Tories were loyal and could be trusted, the party as a whole was factious and disloyal. Equally serious was the manner in which hostile rulers could be encouraged to support Jacobitism, and were themselves encouraged in their stance by a belief in the strength of Jacobitism. Jacobite chances were seen to depend on help from European powers.

The only children of the Emperor Charles VI (1711–40) to survive for any length of time were three daughters, the youngest of whom died in 1730 aged four. Charles hoped to secure the undivided succession of his various territories for his eldest daughter Maria Theresa, rather than for Maria Josepha and Maria Amalia, the daughters of his elder brother, Joseph I (1705–11). This, as much as the stipulations of the indivisibility of the inheritance and the reversion to female in the absence of male descendants, was the most troublesome aspect of Charles's promulgation of the Pragmatic Sanction in

1713, which assigned the succession to his own daughters in default of male heirs, and for the first time asserted the indivisibility of the inheritance. Maria Josepha and Maria Amalia, born in 1699 and 1701, were considerably older than Charles's two eldest daughters, Maria Theresa and Maria Anna, born in 1717 and 1718. Charles had a son in 1716 but he died that year. To reinforce the exclusion of the Josephine archduchesses Charles ensured that their marriages were accompanied by solemn renunciations of all claims to the succession. In 1719 the marriage of Maria Josepha and the heir to the electorate of Saxony, the future Augustus III, was preceded by a renunciation sworn to by bride, groom and groom's father. In 1722 the marriage of Maria Amalia to the heir to Bavaria, Charles Albert, was preceded by a similar renunciation. However, both the Saxons and the Bavarians believed that neither the acts of parents nor renunciations could abnegate inalienable rights. In 1725, to fortify the position of the Bavarians, who had only won the younger of the Josephine archduchesses, Charles Albert's father, Max Emmanuel, forged a copy of the Emperor Ferdinand I's will, purportedly awarding them the Austrian hereditary lands upon the extinction of the dynasty's male line. Charles's continued failure to produce a male heir and his efforts to secure European support for the Pragmatic Sanction helped to make the Austrian succession a more critical issue. Under Charles it increasingly dominated Austrian policy, while powers opposed to Austria resorted to the device of encouraging pretensions upon the succession.

These dynastic weaknesses played a major role in the diplomacy of the decades beginning with the Hanoverian succession in 1714. They led the rulers of the three states to seek guarantees of their position, while at the same time providing a possible means for intervention by hostile monarchs. In the case of the Habsburg dominions they offered the possibility of a territorial recasting of central Europe. Within the Empire, Bavaria fostered the development of a close alliance, a *Hausunion*, between the closely related Wittelsbach electors of Bavaria, Cologne, the Palatinate and Trier and made it clear, in response to Anglo-French efforts in 1725–6 to secure their alliance against Austria, that a commitment to Bavarian pretensions was expected.

Dynastic weaknesses were not the only threat to stability. The Utrecht settlements had left a number of issues unsettled and several rulers unsatisfied and, although the principal sphere of tension was Italy, this affected other powers because of their interests there and their concern about how changes would affect the rest of Europe. A bigger cause of change was the very coming of peace. This dissolved wartime coalitions and created opportunities for new alliances. Within four years of the peace Louis XIV was to approach Charles VI for better relations, Orléans to negotiate an alliance with George I. The French approach to Charles was a tentative one, due in part to Austro-Spanish differences in Italy, stressing common Catholicism, and designed to limit the possibility of Anglo-Austrian action against France. The accession of George I in August 1714 and the replacement of the Tory ministry by a Whig one threatened a reversal of the Austrian isolation that had obliged her to accept the Utrecht settlement, and forced Louis XIV to reconsider his diplomatic position. Because the Whigs had bitterly opposed the Utrecht settlement and played a major role in ensuring the parliamentary rejection of Bolingbroke's plan for improving Anglo-French commercial relations, many assumed in 1714 that the accession of George I and the fall of the Tories would lead to poor relations with France, if not war. The French feared that the new Whig ministry would provoke a conflict, while in Britain French action in support of the Jacobites was believed imminent. Relations between the two countries were very poor in late 1714 and early 1715. The French failure to wreck the harbour of the privateering base at Dunkirk, as stipulated at Utrecht, had already caused tension between the Tory ministry and France. The issue was pressed with vigour by the new Whig government, the French being told that relations depended on a satisfactory settlement of the issue. In itself the destruction of the sluices that prevented the harbour of Dunkirk from silting up was not of great importance, but it was seen as an indication of French willingness to obey and British ability to enforce the provisions of Utrecht. Furthermore, it provided a concrete instance by which French professions of good intentions, in particular in refusing to support the Jacobites, could be judged.

Anglo-French relations reflected negotiations with other powers and cannot be approached simply as a bilateral matter. At first the Whig ministry sought to recreate the Grand Alliance with Austria and the United Provinces, but their failure to do so, which was due in part to strong differences between the Dutch and the Austrians over the Austrian Netherlands, cleared the path towards better Anglo-French relations, a course that the Dutch supported. Had the attempt satisfied Charles's views in Italy and George's as elector of Hanover, there would have been less need for Britain to ally with Orléans, who might in his turn have felt threatened and more obliged to listen to Spanish and Jacobite demands. The French envoy in Vienna was certain in July 1716 that the Whigs wished to fight France in order to win Alsace, Burgundy and Flanders for Charles.

It might appear inevitable that the two weak rulers, George and Orléans, should unite. The Jacobite and Spanish threats made a resolution of Anglo-French diplomatic difficulties urgent. However, distrust was strong in ministerial and diplomatic circles in both countries. The state of Anglo-French relations was linked closely to political struggles in London and Paris. The British ministry watched anxiously the fate of French factional struggles fearing that d'Huxelles or Torcy would defeat Dubois in the battle to influence Orléans or that Orléans himself would fall. George I's suspicions that one of his Secretaries of State, Viscount Townshend, and his brother-in-law Robert Walpole, were dragging their feet over Anglo-French negotiations helped to harm ministerial relations and played a role in George's decision to move Townshend from the Secretaryship, thus precipitating the Whig Split of 1717–20. The negotiation of the Anglo-French alliance was conducted in a strained atmosphere and its frenetic and secretive nature suggests that it is wrong to argue that the alliance was an obvious matter of co-operation for mutual protection. It was to be royal pressure, stemming from Hanoverian vulnerability in the face of the collapse of relations with Peter I of Russia, that persuaded the British ministry to settle with France. By the alliance, signed on 28 November 1716, France guaranteed Hanover and the Protestant succession and undertook to ensure that James Stuart went beyond the Alps, while George promised military support if Philip should seek to rescind his renunciation. Thanks to the Dutch accession on 4 January 1717 the alliance became a Triple Alliance.

The Anglo-French alliance was to persist until March 1731 when, with the Second Treaty of Vienna, Britain reached a unilateral agreement with Austria, that France both resented and refused to support. Though there were periods during the alliance when both powers were far from satisfied with the conduct of the other, especially in 1721–2 and 1728–30, the alliance nevertheless remained the basis of their respective foreign policies. While the treaty was fairly clear in its aims, the maintenance of the essentials of the Utrecht settlement, it was less clear about what should be done to enforce these provisions. Both powers unilaterally developed good relations with third parties, Britain with Prussia in 1723, and often sought to persuade their alliance partner to yield in disputes with other powers, France supporting Russian claims against Britain in 1724. Nevertheless, they avoided supporting the interests of the other powers when they threatened the vital concerns of their partner. This was particularly clear in the case of relations with Spain in the 1720s. France felt little support for the commercial privileges Britain had gained in the Spanish empire at Utrecht, which led to persistent complaints from French mercantile circles, or for her retention of Gibraltar. French support for Spanish pretensions in Italy also reflected wider conceptions of international relations. Though some French ministers supported better relations with Austria and France was to be allied with her in the Quadruple Alliance and to seek to make an Austro-French understanding the basis of the Congress of Soissons in 1728, a major theme of French policy was opposition to Austria, the power that had both gained most from the Utrecht settlement and threatened to dominate post-Utrecht Germany and Italy. Britain was most suspicious of France in the case of Franco-Spanish relations, but the French were willing at moments of crisis to follow the British lead, as in 1718–19 and 1727.

Thus, as in any alliance between major powers, there was tension within the Anglo-French alliance, and this was concentrated on and rendered specific by, relations with third parties. It had been possible to reach agreement in 1716 over constructing the alliance, when it was a matter of mutual guarantees and a defensive mentality. However, attempts to expand the alliance, both in intention and by means of negotiating additional agreements with other powers, proved to be very difficult, and productive of strain and quarrels. The two periods when the alliance worked best were those when it was clearly defensive, in 1716–17 and 1725–7. In the later case the alliance was threatened by a new, dramatic and unpredictable international grouping, the Austro-Spanish alliance, created in the negotiations leading up to the first Treaty of Vienna in the spring of 1725, and fortified the following year by the accessions of Prussia and Russia. This pact represented a formidable military threat, especially to Hanover, and it led to the reassertion of the Anglo-French alliance, first in the Treaty of Hanover in September 1725, and secondly in joint efforts to gain allies and to plan for war. The leading French minister since 1723, the duke of Bourbon, had offended Philip by abandoning the idea of a Spanish marriage for Louis, and he was worried by the possible consequences of an Austro-Spanish alliance. They were also a matter of concern for George I but he was more immediately worried by the possible focusing on Hanover of the hostility of the rising powers of central and eastern Europe. The Austro-Russian alliance of 1726 helped to produce poor Franco-Russian relations, ensuring that negotiations with Russia were no longer a point at issue between Britain and France.

France and Britain appreciated their mutual need, and the unilateral policy-making that had characterized the early 1720s was replaced by co-operation. This was not free of dispute and strains were possibly greater as the attempt to co-operate led to quarrels that had been mostly avoided whilst each power was largely going her separate way in the early 1720s. However the general theme of these years was of an alliance strengthened by outside threat. In 1727 and 1730 the alliance's plans for war with Austria and her allies included as a significant element, to which the British negotiators attached great importance, the movement of a French army into the Empire to protect Hanover from attack. In 1729 and 1730, when Prussian attacks on Hanover were threatened, the French position was again crucial. George ascribed the Prussian decision not to attack in 1729 to the assistance of his allies.

Thus, by the late 1720s Hanoverian security problems had lent new weight to the Anglo-French alliance and posed major problems for British foreign policy, for in 1729–30 French diplomats stressed Hanoverian vulnerability in order to press the British ministry to support French policy initiatives. French pressure to ally with the Wittelsbachs was especially important, for such an alliance would entail unpopular peacetime subsidies and would have committed Britain to a long-term anti-Austrian policy that was at variance with the Anglo-Hanoverian policy of bullying Austria into being an ally on acceptable terms. George II and his ministers did not wish to become tied down in a system for supporting Charles Albert of Bavaria's claims on the Austrian succession. Far from being trapped in rigid conceptions of international relations, neither the British nor the French ministries saw the alliance in the 1720s as much more than a expedient that should be used to further aims as long as it served that purpose, and discarded if there was a change of circumstances. Possibly Stanhope in the late 1710s had genuinely hoped to make the alliance permanent and use it as the basis for the system of mutual guarantees and collective security he so favoured. However, this idea had won little support in British policy-making circles, where suspicion of France was never absent, and it was abandoned with his death in 1721. Thereafter the alliance was seen very much as an expedient, rather than the purpose of foreign policy. This was a more realistic view, given the kaleidoscopic nature of international relations in this period, and the fragility of French support for the alliance. Dependent in the late 1710s on the position of Orléans and his confidential adviser Dubois, who was foreign minister from September 1718 until his death in August 1723, it was based on little more than the life of Bourbon's successor, the elderly Cardinal Fleury (1726–43), a decade later. British policy makers were uneasily aware of this fragility and responded with fear to reports of Fleury's ill health or impending fall. The British ministry was well aware that support for the alliance in France was fragile, just as the French were concerned about the stability of the British government, and the influence of ministers and diplomats deemed anti-French.

Anxious about Hanoverian security, fearful of the prospect of unilateral French and Spanish approaches to Austria, and conscious of domestic criticism of their foreign policy, the British ministry began negotiations with Austria in the early autumn of 1730. Disquiet over both long and short-term French policies played a role, but there was no wish to end good relations with France and the British hoped wrongly that France would accept the new alignment. Unilateral British negotiations with Austria were not new. They had been considered in 1728 and conducted in 1729. The commitment to the French alliance had never been so total as to preclude consideration of better relations with Austria. In 1730–1 the negotiations succeeded because Austria, having lost her Spanish ally in November 1729, felt more vulnerable, the British ministry was willing to make a greater effort to achieve a settlement, probably because of the battering its French alliance had taken in the 1730 parliamentary session over illegal repairs to Dunkirk, and George II was willing to shelve Hanoverian demands, possibly because he realized that the best way to guarantee Hanoverian security was an alliance with Austria that would lead to Austrian restraint of Prussia. By the Second Treaty of Vienna of 16 March 1731 George II, the United Provinces and Charles VI mutually guaranteed each other's territories and the first two guaranteed the Pragmatic Sanction as long as no Bourbon or Prussian marriage was involved. In a separate, later, agreement on the Hanoverian issues George was granted the investitures of Bremen and Verden but Charles refused to support his attempt to maintain his influence and limit that of Prussia in Mecklenburg.

France could not be expected to welcome the guarantee of the Pragmatic, a policy she had strongly opposed in early 1730. However, in August 1731 the Prussian and Russian envoys in Paris told a British diplomat that

> no general pacification can be made whilst France remains in the present situation with regard to the other powers, that she is too considerable to be left alone and if left alone will always be able to embroil matters so far as to endanger the tranquility that it now established among the contracting parties of the last Treaty of Vienna . . . it was necessary to make immediate use of the cardinal's

pacific temper, and not wait till by his death and demise any change of ministry should happen here . . . I agreed that . . . there was no harm in marking out a way for France to enter, with honour for all parties, into the same engagements with the allies of Vienna.[9]

The Austrians, however, were opposed to the British idea of reassuring Fleury about the intentions of the new alliance. A French entry into the new system would have weakened Anglo-Austrian and strengthened Franco-Spanish ties and the attempts to ensure the co-operation of the four powers in 1717–24 hardly provided an encouraging precedent for Austria. In 1731 the possibility of Britain using the Vienna alliance as a stepping stone for a European peace and of persuading France to assent to the new arrangements was lost. Possibly such an attempt would have failed, defeated by French unwillingess to accept a dictated settlement. However, without French consent, no European peace settlement could be secure or long-lasting. Whilst France was isolated her diplomatic efforts, such as the attempts to gain the alliance of Sweden, Denmark, Saxony and Bavaria and to prevent the Imperial Diet accepting the Pragmatic Sanction, were a threat to European tranquility. As soon as France could gain powerful allies who were willing to act, as in late 1733 with Sardinia and Spain, she was to prove a major threat.

The basis for any French accession to the Anglo-Austrian agreement was asumed to be a guarantee of the Pragmatic. France was unwilling to provide such a guarantee, but the eventual solution of the third Treaty of Vienna (1738), the acquisition of Lorraine for the French royal family in return for the guarantee, had been considered before 1733. Should Maria Theresa marry Duke Francis of Lorraine, as she was to do in 1736, the dynastic union of Lorraine and Austria would become a strong possibility, unacceptable to the French. Possibly because of the legacy of Anglo-French bitterness dating from 1731 the British ministry which had pressed Austria to satisfy Spain and accept the introduction of the Spanish garrisons, was unwilling to press Austria to satisfy France over Lorraine. Possibly the effort would have met with Austrian refusal, for there was no equivalent to offer Francis, but the failure to make it was to have serious consequences. When the British ministry attempted to use its good offices to end the Polish Succession War the absence of any substance underlying the mutual assurances of Anglo-French regard was to help ensure its defeat. France and Austria were to settle their differences, including the Lorraine question and the French guarantee of the Pragmatic Sanction, without Britain.

From the Second Treaty of Vienna to the War of the Austrian Succession 1731–40

By 1731 the dynastic weakness that had characterized Austria, Britain and France in 1715 was apparently over. Louis XV was an adult with a son, while the Hanoverian dynasty has survived the Jacobite rising of 1715 and the

[9] J. M. Black, *The Collapse of the Anglo-French Alliance 1727–31* (Gloucester, 1987) p. 205.

succession of George II in 1727 had been peaceful. Charles VI had obtained the alliance and the guarantee of the Pragmatic Sanction of all the major powers bar France. The diplomatic realignment of 1731 had eased some tensions while creating others but circumstances rather than any rigid system determined relations in the following decade. The Second Treaty of Vienna did not lead to an immediate breakdown of Anglo-French relations, though the summer of 1731 saw a war-panic, each power fearing attack from the other. Though relations until the outbreak of formal hostilities in 1744 were poor, fighting was avoided until 1743. Britain did not honour her treaty commitments by supporting Austria against France in the War of the Polish Succession, while France ignored Jacobite requests for assistance until 1744, and refused to support Spain fully in her war with Britain, the War of Jenkins' Ear that began in 1739, by declaring war, as had been feared in London. Both states vied for influence in other countries, particularly in Denmark, Portugal, Sweden and the United Provinces, and competed in colonial and commercial affairs, but they took care to maintain a peaceful rivalry.

A similar rivalry characterized Austro-French relations in 1731–2. It centred on the Empire where on 11 January 1732 Charles VI obtained the support of the electoral college for the Pragmatic Sanction. France encouraged the opposition of Augustus II of Saxony, with whom a subsidy treaty was concluded on 25 May 1732, and Charles Albert of Bavaria and a Saxon-Bavarian treaty was signed on 4 July 1732. These moves, though peaceful, were essentially preparatory for a future conflict over the Austrian succession. That was the prime issue in German diplomacy in 1731–2. War, though, was threatened only by another succession dispute, those to the Rhenish duchies of Jülich and Berg, part of the territories of the childless Karl Phillip, Elector Palatine. The rights of his heirs in the Palatinate, the house of Palatine-Sülzbach, to succeed in Jülich-Berg were contested by Frederick William I, who in 1732 responded to Karl Phillip's ill health by preparing to fight. Karl Phillip's recovery ended the crisis and he was to survive until 1742, being peacefully succeeded at a time when Prussian attentions were concentrated on the larger prize of the Austrian succession.

It is not surprising that disputed successions were the occasions of the two major wars in 1733–48. A disputed succession posed a particular problem for the policies of brinkmanship followed by many major powers, the attempt to obtain benefits by military preparations and the threat of force. A vacant succession lasted only for a certain period before being filled by an election or coronation. This obliged interested parties, such as Russia in 1733 and Bavaria in 1741, to act speedily. Once moves were made it was difficult to retract them lest that was interpreted as a sign of weakness, or to control their consequences. Equally the pressure for action made it difficult to avoid moves that would serve to provoke others or to vindicate claims about the malevolence of supposed intentions.

The Polish succession agitated diplomats well before 1733. The elective nature of the monarchy, the contentious nature of the last election and the conflicting interests of several major powers suggested that the issue might produce war. It was generally accepted that trouble would follow Augustus II's death, but although that was widely reported as imminent in the 1720s, he survived until 1733. The crucial differences between 1733, with its outbreak of a major war, and 1721–32, when serious difference between the powers failed to lead to war, were the willingness of France to fight and the beginning of hostilities in eastern Europe. The international situation was favourable for a French attack on Charles in 1733. British attempts to settle Austro-Spanish and Austro-Sardinian disputes were clearly unsuccessful, the Anglo-Austrian relationship was tense, the United Provinces weak and according to Chavigny, the French envoy in London, the Hanoverian monarchy was in danger of collapsing before Jacobitism, national indebtedness and contentious financial legislation, the Excise Crisis.

That the international situation became favourable for an attack does not mean that it caused it. If it was that simple it is difficult to explain why France had not attacked Austria in 1730, when Britain, Spain and the United Provinces were also committed to do so and Austria's leading ally Russia was affected by domestic political turmoil. The French Council of State decided on 20 May 1733 that war would be declared before they were sure of the support of Sardinia and Spain. Given the significance of royal and national dignity and honour in this era and of dynastic pride, considerations often advanced in the diplomatic correspondence of the period, it is understandable both that Louis XV should support the candidature of his father-in-law Stanislaus Leszczynski for the Polish throne and oppose the attempt to prevent it. On 17 March 1733 Louis declared that he would not tolerate any interference with the free choice of the Polish nation. Royal honour was involved, as it had been for Philip V of Spain in 1725, when Louis XV sent back his intended bride and, as in the latter case, the reaction was violent. The effect of this on French policy is incalculable, as is the wish to take revenge for the diplomatic isolation of 1731, while it is not clear what the relation between the domestic political problems of 1732 and the aggressive diplomatic strategy of the following year may have been. That France went to war probably owed more to a conviction that she must fight for royal honour and to prevent humiliation and isolation than to any wish to establish her power in eastern Europe. The conviction that France was prepared to fight led Charles Emmanuel III of Sardinia and Philip V to reject attempts to keep them allied to Britain and Austria.

On 10 October 1733 Louis XV declared war on Charles VI, holding him responsible for the actions of his Russian ally. Lorraine was overrun and the Rhenish fort of Kehl seized that year but the French concentrated their war effort in Italy. A Franco-Dutch neutrality agreement of 1733 prevented the French from attacking the Austrian Netherlands, and concern about the reaction of neutral Britain and the United Provinces may well have limited French operations in the Empire. In early 1734 fears had been expressed that a French army would invade Saxony. The opening of the campaigning season in 1734 witnesed a successful French campaign in the Moselle valley that left

Belle-Isle's army threatening Coblenz and ready to cross the Rhine, while Berwick's army had outflanked the Austrian defensive positions further up the river. However, these promising developments were not followed up, the French devoting the rest of the campaign to the successful siege of the Rhenish fortress of Philippsburg.

Prefiguring the later failure of numerous rulers to fulfil their guarantees of the Pragmatic Sanction, a number of powers, principally Britain and the United Provinces, failed to come to Charles VI's assistance in 1733–5. Arguing that the merits of the combatants' cases had to be considered, they were more concerned by their domestic situation. Their governments feared the costs of a war while the Walpole ministry was concerned about the general election due in 1734 and the danger of French support for the Jacobites. However, the British response was not one of passivity. Over the previous decade the ministry had shown that they did not wish their alliances to lead them into actual conflict. They were prepared, as in 1726–7 and 1729–30, to carry out major military preparations, in particular to prepare large fleets, but they preferred to negotiate, albeit to do so supported by the threat of military intervention, rather than to fight. A substantial naval armament was prepared, both in 1734 and 1735, and the policy of the late 1720s of negotiating subsidy treaties was resumed. The increase in military strength enabled the ministry to offer its good offices in finding terms upon which the war could be be ended, with the implicit threat that a refusal to accept either good offices or the subsequent terms would lead to conflict. When in 1735 Spain threatened to invade Portugal Britain sent a substantial squadron to the Tagus to protect her ally. The British also intervened actively to prevent other powers from supporting France, influencing Danish and Swedish policy, to foster antagonism between Spain and Sardinia and to coax the United Provinces into military preparations. The French had no doubt that British diplomacy was actively thwarting their schemes. Fleury's decision to accept and seek to manipulate Britain's decision to use her good offices, rather than to ignore it contemptuously, reflected his appreciation of British determination to influence the conflict.

The negotiations at The Hague in the winter of 1734–5 failed, but British neutrality was aided by French moderation. France did not support the Jacobites or make military moves against the centres of government of her enemies, as she had done in 1703–4 and was to do in 1741 (Austria) and 1744 (Britain). The peace she negotiated did not stipulate excessive Bourbon gains. Stanislaus's acquisition of Lorraine with its reversion to France did not represent a fundamental alteration in the balance of power, a difficult concept to apply with precision anyway. Lorraine had been militarily vulnerable to France for a long time, having been gained by them at the start of every major war. The territorial changes in Italy were not as detrimental to Austria as had been feared. The British ministry has been attacked for failing to enter the war, but it is difficult to support claims that this was an error. Austrian weakness in the early 1740s reflected her unsuccessful war with Turkey

(1737–9), the unpredictable policy of Frederick II and the Russian inability to help, rather than any earlier British failure to support her. The experience of the War of the Spanish Succession suggests that had Britain joined in, she would have found Austria committing her energies to Italy and demanding subsidies, whilst leaving Britain with the difficult task of holding the Austrian Netherlands against the principal French war effort, as was to happen in 1745–8.

It could be suggested that British non-involvement encouraged France and Spain to form a low estimate of British strength, and led to Spanish intransigence in 1738–9 over British commercial grievances in the West Indies and the subsequent Anglo-Spanish conflict, the War of Jenkins' Ear (1739–48). It has been suggested that Britain's isolation in this war, for both Austria and the United Provinces remained neutral, was due to her neutrality in the War of the Polish Succession. However, the Bourbons were well aware of British naval power and in 1738 Spain settled her differences with Britain by the Convention of the Pardo, a measure that Walpole was able to carry through Parliament in early 1739 but which ultimately collapsed due to the inability to compromise over the intransigent attitude of the British South Sea Company. The French unwillingness to join Spain suggests that the Bourbons were neither as united nor as strong a threat to the European system as anti-Bourbon publicists claimed. Fear of French intervention and a wish to retain their Spanish trade explained Dutch neutrality in 1739 despite what the British felt to be clear treaty obligations. The Austrians, linked to France and busy in the Balkans, were in no position to attack Spain in Italy. Despairing of Austrian power and intentions the British had already shifted their hopes to Prussia and Russia. It was expected that the future Frederick II, who secretly received funds from his uncle, George II, would support Britain when he came to the throne. The exchange of envoys with Russia in 1732 was followed by a commercial treaty in 1734 and by a British diplomatic initiative launched in 1738 to negotiate an Anglo-Russian alliance. That such a treaty was not signed until April 1741 was due to Russian, rather than British obduracy.

The greatest shift produced by the War of the Polish Succession was not, however, that in British policy but rather the Austro-French *rapprochement* of 1735–40. The preliminary treaty signed by Austria and France, which led to the Third Treaty of Vienna of 1738, produced an entente between the two powers centred on a French guarantee of the Pragmatic Sanction. French diplomatic support for Austria forced an unwilling Sardinia and, in particular, Spain to accept an Italian settlement less favourable than they had militarily secured. The aggressively anti-Austrian French foreign minister Chauvelin was dismissed in February 1737 and the most vociferous contender for a share of the Austrian inheritance, Charles Albert of Bavaria, was consigned to a diplomatic limbo, his freedom of manoeuvre destroyed by the understanding of his two powerful neighbours. Many eighteenth-century wars ended in secret unilateral negotiations, but the terms France accepted in 1735 were completely unacceptable to her allies and, by unilaterally abandoning them, she destroyed the alliance that supported her in the War of the Polish Succession, not that Sardinia and Spain had failed to engage in secret diplomacy. Distrust between the powers that had plotted or acted against Austria in 1732–5 made a successful resumption of such action appear less likely. In 1738 Fleury told the Bavarian minister, Count Törring, that he knew as little of the views and schemes of Elizabeth Farnese as of those of the Great Mongul (*sic*). When France guaranteed the Pragmatic Sanction she had saved the prior rights of third parties such as Bavaria, and on 16 May 1738 France secretly signed an agreement with Bavaria promising to support her just claims. Nevertheless, French conduct in the negotiations over the Jülich-Berg inheritance in the late 1730s, in which she backed the partition of Berg, was scarcely designed to encourage the Wittelsbachs. Törring was pessimistic about the possibility of French support while Fleury was in control of policy, and informed him that Charles VI was too closely linked with France to be separated from her. Fleury replied that he could not be sure of future developments, but was adamant that Austro-French ties were limited to friendship. However, the late 1730s did not witness a repetition of the French diplomatic offensive against Austria of 1731–3, and it was in line with his general policy that Fleury responded to Charles VI's death on 20 October 1740 by assuring the Austrian envoy Prince Liechtenstein that Louis XV would observe all his engagements with Austria.

The War of the Austrian Succession 1740–8

It is not clear what France would have done had the recently crowned Frederick II not attacked Maria Theresa by invading her duchy of Silesia on 16 December 1740. Fleury was already aware that other rulers, especially Charles Albert of Bavaria and Philip V, saw the death of Charles VI as an opportunity for action, but his early plans were restricted to a plan to deny the Imperial election to Francis of Lorraine, rather than to eternalize the glory of Louis XV by heeding Providence's call to re-establish a just European balance of power, as Charles Albert suggested. The Prussian invasion of Silesia dramatically altered the situation by substituting action for negotiation and by forcing other European powers to define their position. It is possible to suggest that France would have gone to war with Austria anyway, but it was equally the case that France in 1740 was moving towards war with Britain in order to prevent the latter from conquering Spanish territories in the West Indies and, by defeating Spain, destroying any maritime balance of power. War between the two powers was widely anticipated and in August the French sent a fleet to the West Indies to prevent British conquests. Once ships had put to sea in the eighteenth century it was difficult to prevent hostile acts. The absence of the anticipated naval war between the two powers cannot be simply ascribed to the death of Charles VI, but was partly due to the unwillingness of both powers to push confrontation to the point of conflict. The British ministry chose to regard neither the dispatch of D'Antin's fleet to the West Indies nor reported French fortification of Dunkirk, in clear breach of treaty obligations, as a cause of war, although they believed it imminent and were under domestic pressure to take a strong stance. Despite their concern over British operations the French did not attack Britain in the West Indies. As in the War of the Polish Succession, when France had taken care to avoid hostilities, so in 1740 an uneasy balance, short of war, was maintained.

Frederick II was unable to achieve such a balance. His invasion of Silesia, where his dynasty had territorial claims, was not intended as the opening move of a major European war, a step that would precipitate attempts to enforce claims on the Austrian inheritance by other rulers. Frederick hoped that Maria Theresa would respond to a successful attack by agreeing to buy him off, and in many respects his invasion can be seen as the action of an opportunist, seeking to benefit from a temporarily favourable European situation. Frederick offered, in return for Silesia, a guarantee for all the other German possessions of the Habsburgs, troops to serve in Italy or the Low Countries, support for Francis of Lorraine's imperial candidature (as a woman Maria Theresa was not eligible to be Emperor) and a cash indemnity. Subsequently Frederick proposed a partition of Silesia. He hoped that Anglo-French hostility would lead both powers to bid for his support.[10] Frederick's opportunism can be regarded as a rash move, for though the conquest of Silesia proved relatively easy, its retention in the face of persistent Austrian hostility was to be a major burden for Prussia. The French envoy felt that Frederick had attacked carelessly, without either allies or negotiations to obtain them.

Combined with a duplicity characteristic of many rulers of the period, including his more religious father, was the rashness that led Frederick to declare that he would sooner perish than desist from his undertaking. The attack on Austria was to some extent fortuitous. In the autumn of 1740 Frederick had expressed more interest in Jülich-Berg and, just as he toyed with approaches from Britain and France, so he was clearly unsure whither to direct his aggressive instincts. Had Charles VI died a year later, then it is quite possible that Frederick would have invaded Jülich-Berg already, as his father had planned to do in 1732 and 1738. The consequence might have been a major war but one that pitched France, a traditional patron of the Wittelsbachs, against Protestant Prussia, as had been envisaged in the late 1730s. Thus the combination of Frederick's aggression, rash or prudent, and the European situation at his accession did not make a War of Austrian Succession precipitated by Prussian action inevitable. Frederick was helped by the death of the Tsarina Anna, three days before Charles VI, and the succession of her two-month-old great-nephew Ivan VI and a weak and divided Regency. Frederick predicted that her death would leave the Russians too concerned with domestic affairs to think of foreign policy.[11]

[10] *Politische Correspondenz* I, 90
[11] *Politische Correspondenz* I, 91

Edward Finch, the British envoy in St Petersburg, claimed that the death of Charles made Fleury's attitude crucial,

> Guarantys like young beauties with small blemishes in their character have now a fine opportunity to reestablish their reputation and there is in particular an old gentleman of our acquaintance who has it in his power to leave behind him a memory for ever to be had in the highest veneration or execration. Since the fate of Europe may greatly depend on his faith or ambition, and by the proofs he now may give of all his constant professions of being that Peace Maker who according to the promise is to see God . . .[12]

However, Fleury was affected by pressure at court from aristocratic circles eager for conflict while Prussian aggression helped to precipitate a major war. Despite British pressure, the Austrians were unwilling to accept Prussian claims, arguing that the cession of Silesia would be followed by demands on the Habsburg lands from other rulers. The failure to settle Austro-Prussian differences speedily had the same effect. Frederick overran Silesia and defeated the Austrians at Mollwitz on 10 April 1741. Maria Theresa's refusal to cede Silesia led Frederick to sign the Treaty of Breslau with France on 5 June. He renounced his claim to Jülich-Berg and agreed to support the Imperial candidature of Charles Albert in return for a French guarantee of Lower Silesia and French promises of military assistance for Bavaria and diplomatic pressure on Sweden to attack Russia. France and Frederick encouraged other powers to act, and they did so realizing the opportunities presented by what appeared to be a Europe in flux. On 15 August 1741 French troops began to cross the Rhine and on 19 September Marshall Belle-Isle, the principal French protagonist for war, obtained an offensive alliance between Charles Albert and Augustus III of Saxony. Charles Albert was to become Emperor and receive the Habsburg provinces of Bohemia, Upper Austria and the Tyrol. Augustus was to become king of Moravia and to gain Moravia and Upper Silesia. The threat of a French invasion of Hanover led George II to abandon his attempt to create an anti-French coalition and on 25 September 1741 to promise his neutrality and his support for Charles Albert's imperial candidacy.

The Habsburgs appeared prostrate, an impression reinforced by signs of support for Charles Albert in Bohemia and Austria. Their traditional allies, Britain and the United Provinces, were weak and disunited domestically and unwilling to aid Austria with troops, while Austria's allies of the post-1726 period, Prussia and Russia, were respectively an enemy and affected by ministerial and dynastic instability. In contrast, a well-developed and well-motivated alliance was able to give military teeth to French diplomatic conceptions. On 14 September Linz fell, and Charles Albert received the homage of the Upper Austrian Estates. On 21 October French and Bavarian troops camped at Saint Polten and Vienna prepared for a siege. Maria Theresa and her ministers had already left for Hungary. However, Charles Albert, fearing that Augustus and Frederick would seize Bohemia, decided to revert

---

[12] Finch to Trevor, 15 Nov 1740, Aylesbury, County Record Office, Trevor mss vol. 24.

to Belle-Isle's original plan to concentrate efforts on gaining Prague, which fell on 26 November to Bavarian, French and Saxon forces. Charles Albert was proclaimed king of Bohemia at Prague on 7 December and crowned as Emperor Charles VII at Frankfurt on 12 February 1742, the first non-Habsburg Emperor since 1437.

And yet France failed in her attempt to create a new territorial order in the Empire. This was due to a variety of factors including underrated Austrian resilience and Russia's refusal to enter the French system as the French envoy in St Petersburg La Chetardie hoped. Unable to dominate Europe militarily on her own, France was forced, as was every other power considering a major conflict, to seek the assistance of others, but the very resort to war made it less easy to retain the support of allies. Powers that were willing to accept subsidies regularly in peacetime and in return promised support proved only too willing to vary their policies to meet wartime exigencies. War made the position of second-rank powers more crucial and accordingly it led to an increase in bids for their support, a significant corrosive of alliances that tended to lack any ideological, religious, sentimental, popular or economic bonds. The British envoy in Turin complained in December 1741 that 'the general system of politics at present reaches no farther with most princes, than to come in for a share of the spoil',[13] and on 9 October 1741 British mediation helped to produce the secret Austro-Prussian Convention of Kleinschnellendorf by which the ground was laid for a separate peace in which Austria would cede Lower Silesia. Though Frederick's path from there to the Peace of Breslau, concluded on 11 June 1742, by which he gained most of Silesia was far from straight, his betrayal of France fatally weakened her cause. Augustus followed him into the Austrian camp on 23 July. Remarking in November 1741 that experience should have taught people to distrust guarantees, Frederick observed that all men were fools.[14]

It was not Frederick alone, however, who was responsible for the collapse of the French cause. Far from the fall of Prague being followed by the collapse of the Austrians, they recaptured Linz in late January 1742, Munich on 12 February and in July began to besiege Prague, which the French abandoned on 16 December. The replacement of Walpole by the bellicose Carteret in February 1742 was followed by the arrival of British troops in the Austrian Netherlands on 20 May and the abandonment of Hanoverian neutrality. Carteret hoped to recreate the Grand Alliance and believed that a strong Austria was essential. Seeking to benefit from the new more interventionist British policy, Charles VII sought help in negotiating a peace with Austria, arguing in June 1742 that the growth of Bavarian power could help to provide Britain with a counterweight to France, more effective than Austria, and in August that Austria must satisfy his just rights and pretensions. Alongside Charles's complaints about his rights was his vision of a new order in central

---

[13] PRO. SP. 105/282 f. 29.
[14] *Politische Correspondenz* I, 411.

Europe. He argued that instead of preserving the preponderance of a single member of the Empire, who could become dangerous, it was necessary to preserve the power of the entire Empire. In September he claimed that neither the theory of a balance of power nor the guarantee of the Pragmatic Sanction could protect just rights, but that only the force of the entire Empire united with that of the neighbouring powers could form and support the balance. He argued that experience had revealed that the preponderance of a single family led to abuses including blows to the states and constitution of the Empire.

Charles's hope of an Empire led by the Wittelsbachs was as implausible as his peace demands of December 1742 which included Upper Austria, Passau, much of Bohemia and the Tyrol, and Neuburg and Sülzbach from the Palatine branch of the Wittelsbachs in return for an equivalent in the Austrian Netherlands. Defeat obliged Charles's language to be that of rights, not power, a marked contrast to that of Frederick II. However, the prospect of major territorial changes, such as the British idea in 1743 that Charles join the Anglo-Austrian alliance and, in return make gains in Alsace, was rendered increasingly unlikely by the progress of the war. George II led an Anglo-German army into the Empire in 1743, defeating the French at Dettingen on 27 June but his attempts that year, and those of the Austrians under Francis's brother Charles of Lorraine in 1744, to make a major impact on France's eastern frontier were unsuccessful. As after 1704, the Austrians dominated the Empire but the French held their Rhine frontier, helped in August 1744 by Frederick II's invasion of Bohemia. He began the Second Silesian War (1744–5) because of his concern about Austrian strength and when it ended on 25 December 1745 with the Peace of Dresden he retained Silesia, having demonstrated once more his ability to defeat Austria and having overrun Saxony. Unlike in the War of the Spanish Succession, the French retained the initiative in the Low Countries, while the control of Britain itself became an issue. The French decision to risk an invasion of Britain in 1744 was a measure of how determined they were to prevent the British from blocking their continental schemes. Dependent on favourable winds and tides, amphibious operations were notoriously difficult and the French scheme was defeated by bad weather but it was a reminder of the extent to which limited military forces obliged the British to keep much of their navy in home waters.

The Jacobite rising of 1745 led by James III's son Bonnie Prince Charlie helped France considerably. British and British-subsidized troops had to be transported from the Austrian Netherlands, and their failure to defeat the outnumbered prince in late 1745 ensured that they could not be sent back to the continent in time for the start of the 1746 campaign. George II was fortunate that Ireland was quiescent and that the French did not invade, as had been feared. On 24 October 1745 Louis XV signed the Treaty of Fontainebleau with the Pretender, by which he recognized him as king of Scotland and promised to send military assistance and to recognize him as king of England as soon as this could be shown to be the wish of the nation. An expeditionary force under the duke of Richelieu was prepared at Dunkirk, but delays in its preparation, the Jacobite retreat from Derby, and British control of the Channel led to its cancellation. The French had better success in the Low Countries. British hopes that they could serve as the base for an invasion of France proved misplaced as the French under Marshal Saxe won the battle of Fontenoy and captured much of the Austrian Netherlands in 1745. In 1747 France declared war on the United Provinces and British hopes that the coup that brought William IV of Orange to power in the provinces of Zeeland and Holland would revitalize the Dutch were proved wrong, the major fortress of Bergen-op-Zoom falling to the French in September. The danger that the United Provinces would be overrun – in 1748 the French took Maastricht – helped to lead the British to negotiate for peace seriously.

Negotiations had in fact been conducted during much of the war, but most of the powers had fought on, hopeful of success, fearful of the consequences of abandoning their allies and distrustful of their enemies. 1745 had brought peace to the Empire with the Peace of Dresden and the death of Charles VII in January 1745. The succession of Maximilian Joseph freed Bavarian policy from the burden of commitments and expectations associated with Charles and bound up with his French alliance and Imperial status. Austrian strength helped to persuade the new ruler to sign the Treaty of Füssen, abandoning France, on 22 April 1745. France supported Augustus III for the vacant Imperial throne but Maria Theresa's husband was elected as Francis I. For Austria thereafter the war centred on Italy. Britain, despite her naval victories over France and the capture of Louisbourg in Canada in 1745, was most concerned about the Low Countries, while France, her foreign trade harmed by the British, her economy hit by a poor harvest and her finances by the costly war, wanted peace. The French were also concerned at the prospect of British-subsidized Russian intervention on the Rhine. Britain and France were responsible for the Treaty of Aix-la-Chapelle, the preliminaries of which were signed on 30 April and the definitive treaty on 18 October 1748. Neither Austria nor Sardinia were happy about the terms and they did not sign until 23 October and 20 November 1748. There was to be a restoration of all conquests and in comparison to the wars of the Spanish and Polish successions relatively little land changed hands. Despite Austrian reluctance, Charles Emmanuel III received the lands he had been ceded at Worms, bar Piacenza, while Don Philip gained Parma, Piacenza and Guastella. The Pragmatic Sanction was renewed for the remaining Habsburg territories, while the French had to agree to recognize the Protestant succession in Britain and to expel Bonnie Prince Charlie. The disputed Canadian border was referred to commissioners. In August 1745 the French had demanded Furnes and Ypres in a secret approach to the Austrians, to which they added Nieuport and Tournai a month later, but in 1748 they agreed to restore the whole of the Austrian Netherlands, while suggestions that the British gain Ostend were abandoned.

Like all compromise peaces, that of Aix-la-Chapelle was criticized. In

Britain the return of Louisbourg was seen as a fatal indictment of the consequences of subordinating policy to the interests of allies, while in France there was criticism of an inglorious peace that had failed to bring any gains. The war has generally received less attention than the succeeding Seven Years' War but in fact it was in many ways more decisive. The last attempt in *ancien régime* Europe to drastically reorder central Europe had ·been defeated. Bavaria had failed to become a great power, while Prussia had succeeded, though this verdict was to be challenged in the Seven Years' War. The Protestant Succession had survived its most major challenge, and a new and lasting territorial settlement was created in Italy. The attempt to contest the Russian position in the eastern Baltic had been unsuccessful and was not to be repeated until 1788. Thus the war and the subsequent peace set the territorial division of much of Europe for the remainder of the *ancien régime*.

Consolidating the Old System

The duke of Newcastle, the British minister with most influence in the field of foreign ministers after the fall of Carteret in 1744, had been determined that the Anglo-Austrian alliance should survive the end of the War of the Austrian Succession, in contrast to the period after the War of the Spanish Succession. Although he had become a Secretary of State in 1724, during a period of alliance with France, Newcastle had become convinced that French power was a threat both to Britain and to European liberties, conceived of as the existing international system. Looking back to the wars of 1689–1713, he felt that Britain must intervene actively on the continent to resist French initiatives and he argued that the diplomatic framework of this intervention should be the Old System, a term he first used in 1748 to describe the alliance of Britain, Austria and the United Provinces. Newcastle devoted his energies in the post-war years to strengthening this system. It is easy to overlook these efforts if attention in the mid eighteenth century is devoted to tensions and developments that appear to prefigure the Diplomatic Revolution of 1756, but it is necessary to query any attempt to make that 'Revolution' appear inevitable. To many contemporaries the European system in the years after 1748 was relatively stable, indeed a continuation of that of the war opposing France and Prussia to Britain, Austria and Russia. The principal departure was the Austro-Spanish alliance of 1752, the successful culmination of several years of effort on the part of Britain to separate Spain from France.

Newcastle's determined attempt to strengthen the Old System helped to lead to the failure of two other diplomatic possibilities. The mission of Henry Legge to Berlin in 1748, an attempt to improve Anglo-Prussian relations, was downplayed by Newcastle who made it clear that improved relations could only be subsidiary to Britain's alliances with anti-Prussian Austria and Russia, a view that Frederick found unacceptable. Puysieulx, French foreign minister in 1747–51, sought better relations with Britain and hoped that Anglo-French co-operation would ease tensions whether in the Baltic or North

America. Frederick was to be very caustic about what he saw as a craven French failure to resist Anglo-Austrian plans in the Empire and the western Mediterranean. Within British ministerial circles there was considerable disagreement as to the best policy to follow.

There was support both for better relations with Prussia and for welcoming French approaches. As in 1713–16 the direction that British policy was to take was in part dependent on political rivalries that were not due to foreign policy differences. Although there was no reason in 1748 to believe that an alliance with France would be negotiated as it had been three years after the War of the Spanish Succession, there was equally little reason why Anglo-French relations should not have developed as their Anglo-Spanish counterparts were to, with a commercial treaty settling outstanding differences in 1750 and good political relations in the early 1750s. France did not appear poised for war with either Britain or Austria and her links with Frederick were not so close as to preclude better Anglo-French relations. Aside from views on particular diplomatic options the view was also held within the British ministry, especially by Newcastle's brother Henry Pelham, First Lord of the Treasury 1743–54, that expensive foreign commitments, particularly the payment of subsidies to allies, should be avoided.

Newcastle defeated these alternative views and brought an active anti-French and pro-Austrian direction to British policy, leading to the resignation of his co-Secretary of State, the duke of Bedford, in 1751. Clearly hoping to dissuade future French aggression, Newcastle sought to have the Barrier in the Austrian Netherlands restored and actively sponsored the Imperial Election Scheme, a plan for the election as king of the Romans, and therefore next Emperor, of Maria Theresa's son Joseph, the future Joseph II. The support of most of the electors was obtained, in part through the payment of British subsidies, but unanimity could not be obtained in large part due to the opposition of Frederick and Newcastle was hesitant about the idea of a majority election. He was not helped by a lack of enthusiasm on the part of Maria Theresa who objected to the idea of obtaining votes by concessions. The plan collapsed in 1752 and an attempt to revive it in 1753 was unsuccessful. Similarly, the attempt to recreate an effective Barrier failed, in large part because Austria did not accept British priorities, while excessive Russian financial demands hindered a British attempt to create an alliance that could prevent Frederick from threatening Hanover.

Despite these failures Newcastle's system was still in place in 1754. Although it was affected by serious disagreements and the United Provinces was weak, it had been strengthened by the Italian settlement of 1752 and neither France nor Frederick was in a position to challenge it. Suggestions such as those of the crown princess of Sweden, Frederick's sister, in April 1749 that a counter-league of Prussia, Sweden, France, Spain, Sardinia, Denmark, Turkey and Saxony be created to balance the Old System, proved unrealistic. Frederick was reduced in 1752 to asking for French pressure on the Turks to declare war on Austria or Russia. International relations were of course unpredictable, as Frederick noted in July 1752 when explaining why he did not wish to make plans for the succession to the healthy Augustus III of Saxony-Poland,[15] but a striking feature of the correspondence of the period is the sense that between them Britain, Austria and Russia dominated Europe. Frederick felt that he was having to respond to apparent threats such as the Imperial Election Scheme or in 1752–3 the prospect that Maria Theresa's brother-in-law, Charles of Lorraine, would become next king of Poland and make it a hereditary kingdom to the great benefit of Austria.[16] Puysieulx's successor Saint-Contest complained in December 1753 that ambitious views were being falsely ascribed to France by powers that indeed were making plans against her.[17] Newcastle's system was to collapse in 1755–6, in large part because he sought to use and extend it without considering sufficiently the views of his allies but this clash of interests should not detract from its apparent strength in 1748–54 nor from the fact that the War of the Austrian Succession was not immediately followed by a diplomatic realignment as the Spanish and Polish Succession wars and, to a lesser extent, the Nine Years War and the War of the Quadruple Alliance had been.

THE DIPLOMATIC REVOLUTION 1755–6

The crucial new developments that constituted the Diplomatic Revolution were the alliances between Britain and Prussia, and France and Austria, both negotiated in 1756. Neither was completely new. George I had been allied to Frederick William I as recently as thirty years earlier. Negotiations for an alliance between the powers had been conducted on several occasions since including 1730, 1740 and 1748. In one sense the alliance was an obvious consequence of the attempt to supplement or replace good relations with Austria that had characterized British policy towards Prussia and Russia for a number of decades. An Austro-French alliance was more novel though there had been approaches for good relations over the previous forty-one years, largely on the part of France. Aside from Louis XIV's probe at the end of his reign, Fleury and the Austrian chancellor Sinzendorf developed a good working relationship at the Congress of Soissons in 1728 that, however, led to nothing because the Austrian ministry preferred Eugene's policy of alliance within the Empire and with Russia and Spain, Fleury and the Austrians co-operated from late 1735 until early 1741 and there had been a number of

[15] *Politische Correspondenz* IX, 161.
[16] AE. CP. Prusse 171 f. 112–13.
[17] Paris, Archives Nationales KK 1400 pp. 390–1.

attempts, for example in December 1745, to settle the War of the Austrian Succession on the basis of an Austro-French understanding. From 1745 the Saxons had sought to create an anti-Prussian Austro-French alliance, just as Hanover was a source for plans for an anti-Prussian alliance of Britain, Austria and Russia. Dynastically linked to France by the marriage of the dauphin to Augustus III's daughter Maria Josepha in February 1747, the Saxons, under the extremely flexible Count Brühl, sought to turn Louis XV against his Prussian ally, a policy that was to succeed eventually in 1756. Saxon talk of the need for a Catholic alliance helped to lead to Austro-French discussions in 1748, but Maria Theresa responded to French advances by making the unacceptable suggestion that Louis abandon Frederick. The Franco-Prussian alliance was an insuperable barrier to an Austro-French understanding in 1748 and was to hinder attempts to improve relations in the following years by Count Kaunitz, Austrian envoy in Paris 1750–3. These varied negotiations in the decades prior to 1756 indicate the extent to which it is misleading to think of the events of that year as shattering a rigid system dominated by geo-political considerations. In 1748 Marshal Richelieu suggested to Puysieulx that better Austro-French relations would not be too difficult to achieve even though they would '*absolutely* change the system of Europe'.[18]

If developments in the years immediately after 1748 scarcely suggested that Anglo-Prussian and Austro-French reconciliations were imminent, there were, nevertheless, indications that both the Old System and the Franco-Prussian alliance were under strain. British determination to use her allies to limit French influence clashed with the Austrian wish to direct their attention to the reconquest of Silesia. Such intentions were, however, a feature of most eighteenth-century alliances and there is no reason to believe that the so-called Diplomatic Revolution would have occurred in the form it did but for the chain of events that began in the Ohio valley in 1754. Kaunitz did not want to break with Britain and as late as 1755 he was still devoting considerable attention to the British alliance because he feared that his *rapprochement* with France would fail. Although the British did not support the idea of a war to reconquer Silesia and refused Austrian pressure to thus commit themselves, Anglo-Prussian animosity was more obvious in Europe in the early 1750s than its Anglo-French counterpart and fear of Prussian aggression towards Hanover encouraged Britain to turn to Russia and Austria for promises of assistance in 1753 and 1755.

This fear was lent urgency in 1755 by the breakdown of Anglo-French relations over the frontier between the French colony of Canada and the British North American territories. The commissioners to whom disputes had been referred at Aix-la-Chapelle had failed to settle them and as the agents of both powers jockeyed for position, each fearful that the others would gain a strategic advantage, fighting broke out. In July 1754 a force of Virginia militia under George Washington sent to resist French moves in the Ohio region was

---

[18] Paris, Archives Nationales KK 1372, 8 July 1748.

defeated by the French. Newcastle feared that if the French consolidated their position there they would be able to drive the British from America when war resumed, as he assumed it well might. As a result he insisted that action be taken to rectify the situation in North America, though he did not want a full-scale war. Thanks to Newcastle and George II's son the duke of Cumberland it was decided in September 1754 to send two regiments to Virginia which were to drive the French from the Ohio in early spring and then take action in other border disputes. Newcastle trusted in the pacific nature of the French ministry and the poor state of Franco-Spanish relations but he was soon dismayed by pressure from within the British ministry, principally from Cumberland and the Secretary-at-War Henry Fox, for a wide-scale aggressive attack on the French in America. Warned by British military preparations, the French began to prepare to send reinforcements, while negotiating with the British at the same time. The British ministry was forced to consider the possibility of a war with France in general and of a French invasion of Hanover, and in early 1755 sought promises of Austrian and Dutch assistance. Anglo-French negotiations revealed the incompatible nature of their territorial demands as preparations for war were stepped up. General Braddock with the British reinforcements sailed for America on 16 January 1755, being followed on 23 April by a fleet under Admiral Boscawen that was designed to prevent the arrival of the French troops that had embarked at Brest on 15 April. In early June Boscawen attacked the French fleet carrying the troops, though he only captured three ships in the fog. When the news reached Paris in mid July the French foreign minister Rouillé, claiming that 'the glory of the king, the dignity of the crown' and the protection that Louis XV owed to the life, honour and fortune of his subjects would not allow Louis to overlook Boscawen's action, ordered the French envoys to leave London and Hanover.

War was not declared until May 1756 but in the meantime both powers committed hostile acts, the British seizing all the French ships they could find on the open seas, beginning operations in Nova Scotia in June 1755 and sending Braddock to defeat the following month. The prospect of a French attack on Hanover or mainland Britain and of action by France's ally Prussia obliged the British ministry to seek firm commitments of support from Britain's allies, the envoy in the Hague writing in August 1755, 'If we can checkmate France in Europe, and be successful in America, the war may be sooner ended than most people dare as yet to imagine.'[19] However fear of French attack and a lack of interest in the British cause in America kept the Dutch neutral while Kaunitz had no intention of helping Britain. Refusing to reinforce the Austrian Netherlands, he made only vague offers to protect Hanoverian neutrality. Nevertheless the willingness to offer a substantial subsidy produced an Anglo-Russian treaty on 30 September 1755. This arose from the common antipathy of both powers to Frederick and was intended by the British to prevent him from attacking Hanover, but thanks to his fear of

[19] BL. Add. 35364 f. 52.

Russia it helped to lead Frederick to pay heed to suggestions, made that autumn through the duke of Brunswick, that he agreed to remain neutral in any Anglo-French conflict. The Anglo-Russian treaty promised mutual assistance in case of attack, provided for British subsidies and stipulated that for four years Russia was to maintain an army near the Livonian frontier from which it could threaten East Prussia. Alliance with Britain would apparently free Frederick from this threat, whereas if he provided France with assistance he would face Russia and possibly Austria as well. As a result Frederick, unimpressed anyway by French policy, accepted British proposals and by the Convention of Westminster of 16 January 1756 the two powers agreed to guarantee their respective possessions and to maintain peace in the Empire by jointly opposing the entry of foreign forces.

This was presented by the British to the Austrians as freeing Austria from any apprehension from Prussian attack and therefore allowing her to concentrate on resisting France, but in fact the Convention destroyed the system Britain had been seeking to create and thus ensured that the war would extend to the continent and that Britain would be vulnerable there. This was because the Anglo-Prussian *rapprochement* led Britain to lose the alliance of Russia, Prussia that of France. Tsarina Elizabeth and her Chancellor Bestuzhev had seen the British alliance as a step that would further their plans for war with Frederick. Seeing him as a challenge to their influence in eastern Europe, they sought to revive the schemes that had existed during the War of the Austrian Succession for a joint attack by Austria, Hanover, Russia and Saxony. Austria was to regain Silesia while East Prussia would be ceded to Augustus III in return for Courland and Poland east of the Dvina and the Dnieper to Russia. The prohibition in the Anglo-Russian treaty of 1755 of separate negotiations with the 'common enemy' was seen as referring to Frederick and Russian anger with the Convention of Westminster led them to refuse to ratify the treaty. Bestuzhev told the British envoy in February 1756 that he had been able to secure Elizabeth's consent to the treaty only by stressing that it was aimed against Prussia. Frederick's hope that the British would be able to restrain Russian animosity, of which he was well aware, were to prove misplaced, and the Russians were taken by their animosity to Frederick and alliance with Austria towards better relations with France, a power seen correctly in St Petersburg as hitherto determined to resist Russian influence in eastern Europe.

The Convention of Westminster also helped drive France towards Austria. Despite Kaunitz's efforts, relations between the two powers had not improved significantly. On 10 August 1755 Starhemberg, the Austrian envoy in Paris, wrote to Kaunitz that he was certain France would attack Austria as part of the developing international crisis. Three days later his opposite number in Vienna, Aubeterre, reported that if France attacked Hanover Austria would act, adding that Maria Theresa would never abandon George II. A month later Rouillé responded to Austrian assurances that they would not participate in the Anglo-French war with scepticism, asserting that Austria would always depend on Britain, while Aubeterre reiterated his view that Austria would never abandon Britain and would help her in the war. Alongside the formal diplomatic approach, Kaunitz also approached Louis through his influential mistress Madame de Pompadour. Louis was tempted by the idea of dividing Britain from her traditional ally. He also found Frederick an irritating and presumptuous ally. However, it was not clear that Austria would be more reliable and in September 1755 Pompadour told Starhemberg that Louis and his ministry assumed that British aggression stemmed from their certainty of assistance from their allies.

The situation was changed by the Convention of Westminster. The Prussian envoy in Paris had warned Frederick in November 1755 that the French government was very worried by reports of Anglo-Prussian negotiations and indeed they appeared to justify the Austrian claims that month that the Prussian alliance was not a natural one for France. Frederick does not appear to have appreciated the reaction in France: on 20 January 1756 he told the French envoy Nivernais who had been sent to renew the Franco-Prussian treaty that he was keen to do so. In fact French anger led Louis's council to decide on 4 February not to renew the alliance with Prussia. The Convention also angered the Austrians, whose plans for an attack on Silesia it hindered, leading to renewed efforts on their part. Maria Theresa wrote to her brother-in-law on 10 February that the new British engagements were directly contrary to her interests which, she claimed, could never be reconciled with Prussia. She ordered her envoy in St Petersburg to hinder the implementation of the Anglo-Russian subsidy treaty and on 6 March wrote to Starhemberg that she was ready to accept a French attack on Hanover for the sake of alliance with France. On 1 May the two powers signed a defensive alliance, known as the First Treaty of Versailles. It specifically excluded the Anglo-French war which had passed its phoney stage on 18 April 1756 when French troops landed on Minorca. Maria Theresa promised her neutrality and, as Starhemberg pointed out, Austria benefited most from the defensive agreement because her position made her more vulnerable to attack than France. On the other hand it appeared to free France for war with Britain by destroying the Old System, while the treaty stipulated that if a British ally attacked France Austria would help her.

The new alliance also helped Russian plans for war with Prussia as it appeared increasingly likely that such a conflict would benefit from Austro-French support, not least crucial financial support. On 26 March 1756 the newly established Russian 'Conference at the Imperial Court' produced an extensive plan for war with Prussia. Austrian hesitation about the extent of likely French assistance, for France was not bound by the Treaty of Versailles to an offensive war to gain Silesia, led Kaunitz to persuade Elizabeth to delay the attack until 1757. Frederick, well aware of Austro-Russian military preparations, decided to ignore British advice to restrict himself to defensive moves and instead to launch a pre-emptive strike. In order to deny a base to the gathering coalition against him, Frederick invaded Saxony on 28 August

1756. This was a dangerous move. Louis XV felt obliged to succour his heir's father-in-law and this added a powerful motive to French antipathy to Frederick. Indeed Frederick helped to precipitate both a hostile Franco-Russian *rapprochement*, and an expansion of the Austro-French alliance. Elizabeth acceded to the First Treaty of Versailles on 30 December 1756 and concluded an offensive alliance with Austria the following month. Meanwhile plans were drawn up for territorial changes that could result from the new alignment. The French sought gains in the Austrian Netherlands and suggested that Hanover lose Bremen and Verden. The possibility that the elector Palatine gain Prussia's Rhenish possessions was discussed. Frederick was willing to suggest to George II in December 1756 that Hanover acquire the bishoprics of Osnabrück and Paderborn but his hopes were increasingly desperate. He speculated about the chances of Elizabeth dying or Louis changing policy and he pressed the idea of a Protestant league. Frederick was, however, fully conscious of his vulnerable position and on 4 January 1757 he wrote to his sister the queen of Sweden, comparing himself to Charles XII at the beginning of his reign when three neighbouring powers had plotted his fall. In fact serious differences still separated his rivals, including French unhappiness about Russian troops operating on Polish territory and thus limiting Polish liberties, Elizabeth's anger about France's unwillingness to drop her Turkish alliance and Austrian opposition to French determination to extend the war to Hanover. Nevertheless, the pressure of the war that was already being waged drove them together to a considerable extent, even if Austria and Russia never joined France in her war with Britain. On 1 May 1757 an Austro-French anti-Prussian offensive alliance was reached in the Second Treaty of Versailles. The Diplomatic Revolution was complete. France promised an army of 105,000 and a substantial subsidy to help effect a partition of Prussia.

THE SEVEN YEARS' WAR 1756–63

The central facts of the war were the survival of Prussia in the face of Austria, Prussia, Russia, the Empire and, from March 1757, Sweden, and Britain's successful maritime and colonial war against France and, from January 1762, Spain. The long-term significance of both was considerable. Britain became the dominant European power in North America and India, while Prussian survival ensured that control of the Empire (Germany) by Austria and of eastern Europe by Russia would not go unchallenged.

British War

The war began badly for Britain with naval humiliation and the loss of Minorca to a French invading force under Richelieu in 1756, and widespread fears that the French would invade Britain itself that year. The early stages of the struggle in North America were not conspicuously successful, Louisbourg not falling in 1757, and in that year Richelieu overran Hanover forcing the defeated duke of Cumberland to sign the Convention of Kloster-Zeven which dissolved his army, left Hanover under French occupation and exposed Prussia's western frontier. In comparison Clive's victory at Plassey on 23 June 1757 which opened the way for British dominance over Bengal appeared a minor triumph. Prussian victories and George II's repudiation of the Convention saved the Anglo-Prussian relationship. Under a subsidy treaty signed on 11 April 1758 both powers agreed not to carry on separate negotiations, the British agreed to pay a subsidy of £670,000 and George II, as king and elector, promised to maintain an army of 55,000 in Hanover, to cover Frederick. Under this treaty, renewed in 1759 and 1760, Britain provided valuable financial and military assistance to the outnumbered and financially exhausted Frederick. Victories such as Minden in 1759 also denied the French control of Hanover, which would otherwise have served as a bargaining counter in negotiations rather as the Austrian Netherlands had done in 1748.

A more crucial triumph was the successful defeat of the French invasion plan of 1759. Choiseul, who became French foreign minister on 3 December 1758, proposed a joint attack with Russia and Sweden. Plans for Russian and Swedish forces to be transported on a Swedish fleet to Scotland were thwarted by the opposition of the two powers, but instead French landings of 100,000 troops in Essex and Glasgow and on the south coast were planned. British naval victories at Lagos (19 August) and Quiberon Bay (25 November 1759) destroyed the Toulon and Brest fleets and Choiseul's hopes of establishing the Jacobites, a change that would have been as dramatic as the schemes for a partition of Prussia. These victories contrasted with the failures of the British attacks on the French coast to divert forces from the war with Frederick as William Pitt, Secretary of State for the Southern Department 1757–61 and with Newcastle effectively joint-head of the ministry, had hoped. Cherbourg was temporarily seized in 1758 and its fortifications destroyed. Belle Ile off the Breton coast was captured in 1761 and held until the peace. However, whereas Britain could be threatened by invasion with serious strategic consequences, as in 1731, 1744, 1745–6, 1756, 1759 and 1779, France was not thus affected, despite the hopes of British politicians. This reflected the greater vulnerability of Britain to amphibious attack and the smaller size of its armed forces, both the regular and militia. Britain suffered the disadvantages of seeking to act as a great European power without possessing one of the basic requirements, a large army.

British amphibious forces were more successful outside Europe, not least because French naval weakness left them with the initiative. All the major centres of the French empire bar New Orleans were captured: Louisbourg and the West African slaving base of Goree (1758), Guadeloupe and Quebec (1759), Montreal (1760), Pondicherry (1761) and Martinique (1762). British success depended in part on Spanish neutrality but Charles III (the former

Don Carlos), who succeeded his childless half-brother Ferdinand VI in 1759, was concerned about a fundamental shift of oceanic power towards Britain. His attitude helped to encourage French firmness in the face of stiff British territorial demands during abortive Anglo-French peace negotiations in 1761. On 15 August the Third Family Compact and a Secret Convention were concluded obliging France to support Spain in her commercial and colonial disputes with Britain, and Spain to declare war by 1 May 1762 if peace had not been concluded. Attacks on Gibraltar, Ireland and Jamaica were discussed as was pressure on Portugal to abandon her British alliance.

Pitt responded to this new alliance by proposing a pre-emptive attack on Spain, resigning on 5 October 1761 when his plan was rejected. However, the failure of negotiations led to a British declaration of war on 2 January 1762. The Spaniards proved far worse prepared than they had assured the French and lost Havana and Manila to British amphibious attacks in 1762. Charles III hoped that gains in Portugal would compensate him for losses elsewhere and his invading forces had some success in April and May. A British expeditionary force helped to stiffen the Portuguese defence and on 17 August 1762 Choiseul informed his envoy in Madrid that it would be good for Spain if peace could be negotiated and that the moment had been lost for the conquest of Portugal.

Anglo-French discussions through Sardinian intermediaries in the winter of 1761–2 reflected the financial exhaustion of both powers, their desire for an end to the war and their unhappiness with their allies. They led to preliminaries of peace, signed at Fontainebleau on 3 November 1762 and confirmed by the Peace of Paris of 10 February 1763. France agreed to restore the territory of Britain's German allies with the exception of Prussia: Hanover, Hesse-Cassel and Brunswick; to return Minorca and to recognize Britain's gains of Canada, Senegal, Grenada, Tobago, Dominica and St Vincent. Britain returned Guadeloupe, Martinique, St Lucia, Goree, Belle Ile and Pondicherry to France and left the French a part of the valuable Newfoundland fishery. Havana and Manila were restored to Spain but she yielded East and West Florida to Britain, receiving Louisiana from France in compensation. Spain's commercial grievances against Britain were not redressed. Claims that were not satisfied included the British attempt to gain New Orleans and Portuguese demands for acquisitions from mainland Spain. The terms were criticized in Britain by, among others, Pitt on the grounds that they were too generous to the untrustworthy Bourbons and indeed in April 1763 the French began to gather information that might help in an invasion of Britain. However, the terms secured a large majority in Parliament and the success of the ministry in negotiating peace was popular. Furthermore, there was the risk that if Britain fought on she might become dangerously isolated, for the Anglo-Prussian alliance had collapsed in early 1762 amidst recriminations about unilateral negotiations. This reflected the absence of any long-term shared interest to bind the two powers together. Hanoverian security had brought them together but it became less important as an influence on British policy with the accession of George III in 1760 and was, anyway, not guaranteed by alliance to the maverick Frederick. As with so many alliances in the century, the prospect of a negotiated peace exposed serious strains. The British ministry failed to adapt the alliance to meet the consequences of the Anglo-French peace that they needed but it is unclear whether it could have survived in a post-war world in which both powers would have sought to manoeuvre to best advantage: Frederick without being tied to Britain's animosity towards the Bourbons and Britain without being tied to his opposition to Austria.

The Prussian War

Frederick's survival was the product of good fortune and military success, not only a number of stunning victories such as Rossbach (1757) over the French, Leuthen (1757) and Torgau (1760) over the Austrians and Zorndorf (1758) over the Russians, but also the advantage of fighting on interior lines against a strategically and politically divided alliance. Russian interests centred on East Prussia and Poland, the Austrians were most concerned by Silesia and, after Rossbach and the repudiation of Kloster-Zeven the French devoted their efforts to the Westphalian conflict with the British-financed and partly-manned Army of Observation. Frederick's task was far harder than in the First and Second Silesian Wars not only because of the number of his enemies, including crucially Russia, but also because he was very much the major target of Austrian action, as he had not been during the War of the Austrian Succession. Thus the opportunistic diplomacy which Frederick had used so skilfully during the 1740s was of little value during the Seven Years' War. Indeed an obvious feature of the conflict in comparison with the earlier war was the lesser role of diplomacy. There were fewer combatants in the Seven Years' War and they were, for at least the first few years, relatively more determined. The issues at stake and the strength of the anti-Prussian alliance thwarted British attempts to recruit Bavaria and Sardinia. George II might hold out to the Bavarian envoy in January 1757 the idea that the Imperial crown could return to the Bavarian house but it was clear that the prospect of gaining great power status was no longer an option for second-rank rulers, as it had been in the 1740s. There were no longer two roughly equal alliances competing nor would any partition of Prussia benefit such rulers as that of Austria had seemed to offer.

Although Prussia survived the war, indeed in a better shape than Saxony whose army had been forced to capitulate on 16 October 1756, it was not without serious difficulties. The summer and autumn of 1757 was a period of particular difficulty with a Russian invasion of East Prussia, a Swedish invasion of Pomerania, the French conquest of Hanover, the raising of the siege of Prague and the end of the Prussian invasion of Bohemia after the Austrian victory at Kolin (18 June) and the Austrian capture of Berlin and most of Silesia. Frederick saved the situation at Rossbach and Leuthen. In 1758 the Russians captured East Prussia, which they were to hold for the rest of the war, but Frederick's victory at Zorndorf blocked their invasion of Brandenburg. The following year the Russians defeated Frederick at Kunersdorf but failed to follow it up by concerted action with Austria. In 1760–1 the Austrians consolidated their position in Saxony and Silesia while the Russians overran Pomerania. Frederick was saved by the death of his most determined enemy Elizabeth on 5 January 1762 and the succession of her nephew Peter III, the duke of Holstein-Gottorp. Frederick was his hero and he speedily ordered the Russian troops to cease hostilities. On 5 May 1762 a Russo-Prussian peace restored Russian conquests and obtained Prussian support for a war with Denmark to restore the position of Holstein-Gottorp. Sweden followed Russia, concluding peace on 22 May. Peter's assassination in July and the succession of his wife Catherine II ('the Great') was followed by a cooling in Russo-Polish relations and the abandonment of plans for war with Denmark, but Catherine did not wish to resume the war with Frederick. Austria, isolated, was driven from Silesia. Prussian success against Austria and the death of Elizabeth permitted a peace to be signed at Hubertusberg on 15 February 1763 on the basis of the *status quo ante bellum*, terms that satisfied both Prussia and Russia.

The two peaces of 1763 ended a period of warfare that had lasted for three decades and involved most of Europe. They were followed by three decades mostly of peace in western, central and northern, though not eastern, Europe. In part this was due to the financial exhaustion produced by the wars, though that did not prevent Britain, France, Austria and Prussia from going to war in the late 1770s and Russia from doing so in 1768. The willingness to fight arguably reflected the fact that matters had been settled or nearly settled in the mid-century wars. The Wettins of Saxony had retained the Polish throne in 1733; the Habsburgs had survived the coalition assembled against then in 1741; the Russians had retained their dominance of eastern Europe; the British had defeated the Bourbons in the struggle to control the oceans, had driven the French from Canada and defeated them in India; Prussia had nearly been crushed by the Austro-Russian alliance. With the exception of Britain, these conflicts had been waged with scant reference to opinion outside the higher echelons of courts and governments. On 31 January 1757 Starhemberg reported that French public opinion was strongly against Austria and the Austrian alliance, but it was to last to 1791. In that year the developing vortex of disorder and governmental weakness in France was to suggest new directions in foreign policy that would even bind Austria and Prussia together in counter-revolutionary action but, until then, international relations were largely set in their mid-century mould.

III

1763–1793

INTRODUCTION

In many respects European international relations were very stable in this period. Despite periods when probings took place to create better relations, both Anglo-Bourbon and Austro-Prussian enmity remained reasonably constant. Austria continued to be the leading power in the Empire, and Russia in the Baltic and eastern Europe though both were challenged by Prussia and it was Prussia that was crucial to 1789–91 plans for a territorial reorganization of eastern Europe to reduce their power. Italy remained under the control of the Bourbons and the Habsburgs, effectively keeping the peninsula stable and leaving Sardinia with little role in international diplomacy. France absorbed Lorraine on the death of Stanislaus Leszczynski in 1766 and in 1768–9 purchased and annexed Corsica, the rebellious dependency of the republic of Genoa, but she had in effect abandoned earlier traditions of eastward expansion, a necessary cause and consequence of the alliance with Austria which lasted until 1791. As a result the Low Countries were free from external war from 1748 until 1792, though both the Austrian Netherlands and the United Provinces were affected by civil war in the late 1780s, which led to a Prussian invasion of the latter in 1787 to restore order. Similarly the Rhineland and the western areas of the Empire were peaceful from 1763 until 1792.

Nevertheless, stability did not preclude change. In eastern Europe Russian strength was displayed in wars with the Turks in 1768–74 and 1787–92 and intervention in the Crimea in 1782–3 and led to the annexation of the Crimea and the territory east of the Dniester and the establishment of Russia as a Black Sea power. The anxious French response to the fate of the Crimea and the British concern about Russian conquests which nearly led in the Ochakov crisis of 1791 to war between the two powers marked the beginning of the 'Eastern Question', the acute concern of western European powers in the apparent Russian succession to the Turkish Empire. In the short term more anxiety was aroused by the First Partition of Poland of 1772, an unprovoked despoliation of the country by Austria, Prussia and Russia that suggested that other vulnerable countries would encounter a similar fate, to the destruction of any notions of a balance of power or of international legality.

Britain's loss of the Thirteen Colonies in North America also appeared to usher in a new age. The successful rejection of the authority and power of a European colonial state and the creation of a strong republican trans-oceanic country inhabited by people of European descent was unprecedented and suggested that the combination of new ideologies and political mismanagement might sap traditional links and loyalties throughout the European world. France, Spain and the United Provinces had intervened in the War of American Independence to help the rebels but, though the war led to some traditional territorial changes between the European powers, Britain losing Minorca and Florida to Spain, and Tobago and Senegal to France, the major consequence of their intervention was to aid in the creation of a new state that owed nothing to the world of kings and courts. It was unclear how far the British empire would disintegrate in the 1780s. There were fears that British India and Ireland would be lost.

In fact British naval successes in the closing year of the American war, Bourbon financial exhaustion, and the stabilizing policies of William Pitt the younger, the son of the Seven Years' War Pitt, who was Prime Minister from December 1783 until 1801, helped to maintain the British empire and to strengthen it in the post-war world so that it survived the challenge of revolutionary France better than might have been predicted in 1780, when, in the Gordon Riots, a mob took over London.

Domestic disorder was to become an increasingly important element in international relations from the late 1780s. Rebellions in the Austrian Netherlands and Hungary affected Austrian conduct and Prussia sought to exploit them, prefiguring the attempts of revolutionary France to exploit revolutionary feeling elsewhere, but without the potent though at times weakening element of ideological affinity. However, alongside new developments traditional rivalries continued. Austria, Prussia and Russia watched each other's activities anxiously as Poland was partitioned into extinction in 1793 and 1795 while Britain, which had remained aloof from the crusade against revolutionary France in 1792, went to war with her in early 1793 over threatened French control of the Low Countries.

THE POLICIES OF THE PARTITIONING POWERS 1763–74

Eastern Europe had been dominated by four powers, Austria, Prussia, Russia and Turkey since the defeat of Sweden and the weakening of Poland during the Great Northern War, though this dominance was dependent on the maintenance of these changes, a task essentially fulfilled by Russia in the decades after 1721. A persistent challenge was mounted by France, publicly with support for Stanislaus Leszczynski in Poland, culminating in the expeditionary force sent to Danzig (Gdansk) in 1734, for Turkish demands that Russia stay out of Poland and for Swedish wishes for *révanche* against Russia. Privately the challenge stemmed from the *secret du roi*. This secret diplomacy of Louis XV began in the early 1740s with support for a plan that his cousin, the prince of Conti, become next king of Poland and it broadened out into a wish to recreate a powerful alliance of Poland, Sweden and Turkey that could serve French interests against Austria and especially Russia, which was seen in France as a disruptive alien force in Europe. These schemes had to be suspended during the Seven Years' War, when France's supporters in Poland became disillusioned by her willingness to accept Russian pretensions there, but it was to be revived after the war. Differences between Austria, Prussia and Russia were arguably more important as a challenge to the order created by 1721. When the three had co-operated, in 1726–32, eastern Europe had been particularly stable but Austro-Prussian and Prusso-Russian animosity had kept the situation precarious since the early 1740s. It was not precarious in the sense that major territorial changes had proved readily possible – Austria and Russia had survived the attacks of 1741, Prussia plans to attack her during the War of the Austrian Succession, and the third Silesian War. However conflict seemed a constant possibility and the uneasy jockeying of the powers led them to view all developments as matters that they had to influence in their own interest. They thus ensured that changes in Poland, Sweden and Turkey could not be viewed without concern. This was true both of internal changes and of territorial gains by one of the major powers, which led the others to press for equivalents. This concern remained after 1763 and was more important than the shifts in alliances between the three powers.

From Hubertusburg to the Outbreak of the Russo-Turkish War 1763–8

None of the eastern European powers had benefited territorially from the Seven Years' War and all had emerged financially exhausted and anxious to introduce domestic reforms that would revive and strengthen their states. The death of Elizabeth and the brief reign of Peter III had injected a major element of inconsistency into Russian policy and many other rulers felt that Catherine II's position was an unstable one. The first crisis was inspired by a traditional cause, the death of a king of Poland, Augustus III, on 5 October 1763 and manoeuvres over his succession. These started before his death and related to the possibility of resisting what the French envoy in Vienna, Chatelet, termed 'the despotism that the court of St Petersburg seeks in Polish affairs'.[1] Austro-Russian relations were cool after the Russian abandonment of Austria in 1762 and in July 1763 Kaunitz proposed united pressure by Austria, Britain and France on Prussia and Russia over Poland. That month the Saxon envoy warned Chatelet that if measures were not taken to oppose Prussia and Russia, the Saxons would in light of their strength have to abandon their pretensions. However, Britain, seeking better relations with Russia, was not interested in opposing her over Poland, her attitude from the early 1730s until the late 1780s while Austria and France were less determined than Prussia and Russia. Seeking a pliable monarch, Catherine supported the candidature of a former lover, the Polish noble Stanislaus Poniatowski, rather than a Saxon candidate who might make the throne appear hereditary. Frederick correctly saw Catherine's anxiety about opposition as an opportunity to assuage his fears of Russia by negotiating a defensive alliance, the treaty of 11 April 1764. This freed Catherine to dominate Poland while blocking any Austrian attempt to regain Silesia.

The new alliance served as the basis for the 'Northern System', advanced by Nikita Panin, who became Russian foreign minister in October 1763, a scheme that sought to maintain the Russian position in eastern Europe and dissuade France and Sweden from revisionist efforts by creating a collective security system of alliances that was to unite Britain, Denmark, Prussia and Russia. They were to co-operate in preventing anti-Russian policies and the reintroduction of strong monarchy in Sweden, the country that appeared to most threaten the Russian *status quo* after the Polish election had been settled in Poniatowski's favour. Russo-Danish treaties were negotiated in 1765 and 1767 but Britain stayed out of the system as a result of Frederick's opposition and British unwillingness to meet Russian demands for subsidies and the extension of any defensive guarantee to cover a Balkan war. Thus Russian foreign policy came to centre on a Prussian alliance that satisfied Frederick's desire for security while Prussia recovered from the punishing Seven Years' War, but that offered little to Russia if her attention was redirected towards Turkey.

[1] AE. CP. Autriche 295 f. 8.

Poniatowski was as much a disappointment for Catherine as Adolf Frederick of Sweden had been for Elizabeth; his rule prompted the idea that the Russian policy of an effective protectorate over Poland might require replacement. Catherine felt obliged to intervene to limit his independence and to block his moves to introduce reforms that might strengthen Poland. She used the position of the Dissidents, non-Catholic Poles, as an excuse and sent troops to influence the Diet of 1767–8. The Russian envoy Repnin behaved like a pro-consul, arresting five leading politicians in October 1767 for criticizing Catherine. Russian pressure led the Diet on 24 February 1768 to approve the Perpetual Treaty, by which Poland and Russia mutually guaranteed their territories, while Poland undertook to safeguard the rights of the Dissidents and placed her 'constitution, the form of her government, her liberties and her rights' in Catherine's hands. Kaunitz claimed that December that she had almost succeeded in making Poland a Russian province like Courland. Polish resistance issued in February 1768 in the formation of the Confederation of Bar and the outbreak of fighting. Turkey, concerned about the potential consequences of Russian control of Poland in any future war and encouraged by Choiseul, who had been pursuing a markedly anti-Russian policy since the spring of 1766, responded to the violation of her territory by Russian forces pursuing Polish confederates by declaring war in October 1768.

The First Partition of Poland and the Russo-Turkish War 1768–74

Despite initial unpreparedness, the Russians were soon beating the Turks, overrunning the Crimea, Moldavia and Wallachia and destroying the Turkish fleet at Chesmé in July 1770 with ships that had been sent from the Baltic, becoming the first Russian fleet to enter and winter in the Mediterranean. Though their attempt to use naval power to drive the Turks from the Aegean and to inspire a rebellion that would drive them from Greece was unsuccessful, Russian naval power had a serious economic effect on the Turks while other Mediterranean powers were forced to consider the possible implications of Russia spreading her power. When her warships at Zante disregarded Venetian quarantine and other regulations in 1773, observers wondered what military, political and commercial consequences might flow from Russian gains from the Turks, including a possible base in the eastern Mediterranean.

Russian success alarmed both Austria and Prussia, Kaunitz arguing in December 1768 that Austria had more to fear from Russia than Prussia, that Catherine sought a Greek empire, and that Russia could only be a safe ally when she was pushed back to her former frontiers. Austrian ministers were concerned about Russian gains in the Danubian principalities, traditionally an area of their interest, while the Prussians were anxious about both the unbalancing consequences of an excessive growth of Russian power and the possibility of Austro-Russian co-operation against the Turks. These twin fears produced warmer Austro-Prussian relations in 1769–70 and meetings between Frederick II and Joseph II at Neisse and Neustadt in August 1769 and September 1770 respectively. Frederick told Joseph at Neisse that it was necessary to stop Russia, while Kaunitz assured Frederick that Austria had renounced the idea of reconquering Silesia and that if Russia gained Azov and the Crimea her greater strength would threaten Prussia and Austria. Kaunitz instructed the Austrian envoy in Constantinople in November 1769 to assure Turkey of Austria's benevolent neutrality and in early 1770 Kaunitz proposed joint Austro-Prussian mediation of the Balkan war, a mediation that was to be supported by military preparations and a demonstration of strength. As the Turks indicated a willingness to accept mediation, such a step would be clearly anti-Russian. That December Frederick suggested to Swieten, an Austrian envoy, that the Crimea be made independent of both Turkey and Russia to which he replied that this would eventually lead to Russian annexation and dominance of the Black Sea. Insisting that Russia be stopped, Swieten stated that Austria would fight rather than see Turkey destroyed, to which Frederick replied that Russia's success had to be rewarded with some gain, a point he had already made, for example at Neisse. However, Frederick found Catherine's demands, outlined that month, intolerable. They included territorial gains especially Azov, free navigation of the Black Sea, Crimean independence, an Aegean base and the occupation of the Danubian principalities for twenty-five years. The Austrians persisted with their plan for an armed mediation with Prussia and took hostility to Russia to the point of signing a defensive alliance with the Turks in July 1771 which, though unratified, led to their acquisition of the poor Turkish province of Bukovina in 1775.

However, neither Austria nor Prussia really wanted war, and their ability to co-operate was compromised by distrust. Frederick's solution was an agreement to offset any threat to the balance of power posed by Russian gains by allowing Austria and Prussia a share with Russia in a partition of Polish territory, hitherto a sphere in which neither had had much influence. A settlement of Polish disputes was clearly going to have to be part of any eastern European pacification. The French had sought to use the Polish situation to help the Turks. French agents were sent to the Confederates and in August 1770 Choiseul chose General Dumouriez as an agent charged with creating a confederate army that would, with French help, be able to assist the Turks. In common with others who had sought to turn eastern European insurrectionary movements against Austria, Russia and Turkey, Dumouriez was disappointed to find the Confederates divided, badly armed and disciplined and less numerous than he had hoped, but French plans lent force to the Russian desire to regain control of Poland. A partition would ensure that the settlement was to the benefit of all three powers. A partition had been sent for discussion to St Petersburg by Frederick in February 1769, but it had been dismissed as impracticable. Pursuing his anti-Russian theme, Kaunitz had suggested to Frederick at Neisse that Catherine withdraw her forces from

Poland and that the three powers should jointly guarantee the peace of Poland, but Frederick became more interested in the idea of partition as the result of a favourable visit by his brother, Prince Henry, to St Petersburg, a visit that worried Kaunitz greatly. Despite Panin's opposition, Catherine in the autumn of 1771 accepted the idea of a partition which she hoped would defuse tension with Austria and Prussia and allow Poland to be quietened.

Despite Austria's forcible annexation of the county of Zips and of three areas in the Carpathian foothills in 1769–70, there was opposition in Vienna to the idea of a partition that would benefit Prussia and which Maria Theresa regarded as a crime. When in May 1770 Frederick had suggested to an Austrian envoy that Austria might gain Bavaria, he had been told that Austria had never usurped anyone's territory and his suggestion that she could seek Parma and part of the Venetian republic had similarly been rejected. However, the danger that Prussia and Russia might make gains without any Austrian equivalent was sufficient to lead to a change of heart. In February 1772 Prussia and Russia agreed to the acquisition of Polish territory and by conventions signed in St Petersburg on 5 August 1772 precise shares were allocated. The presence of Russian troops in Poland and the danger of further losses led the Polish Diet to accept the partition on 30 September 1772. By it Poland lost nearly 30 per cent of her territory and 35 per cent of her population. Austria gained Galicia and over 2½ million people, Russia a less populous area in Polish Livonia and White Russia while Frederick gained Polish (Royal) Prussia, linking East Prussia to Brandenburg.

The partition was greeted with outrage and fear. D'Aiguillon told Mercy, the Austrian envoy in Paris, that the defensive provisions of the Austro-French alliance could not extend to these new gains, while Mercy's counterpart, Rohan, and his government complained about the Austrian failure to consult France. George III termed the declaration of the partitioning powers 'revolting and unjust', and expressed his hope that their alliance would not last. However, when Stanislaus appealed for his support, George replied that he could see no other remedy but that of divine intervention. It was feared that the partitioning powers would seize other territories, Prussia possibly acquiring Danzig and Swedish Pomerania and Russia intervening to reverse Gustavus III's Swedish *coup* of August 1772. One of the British Secretaries of State, the earl of Suffolk, responded to reports that the Prussians might attack Hanover, by telling the Wittelsbach envoy, 'if the triple alliance continues one could say that these three powers are the sovereign masters of the continent and could partition it as they wish, and I am very afraid that they already have plans to achieve this'.[2] These fears persisted. In 1773 the duke de Broglie, formerly envoy in Warsaw and the director of the *secret du roi*, painted for Louis XV a bleak picture of the consequences of the new alliance,

> Poland will remain partitioned, the Turks defeated, Gustavus will probably be dethroned; all of Germany will only exist at the discretion of the Emperor and the

[2] Munich, Bayr. London 250, Haslang to Beckers, 29 Dec. 1772.

king of Prussia, who will despoil the princes one by one. Italy will be threatened with oppression under the specious pretext of Imperial rights, and all of Europe will be subject to the influence of three rulers, united in order to subjugate or overturn it.[3]

As far as the Balkans were concerned such fears were largely misplaced. Agreement over Poland ensured that Austria dropped her support for the Turks and the scale of Russian demands led to the failure of Russo-Turkish negotiations in 1772–3. When military operations were resumed in 1773, however, the Turkish empire did not collapse, not least because of the diversion of Russian forces to deal with the Pugachev rising, a peasant-Cossack rising of 1773–4 that indicated the potentially serious political consequences of a brutal social regime, as the Transylvanian rebellion of 1784 was also to do. By the treaty of Kutchuk-Kainardji of 21 July 1774 Russia gained several Crimean fortresses and territory to the north of the Black Sea and in the Caucasus, was allowed to fortify Azov and to navigate on the Black Sea. Russia also gained the right to protect those associated with a new Orthodox church in Constantinople, a provision that was to be extended to wide-ranging demands to protect Orthodox Christians, and obtained the independence of the Khanate of the Crimea, a move that was assumed correctly to be a preliminary to Russian annexation. Sir James Porter, a former British envoy in Constantinople, remarked in October 1774 that the new Russian possessions in the Crimea 'will hold any navy in Europe . . . they may soon have one superior to the Turks in which case with a fresh north-east wind they may be masters of Constantinople in 48 hours besides they may throw aside the chimerical independence of the Tatars'.[4] Though indeed the Crimea was to be annexed in 1783, the final stage in the destruction of the buffer zone between Russia and Turkish centres of power, assumptions about Russian naval power were to be proved exaggerated by the war of 1787–92, while for the rest of Europe the crucial aspect of Kutchuk-Kainardji was the Russian failure to obtain their earlier goals in the Danubian principalities, let alone the Aegean.

A New European System?

Arguably the best comment on the fears provoked by the First Partition was the absence of significant territorial changes in the following two decades. The Austrians did not increase their power in Italy, the Bavarian Exchange Scheme was thwarted, Russia did not succeed in intimidating Gustavus III. In large part, however, this relative stability reflected the anticipated collapse of co-operation between the three powers which led to the War of the Bavarian Succession of 1778–9. Thus the immediate consequences of the triple alliance were short-lived. Nevertheless both contemporaries and later commentators

[3] E. Boutaric, *Correspondance secrète inédite de Louis XV sur la politique étrangère* (2 vols, Paris, 1886) II. 497–8.
[4] Bedford CRO. L30/14/314.

argued that it inaugurated a new era in international relations, one characterized by a use of strength to gain territory without consideration of even
tenuous legal claims. Outrage was one response to an apparently novel
situation, as can be noted readily in the diplomatic correspondence of the
period. A Sardinian diplomat claimed in April 1773 that the partitioning
powers had adopted 'new maxims' and ignored the 'solidity of the most
solemn treaties'. The Palatine foreign minister was worried by the rapidity of
new Prussian claims and observed in September 1773 'the policies of governments are in such a confused chaos and their systems are so little followed that
it is impossible to know what to believe'. The British envoy in Paris wrote in
1774 that the triple alliance was 'a connexion so contrary to every political
principle, a connexion begun in and supported by violence . . . every system is
unhinged . . . we see the wisest courts act in direct contradiction to their
essential natural interests'.[5] Such claims of 'new maxims' are, however,
somewhat surprising. Not only had treaties been cynically breached on many
occasions, but the actual or planned despoliation of weak states by more
powerful neighbours, alone or in combination, was far from novel. The
remodelling of territorial control by agreement among some or all of the
major powers, generally without heeding the views of their weaker counterparts, had been a characteristic of the extensive diplomacy over the Spanish
Succession and was a feature of the peace settlements of the period. William
III had told Tallard in April 1698 that they were determining the fate of
countries they did not control. It is possible to present this diplomacy in an
optimistic light by stressing the role of equivalents, considerations of balance
and the desire to achieve a peaceful and 'rational' solution to disputes,
especially in avoiding general war. The reality was also that the pretensions of
the weak were overriden and that such manipulative diplomacy was generally more fertile than successful. Partition plans were less common in the first
half of the eighteenth century than rumoured schemes such as that in
1715–16 of a league of Austria, Spain and Victor Amadeus II to redistribute
the territories of western Europe in the event of the death of Louis XV, or an
anti-Austrian scheme of France, Spain and Russia in 1722, a plan to partition
the Austrian Netherlands in 1724 or the possibility of co-operation between
Austria, France and Spain to despoil Sardinia in 1748. However, the rumours
indicate the extent to which partition plans were considered feasible and
there were anyway a number of such schemes including those of the
anti-Swedish coalitions during the Great Northern War, the plan of 1722 for a
partition of Poland between Prussia, Russia and Augustus II and those during
the War of the Austrian Succession for partitions of Austrian and Prussian
territories.

Numerous suggestions of hostile seizures of territory can be found in the
diplomatic correspondence and they were not only propounded by rulers,
such as those of Russia, who had few dynastic and other legal claims that they

[5] AST. LM. Ing. 79, 9 Ap. 1773; Bayr. Wien 699, Beckers to Ritter, 6 Nov. 1773, London 251, Beckers to Haslang, 25 Sept. 1773; PRO. SP. 78/294 f. 209.

could advance. In 1704 Frederick I of Prussia demanded Nuremberg as his price for abandoning the Grand Alliance, in the early 1740s Spain advanced plans for major territorial changes in Italy, while in 1744 Frederick II, while suggesting major gains for Prussia and Saxony in Bohemia, argued that Charles VII could be compensated for his claims there with the archbishopric of Salzburg and the bishopric of Passau. The Baltic was a region particularly fertile in schemes for new territorial dispositions, some not intended as hostile, such as the Holstein project in 1726 for the acquisition of Russia's conquests from Sweden by the duke of Holstein-Gottorp or the Danish wish to regain Sweden by monarchical election in the 1740s; others required war such as those of 1744 for action against Prussia, leading to the gain of East Prussia by Poland with Russia obtaining an equivalent in eastern Poland, and for the acquisition of Bremen and Verden from Hanover by Denmark which was in turn to return Schleswig to Holstein-Gottorp.

Contemporaries had little doubt of the sweeping changes envisaged by many rulers and consultation of the documents provides little support for claims that attitudes were characterized by 'a stultifying conservatism' and were 'defensive'.[6] Amelot, the French foreign minister, commented on the 'vast ideas' of Charles VII in 1743 while in 1744 the French envoy to Charles, faced with the accusation that French policy would be seen as renewing the idea of a universal monarchy, complained that George II sought to dispose of eastern France 'like the things in his garden at Herrenhausen'. The same year a British diplomat claimed that French support for the Jacobites 'gives a flat lie to the boasted moderation and innocence of her views and must convince every subject of the republic, as well as of England, that not only the possessions of the House of Austria, and the Balance of Power, but even our own liberties and religion, are struck at by that ambitious power'.[7] Minor powers were particular victims of the desire for expansion. Those in the German part of the Empire, especially the vulnerable ecclesiastical principalities and Imperial Free Cities, were protected to a certain extent by respect for, and a disinclination to challenge, the Imperial constitution, guaranteed as it was by the Imperial position of the Habsburgs and by the guarantors of the Peace of Westphalia, particularly France. In northern Italy, however, the situation was less favourable, and the Austrians seized, with scant respect for justice, the Duchy of Mantua and a number of smaller territories. Their limited respect for legal rights was more than matched by the rulers of Savoy-Piedmont whose expansionist schemes were conducted simply with reference to diplomatic opportunity. Frederick II told a British envoy in 1748 that Genoa had been justified in joining the Bourbons because by the Treaty of Worms her territories had been disposed of 'against all the rights of man'. Paradoxically he also revealed that he was willing to support a similarly illegal and unprovoked Hanoverian acquisition of Osnabrück and Hildesheim.[8] The

[6] J. Childs, *Armies and Warfare in Europe 1648–1789* (Manchester 1982) pp. 21, 101.
[7] AE. CP. Bavière 102 f. 78, 110 f. 71; PRO. SP. 84/402 f. 90.
[8] *Politische Correspondenz* VI, 100–1.

fate of Genoese-owned but rebellious Corsica had also been a matter of discussion with it being provisionally allocated in the 1740s to both Don Philip and Sardinia. Francis of Lorraine had complained impotently about the fate of his duchy in 1735.

Possibly the First Partition created such a shock because Europe had been territorially stable since 1748, but it is more likely that the key element inspiring fear was the combination and seeming apparent invulnerability of the three partitioning powers. A sense of balance was lost and that destroyed any element of predictability. It was no longer the case that schemes would be opposed by states that could hope to block them. However it would be wrong to suggest that the shock was felt all over Europe. James Harris, the British envoy in Berlin, commented in November 1772, 'the South of Europe seems to be so little concerned with what is going on in the North',[9] and although Britain, and to a greater extent, France were worried about the actual and possible consequences, both were soon to be more interested in the fate of the maritime and colonial balance of power.

DIVISION AMONG THE PARTITIONING POWERS, 1775–87

Predictions that the tensions between the partitioning powers would divide them became more realistic as the Polish occasion for their co-operation receded in importance. In August 1775 Harris noted, 'I never recollect the North in such a state of tranquillity, glutted with the division of Poland the several powers seemed to be sleeping off their debauch – the moment of their awakening I have no doubt will be serious, every day may produce events, which may certainly change the present system and the smallest change in this system necessarily brings about new alliances'. That March a Wittelsbach diplomat had suggested that it was hardly probable that the powers' large armies would long rest idle, a point also made by others.[10] The principal cause of tension was Austrian concern about Russian intentions in the Balkans, which led an Austrian envoy to tell Frederick II in early 1775 that Austria would oppose any further Russian advance which would, he argued, unbalance Europe. Joseph II was increasingly adopting a more volatile attitude than his mother and co-ruler Maria Theresa. Concerned by this, Frederick sought both to improve his relations with Catherine and to increase French concern about Austrian intentions, instructing his envoy in Paris in December 1776 that Joseph's ambitious views could be used to this end.

---

[9] Bedford CRO. L30/14/176/10.
[10] Bedford CRO. L30/14/176/22; Bayr. London 253, Haslang to Beckers, 10 March 1775; J. Richard, *A Tour from London to Petersburg* (1780) p. 159.

Distrust ensured that the partitioning powers did not plan their policies jointly or create co-operative arrangements akin to that established in the so-called Congress System after the Napoleonic wars. Partly as a result differing views over the first major dispute, the Bavarian Succession, led to war. Neither Maximilian Joseph (1745–77) nor his successor Charles Theodore of the Palatinate had any direct heirs and Joseph II saw this as an opportunity to gain much of Bavaria. After Maximilian Joseph's death on 30 December 1777 he reached an agreement with Charles Theodore by which the latter ceded much of Bavaria and many of his illegitimate children were found posts in Vienna. This was opposed by Frederick II, concerned about any accretion of Habsburg strength, by Charles Theodore's heir, Charles Augustus of Zweibrücken, by the elector of Saxony who had his own claims and by France, which was concerned about Habsburg gains in the Empire. Unwilling to support either side militarily, not least because of her developing commitments to the American cause, France's refusal to support her Austrian ally was a serious blow to the Habsburgs especially as Catherine gave important diplomatic support to Frederick. Frederick attacked in July 1778 but failed to win a decisive victory. The cost and stalemate of the conflict and Maria Theresa's concern for peace led rapidly to negotiations and by the Peace of Teschen of May 1779, Austria gained the Innviertel, a small but strategic area of south-eastern Bavaria that was far less than the gains stipulated in the agreement with Charles Theodore. The peace was concluded under Franco-Russian mediation, leading to an important increase in Russian prestige particularly in the Empire. Harris wrote from St Petersburg, 'Here we distribute peace on all sides, and the Empress enjoys gloriously the effects of her strength and greatness' while a compatriot observed 'the Russians may now be considered as the arbiters of Germany, since it is evident that their conjunction with either power must overwhelm the other'.[11]

The war and a revival in concern about the Balkans led to a diplomatic realignment. Joseph's determination to destroy the Prusso-Russian alliance took precedence over earlier concern about Russian expansion against the Turks and was aided by the death on 29 November 1780 of Maria Theresa who was hostile to Catherine. Catherine gradually shifted her attention in the late 1770s from Panin and his 'Northern System', a policy essentially of defending a beneficial *status quo*, to ambitious anti-Turkish schemes, including the Greek Project, the plan for the expulsion of the Turks from the Balkans and the creation of an empire ruled by her grandson born in 1779 who was symbolically christened Constantine. These schemes were associated with an influential former lover Potemkin who was closely associated with the development of Russia's recent gains from the Turks. Russian intervention in the Crimea, in support of a client khan, Sahin Giray, and the convention of Aynali Kavak (1779) increased Russian control of the Crimea. Catherine supported agreement with Austria in order to facilitate her plans and, though her claims to an

[11] Bedford CRO. L30/14/176/27; Richard, *Tour* p. 159.

imperial title which Joseph found unacceptable prevented the negotiation of a formal treaty, in May and June 1781 the two rulers exchanged letters that in practice constituted a secret treaty of defensive alliance.

The alliance was to be of considerable benefit to Catherine both in facilitating her peaceful annexation of the Crimea and in freeing her from having to fight the Turks alone later in the decade. Instability in the Crimea, where Sahin Giray proved an unreliable client ruler, led to Russian military intervention in 1782 and annexation on 19 April 1783. Vergennes sought British co-operation against the step, just as in March 1777 he had written of the need for Anglo-French co-operation against measures to weaken Turkey, but the British preferred to hope for improved relations with Russia. Catherine's disclosure of the secret Austro-Russian alliance that summer successfully intimidated France and Prussia.

Joseph was less successful in his projects. Compared by Frederick II in August 1781 to a chemist who kept the affairs of Europe in fermentation, he took a number of steps which increased his reputation for unpredictability and disrespect for international agreements. Uninterested in compromise or the views of others and unwilling to honour accepted conventions and privileges, either domestically or internationally, Joseph prefigured to a certain extent the attitudes of revolutionary France, though he proved less willing to push issues to a crisis, In 1780 the tradition that a Wittelsbach should fill the archbishopric electorate of Cologne and the neighbouring prince bishoprics was broken in favour of the election as successor of Joseph's younger brother Maximilian. In 1781 Joseph expelled the Dutch garrisons from the Barrier, but French opposition led him to back down from a threatened war with the Dutch over the opening of the Scheldt in late 1784. Earlier that year he began to press hard the scheme for an exchange of the Austrian Netherlands for Bavaria but, though Charles Theodore was willing, his heir was not and the French, unwilling to support a measure which they saw as likely to strengthen the Habsburgs, refused to support their ally. Russia offered some diplomatic support but was unwilling to intimidate Frederick II who responded to Joseph's plan, at a time when the Emperor was already disillusioned about his prospect of success, and to Austrian pretensions in general by forming a *Fürstenbund*, League of Princes, with other German princes in July 1785. It was a measure of the suspicion aroused by Joseph that the German princes, who had traditionally supported the Emperor or been wary of opposing him and had thus tended to isolate Frederick within the Empire, were willing to publicly form a league against him. Many of the ecclesiastical princes were also unhappy about Joseph's attitude to the Church and suspected him of being willing to support secularization. The *Fürstenbund* was more powerful than the last major league unrelated to external sponsorship, the Wittelsbach *Hausunion* of the 1720s, and it represented a revival of the alliance of 1719–26 between Hanover and Prussia that had opposed the apparent determination of Charles VI to increase imperial authority in the Empire.

The *Fürstenbund* marked the failure to weaken Prussia within the Empire and was to be followed by growing French interest in a *rapprochement* with her and by the Anglo-Prussian alliance of 1788. It helped to bring stability to the Empire in the last years of Joseph's reign as sole ruler (1780–90) but this stability was probably more due to the unwillingness of Joseph's French and Russian allies to provide significant support for his schemes. Just as in Italy, the last years of *ancien régime* diplomacy in the Empire were characterized by territorial stability, a marked contrast to the uncertainty and apparent volatility produced by war and confrontation in eastern Europe. The principal threat to this stability came from Austrian hopes of benefiting from the death of Frederick in August 1786 in order to wage a war of revenge against Prussia. Such hopes were probably unrealistic, but they were to be dashed anyway by the Turkish declaration of war on Russia in August 1787.

WAR AND CONFRONTATION IN EASTERN EUROPE, 1787–95

An escalating Russo-Turkish struggle for influence in the Caucasus and Turkish anxiety about the development of Russian Black Sea naval bases at Kinburn and Sevastopol led the Turks to fear Russian attack but it was actually they who declared war unexpectedly in August 1787, probably because of the rise of bellicose ministers in Constantinople and the apparent opportunities created by Russian harvest problems. Joseph II had sought to prevent a Russian attack but the Turkish declaration of war activated the defensive side of his alliance with Catherine. Kaunitz, whom Joseph had retained as Chancellor while increasing his own role in foreign policy, argued that Austria would have to support Russia both because of her possible need for assistance against Prussia and more particularly to prevent a Prusso-Russian reconciliation, and in order to influence Russian conduct of the war in the Balkans. Joseph unenthusiastically could see no alternative option and in February 1788 Austria declared war having attempted unsuccessfully a surprise attack on Belgrade.

The war was not as disastrous initially for the Turks as many had imagined, and though Russia captured Ochakov in 1788, neither she nor her ally had much to boast of from that campaign. The conflict broadened when Gustavus III took advantage of Russian commitments to declare war in 1788. He saw Russia as a hostile power and hoped by successfully reconquering some of Sweden's former territories to strengthen his position domestically. However, domestic opposition, especially in Finland, hamstrung his efforts and he was only rescued from action by Denmark, Russia's ally, in August 1788 thanks to Anglo-Prussian pressure, including a threatened Prussian invasion. Gustavus

signed a subsidy treaty with the Turks in July 1789 but his failure to defeat
Catherine led to the signature of peace at Verela in August 1790 on the basis of
the frontiers of 1788, Russian recognition of the new Swedish constitution of
1772 and a Russian renunciation of intervention in Swedish politics.

The failures of 1788 had led Joseph II to begin peace negotiations with the
Turks in the winter of 1788–9 but the accession of the bellicose Selim III in
April 1789 caused their failure. However, the Austrian and Russian armies
fought well that campaign, defeating the Turks and capturing Belgrade and
Bender respectively. The prospect of substantial Austro-Russian territorial
gains led Prussia to press for an equivalent from Poland, which was to be
compensated by regaining Galicia from Austria. The prospect of war with
Frederick William II, who was already providing diplomatic support to Selim,
and escalating domestic problems in the Austrian Netherlands and Hungary,
where Prussia appeared willing to support rebellion, led Joseph's successor
Leopold II (1790–2) to decide to defuse the crisis soon after his succession in
February 1790. The possibility of war with Prussia was lessened by a convention with her negotiated at Reichenbach on 27 July 1790 which provided for
an end to operations against the Turks and the summoning of a peace
conference which produced the Peace of Sistova of August 1791 by which
Austria returned her gains.

Catherine was less concerned about the anti-Russian movement of
Austrian policy under Leopold than by a comparable shift in Poland. Russian
control there decreased with the outbreak of war in the Balkans and the Polish
reform movement that had begun after 1772 culminated in the four-year Diet
that began in 1788 and saw the rejection of Russian influence and the issue of
a new constitution on 3 May 1791. This changed Poland into a hereditary
constitutional monarchy and instituted a number of far-ranging political and
governmental reforms. The establishment of a substantial standing army was
also stipulated.

Reform in Poland was supported initially by Prussia, which signed a
defensive alliance on 29 March 1790, and by Britain. Both were concerned to
prevent any Balkan settlement that might leave Austria or Russia too powerful and, having divided Leopold from Catherine, they saw an opportunity to
reduce Russian influence in eastern Europe. Russia was an important commercial partner of Britain and agreement, if not alliance, with her had been
the goal of successive British ministries, not least because of her poor relations
with France. However, relations had deteriorated for a number of years
because of Catherine's hostility towards George III, whom she believed to be
intriguing against her, and because the Russians, far from renewing the
commercial treaty with Britain which had expired in 1786, had concluded
one with France in 1787. Suspicion of Russia led to opposition to her interests
in eastern Europe. This direction was encouraged during the Regency Crisis
produced by George's severe ill-health in the winter of 1788–9 during which
the initiative in the Triple Alliance was increasingly taken by Prussia with its
bold plans for limiting Austro-Russian power while in British foreign policy it

was increasingly taken by the anti-Russian envoy in Berlin, Joseph Ewart. Pitt, who was influenced by Ewart, hoped that Poland would become a larger trading partner than Russia and he sought to impose the *status quo ante bellum* on Catherine. This demand was supported by British preparations for a naval expedition to the Baltic and by an attempt to create a powerful anti-Russian alliance, a move that was weakened by the Russo-Swedish peace and by Leopold's refusal to co-operate. The crisis culminated in the spring of 1791 with the presentation of an ultimatum demanding that Russia not annex Ochakov and the territory between the Bug and the Dniester. However, serious domestic criticism, in part due to skilful action by the Russian envoy Vorontsov, and an absence of ministerial confidence over the issue led to a climb-down which destroyed the Anglo-Prussian alliance and thus British influence on the continent, and left Russia free to settle with the Turks. Further Russian victories led Selim to accept negotiations in the summer of 1791 and by the treaty of Jassy of 9 January 1792 the Turks confirmed the terms of Kutchuk-Kainardji, recognized the annexation of the Crimea and yielded Ochakov and the territory between the Dniester and the Bug.

The failure of the confrontation with Russia led Frederick William II to abandon the Turks and seek reconciliation with Russia. Catherine was furious at the collapse of Russian influence in Poland and worried that reform would lead Poland to radicalism. Freed of the Turkish war she was able to concentrate on restoring her influence in Poland, a course eased by the death on 1 March 1792 of Leopold II who was unenthusiastic about intervention in Poland, and by the outbreak of war between France and Austria on 20 April 1792. Russian troops invaded Poland in mid-May under the pretext of supporting the Confederation of Targowica, a Polish noble league that Catherine had inspired. The outnumbered Poles were forced to submit in July 1792. Catherine's concern that Poland be thoroughly controlled in order to prevent it from becoming a revolutionary base and her wish to keep Frederick William II in the struggle with France led her in December 1792 to accept his demand that he be compensated with Polish territory. By a Russo-Prussian treaty of partition signed at St Petersburg on 23 January 1793 Poland lost about 60 per cent of her territory and about half her population. Most of the gains were made by Russia, which received the western Ukraine, Podolia and the rest of White Russia, while Prussia gained Danzig and Great Poland. Russia forced the Diet of Grodno to ratify the treaty, to reject the constitution of 3 May 1791 and on 16 October 1793 to accept a treaty making Poland in effect a Russian protectorate. A Polish insurrection against the new settlement began in March 1794 but was crushed by the Russians, with Prussian assistance, by the end of the year. Both powers intended to retain their gains in a fresh partition and, though Austria had wished to maintain a Polish buffer state and had stayed neutral, she felt obliged, by the Prussian military advance and by the need to maintain her position with respect to the other powers, to intervene. Austria and Russia agreed on their shares and the more ambitious Frederick William II was coerced into accepting them in 1795. By treaties signed on 24 October 1795 Poland ceased to exist as a state. Though Russia had in exchanging her protectorate for partition lost influence over much territory, she had acquired the largest section of Poland, extending her frontiers considerably further west with the acquisition of Courland, Lithuania and Podlesia in 1795. Her role in eastern Europe was to be further enhanced by the difficulties that French success and expansion created for Austria and Russia.

THE REVIVAL OF FRENCH ACTIVITY AND THE ORIGINS OF THE REVOLUTIONARY WAR, 1789–92

While events in eastern Europe dominated the diplomatic agenda, developments in France in 1789–90 simply enhanced the extent to which the country had already been largely written off as a political force. There was concern in some quarters that the Estates General might lead to the reform of French society and institutions and thus a revival of French strength, but this was swiftly ended by the political turmoil that instead followed. Foreign governments were most interested in the state of the French armed forces and government finances and both these deteriorated with army mutinies, naval indiscipline and depreciation and an increasing loss of confidence. The confused, factious and weak French response to the Nootka Sound Crisis in 1790 appeared to epitomize the collapse of France as a power and her related unreliability and lack of value as an ally. *Émigré* requests for assistance were rejected by, among others, Louis XVI's brother-in-law Leopold II, and only the maverick Gustavus III was prepared to consider intervention. And yet within two years both Austria and Prussia were to be at war with France and by the end of 1792 French forces had overrun the Austrian Netherlands, Savoy and part of the Rhineland.

This change was due to developments in France but also to events elsewhere. In 1790 neither Austria nor Prussia were really in any state to fight France, however weak she might be. Both were principal players in the crisis in eastern Europe and Austria was additionally challenged by rebellions in Hungary and the Austrian Netherlands. The resolution of the eastern crisis the following year enabled a shift in attention to take place. The Austro-Prussian *rapprochement* that followed the Convention of Reichenbach led on 27 August 1791 to the Declaration of Pillnitz, a joint statement by Leopold II and Frederick William II expressing concern at the position of Louis XVI after his unsuccessful flight to Varennes, and the wish that the European powers would act to assist him. Louis's youngest brother the duke of Artois, who had left France after the fall of the Bastille, and his advisor Calonne were both at

Pillnitz though they had little influence there or elsewhere. Though the declaration made action dependent on support by other states and was a disappointment to French *émigrés*, it was important not only because it encouraged French radicals to argue that the revolution was under external threat and must be defended, thus ensuring the process of radicalization under real or apparent threat that is crucial to so many revolutions, but also because it indicated that the two monarchs were concerned. This was more important than the actual provisions of their concern at Pillnitz.

In late 1791 Austro-French relations became increasingly tense as each power sought, in an atmosphere of growing mistrust and uncertainty, to intimidate the other, both convinced that the other would respond by backing down and failing to appreciate that their measures would be taken as warlike steps. Two major areas of tension were the feudal privileges of German princes in Alsace and the protection afforded to the *émigrés* in the Rhineland, particularly by the archbishop-electors of Mainz and Trier. On 4 August 1789 the French extended the abolition of the feudal regime to the Alsatian rights of German princes that had been guaranteed by successive treaties. This was a clash between the national sovereignty of a new political order determined to enforce its decrees universally within its frontiers, and the intention of other powers to retain a more variegated notion of sovereignty in which inherited privileges and corporate rights played a major role. The Imperial Diet declared its support of the princes' claim in July 1791 and Leopold's subsequent backing for it in diplomatic exchanges with Paris that winter aroused anger there. Coblenz in the electorate of Trier had become the central focus of *émigré* activity in 1791 and, as French concern about counter-revolutionary activity and possible intervention in France increased, so more pressure was exerted on the Rhenish rulers to deny the *émigrés* support and hospitality. This led to Leopold indicating his determination to defend the princes from any French pressure. Conventional diplomatic relationships were being compromised by pressures arising essentially from ideological fears. Radical French attitudes appeared to threaten agreements as with German privileges in Alsace and to suggest that sovereign rights would be challenged, as with the Rhenish rulers or the Papacy, whose enclave of Avignon within France had been annexed in September 1791.

In France a political grouping under Brissot saw confrontation with Austria as a means to power. The cause of 'peoples against kings' was a potent one in radical circles not least because kings seemed to be acting against peoples. Increasingly aggressive policies were advocated in Paris and Austrian demands were rejected. Leopold II, who had sought to avoid war and without whom a violent German confrontation with France was impossible, died on 1 March 1792 to be succeeded by his more bellicose son Francis II. On 20 April France declared war on Austria in the hope that a revolutionary crusade would defeat the enemies of the Revolution, consolidating it in France and extending the revolutionary example elsewhere in Europe. A variety of proposals for the reorganization of Europe were advanced including the extension of France to her 'natural limits' and the division of much of Europe into small republics. *Émigrés* from failed revolutions elsewhere in Europe, particularly from the Austrian Netherlands and the prince-bishopric of Liège, Dutch 'Patriots' and radicals from other countries, such as Britain, encouraged deceptive opinions concerning the willingness of their compatriots to rebel and help France, and pressed strongly for French assistance in remodelling the Low Countries.

Initially the war went badly for the revolutionaries with the failure of their offensive into the Austrian Netherlands. Frederick William II, who had signed a defensive alliance with Leopold in February 1792, declared war on France on 21 May 1792, hoping that Prussia would again reap the glory and seizure of the diplomatic initiative that her successful invasion of the United Provinces in 1787 had brought and be rewarded with Polish territory. A Prussian army under the duke of Brunswick invaded France but supply problems and the lateness with which the campaign had begun encouraged him not to persevere when his forces encountered superior French forces in a skirmish at Valmy in September. The French gained the initiative invading Savoy, the Rhineland, and the Austrian Netherlands. An outnumbered Austrian force was defeated at Jemappes in November and their position in the Austrian Netherlands collapsed. Although many of these losses were to be reversed the following year, the Austrians defeating the French at Neerwinden in March and driving them from Mainz in July, it was clear that the war was not going to be a quick police action or a profitable restoration of order in France. The strength of revolutionary France was readily apparent by the end of 1792 and it was to help dictate the diplomatic and political agenda in an increasing amount of Europe for several years.

ANGLO-BOURBON STRUGGLES
1763–83

Although both the Anglo-Prussian relationship and Franco-Russian good relations did not survive the Seven Years' War, both the Austro-French and the Franco-Spanish alliances did. This sustained the difficult position Britain had been in. Hopes that the Austro-French alliance would disintegrate proved misplaced and, whatever the tensions between the two powers, Austria was unwilling to co-operate with Britain against France until the era of the French Revolution. Attempts to negotiate defensive treaties with Prussia and Russia proved unsuccessful and thus the British faced the prospect of renewed conflict with France without allies. Arguably more crucial was the French success in winning the support of the other major maritime powers, Spain and the United Provinces. The United Provinces was a declining naval power, but its naval support had been useful in the Spanish and Austrian Succession wars and in other episodes in the first half of the century such as the attempt to intimidate Spain navally in 1729. In the Seven Years' War the Dutch had been neutral and their complaints about the British attempt to prevent their handling of French trade had been a major grievance. It helped to lead in the War of American Independence to Dutch support for France which led in 1780 to a British attack that was misguidedly intended to provoke a crisis that would sweep William V of Orange into power, as his predecessors had been in 1672 and 1747. The fourth Anglo-Dutch war (1780–4) led to major Dutch losses of shipping but it helped to worsen Britain's relative naval position.

Spain was more important as a naval power and the nearly constant poor relations from 1759 to 1790 posed a serious problem for Britain. They contrasted with the situation earlier in the century when, despite concern over the consequences of the Bourbon succession in Spain, relations between France and Spain had often been poor, in large part because of Spanish expansionist interest in Italy. The Anglo-Spanish conflict of 1718–20 had arisen as a direct result of this interest and Philip V and his wife were more interested in fighting Austria in 1741 than Britain in 1739. They were willing to satisfy British commercial demands for the sake of support in Italy in 1729 and 1731 and the Austrians feared that the British would make a similar offer in 1741. In the second half of the century, however, the Spaniards displayed a greater concern with the trans-oceanic position. This reflected the greater threat apparently posed by the British who now appeared as conquerors rather than interlopers, Charles III's determination to obtain more substantial economic benefits from the empire, and the stability of Italy and the western Mediterranean where the attack on Algiers in 1775 did not indicate any intention to conquer North Africa. The French government was sure that the naval parity with Britain it achieved in 1778 could not be upheld without the addition of the Spanish fleet and Spain indeed played a major role in the War of American Independence. However, there was nothing inevitable about Spanish support for France and the Franco-American alliance of 1778. Charles III was unhappy about the idea of helping American rebels, and offered Britain neutrality in 1778 in exchange for Gibraltar. It was the unacceptable nature of the British response to the Spanish offer to mediate, rather than any immutable consequences of the Family Compact, that led Spain to help France. The Spaniards insisted on French assistance to regain Florida, Gibraltar and Minorca and that the two powers mount a joint invasion of Britain in order to force a quick end to the war, an attempt that the weather helped to make an expensive mistake in 1779.

If Spain was an important ally to France in the American war, with colonial and commercial grievances of its own against Britain, it was, nevertheless, France that was Britain's prime opponent in Europe, on the oceans and in the colonial world. Readjustment of Britain's continental foreign policy in the 1730s so that it centred on finding allies against France, a policy that had been given greater force by the duke of Newcastle after 1748, was not reversed, even though George III and his ministers were less interventionist in European diplomacy than his grandfather George II and his ministers had been. There was concern in London and, to a far greater extent, Paris, about events in eastern Europe and this led to suggestions of co-operation but they were less important than the continued reality of rivalry. In both Britain and France it was assumed that the peace negotiated in 1763 would not last. The British used gunboat diplomacy in 1764–5 to defend their position successfully in colonial disputes in West Africa and the West Indies. However, domestic stress, associated especially with the Wilkesite troubles, ministerial instability and, according to some historians, a maladroit handling of foreign policy, helped to produce a confused and weak policy in the later 1760s which encouraged the assertive schemes of Choiseul and led in particular to the irresolute response to the French annexation of Corsica in 1768. The Falkland Islands crisis of 1770, in which Britain threatened war when Spain expelled a British settlement, led France to the brink of war in support of her ally. The Falklands were seen as a staging post to the Pacific, an area of Spanish commercial monopoly that the British were increasingly keen to penetrate. Louis XV's unwillingness to fight, which led to Choiseul's fall on 24 December 1770 and to the notification of Charles III that France needed peace, defused the crisis and persuaded Spain to accept an agreement on 22 January 1771. By this Spain restored Port Egmont to a British garrison, in return for a secret verbal assurance that Britain would eventually abandon it, as she did, largely on the grounds of cost, in 1775.

D'Aiguillon, Choiseul's successor as foreign minister, 1771–4, was interested in the idea of a *rapprochement* with Britain, in order to resist what he saw as the threat of Russian power to the European system. He set out deliberately to make concessions in colonial disputes in order to improve relations, and in March 1772 proposed concerted pressure on Austria and Russia to dissuade them from partitioning Poland. George III, however, responded coolly and when the French-backed Gustavus III staged a coup in Sweden in August 1772, seizing power from a ministry inclined to Britain and Russia, suspicion of France increased.

Concern about the domestic response clearly played a major role in dissuading the British ministry from heeding D'Aiguillon's approaches, but there were also good diplomatic reasons for British caution. An Anglo-French understanding would have committed Britain to opposition to the most powerful alliance in Europe, fears were raised about the security of Hanover, it was pointed out that the French could do little to help Poland, and British ministers argued that the partitioning powers would not remain united for long. It was easy for observers to suggest that Britain and France might be able to negotiate an understanding, based on France agreeing not to offend Britain in commercial and maritime matters but British ministerial suspicion of France remained strong and, however concerned the government might be about the policies of the partitioning powers, it had no wish to allow France to commit Britain to opposition to them. However poor British relations with the partitioning powers might be, it was more reasonable to hope that they could be improved than that a successful Anglo-French alliance could be created. In addition, it was possible that D'Aiguillon would be replaced by a less co-operative minister as happened in 1774 when the accession of Louis XVI led to his replacement by Vergennes. In such a situation it would be foolish to have alienated other powers simply because Britain and France had held similar views in 1772. These attitudes led the British to use threats in 1773 to dissuade the French from deploying their navy against Russia in the Baltic and the Mediterranean. However, conflict was avoided as both powers sought peace because of their domestic problems and saw no reason to fight.

It was to be the American rebellion that altered the situation. The new ministry of 1774 was less inclined than D'Aiguillon to heed British wishes, but they would not have risked war with Britain had it not been for developments in America where in 1775 discontent had turned into rebellion, leading the British ministry to decide on a military solution. The rebels sought the assistance of France and they found her ministry unwilling to commit itself publicly but ready to provide financial and military assistance. Vergennes hoped that the British would lose America and therefore that a colonial balance of power, lost in the Seven Years' War, would be restored, enabling the two powers to co-operate in limiting the influence of the partitioning states and France to redirect expenditure from the navy. Other French ministers were more interested in the simple idea of weakening Britain. Expenditure on the navy more than quadrupled between 1774 and 1778. Tension over French aid to the rebels, specifically allowing their privateers to use French ports, led Vergennes to press Louis XVI in the summer of 1777 for French entry into the war. The British failure to defeat the Americans that year, culminating in Burgoyne's surrender at Saratoga on 17 October and Howe's futile campaign in New Jersey and Pennsylvania, encouraged the French to intervene and led to the treaties of Alliance and Commerce of 6 February 1778 with the rebels. The notification of the Treaty of Commerce to the British government on 13 March led to the recall of the British envoy in Paris, for George III could not accept the recognition of American independence. As neither power wished to appear an aggressor to her allies, hostilities did not begin until June when the struggle to control Channel waters began.

French intervention was to make the possibly impossible British task of conquering America completely impractical. Until then it had been feasible to imagine that British success might lead to a negotiated end to the war and thus obviate the need for total victory, but the French role made independence a reasonable goal. For France, however, the war brought major financial burdens and in the short term it restricted her chance to affect the Bavarian succession crisis of 1778–9. By going to war she limited her options and mortgaged her future as most eighteenth-century combatants did, but she did so without pressing need and failed in the long term to either appreciably increase her influence in Europe or her relative power overseas.

The British proved reasonably successful in resisting the Bourbons but were defeated in America. Though Minorca and a number of West Indian islands were lost, Gibraltar successfully resisted an active siege and the French failed to defeat the British in India, though their squadron under Suffren and their ally Hyder Ali of Mysore won a number of victories. By 1782 British general superiority at sea was established and the Franco-Spanish naval effort was nearing exhaustion toward the end of the war. Rodney's victory at the Saints in April 1782 saved Jamaica from invasion. However, the previous year French superiority in American waters had forced the blockaded Cornwallis on 18 October to surrender to the French and Americans at Yorktown. The British still held much of America, including New York, Charleston and Savannah, but Yorktown produced a political crisis that brought down the ministry of Lord North, ending twelve years of ministerial stability and bringing to power the Rockingham Whigs who were determined to give independence to America and negotiate peace. As Vergennes was anxious to direct his attention to blocking Russian expansion in the Crimea British willingness to negotiate was matched by France. Rockingham's death on 1 July 1782 was followed by the creation of a new ministry under the earl of Shelburne who was responsible for the more far-reaching aspects of the peace. He saw American independence as an opportunity to create a fruitful commercial relationship between Britain and America that might also bring political co-operation. While retaining Canada, Newfoundland and Nova Scotia for Britain, he yielded the 'Old North West', the lands south of the Great Lakes, to the United States. Bourbon gains were more modest, France receiving Tobago, Senegal and concessions in the Newfoundland fisheries, while Spain obtained Minorca and East and West Florida. Symbolic of the changed relationship was the abrogation of the article in the Peace of Paris giving Britain the right to maintain a commissioner at Dunkirk to prevent the rebuilding of its fortifications. The Dutch yielded the Indian port of Negapatam to Britain and the right of navigation among their spice islands (modern Indonesia). The terms of the Peace of Versailles on 3 September 1783 have to be seen in the wider political and diplomatic context. Britain was isolated but France was exhausted and had failed to conclusively undermine the British empire. Noailles, the French envoy in London, wrote to Vergennes in January 1778 of his hope that the division of the British empire and thus the loss of British power would deny France's continental rivals their principal help, specifically by ending Britain's capacity to subsidize them. In contrast twenty-one months later Robert Liston, the British envoy in Berlin, complained, 'is it possible anyone can be blind to the danger that threatens the peace of Germany and indeed the system of Europe from the aggrandizement of France, the proportional degradation of England? I am afraid this danger is seen at a great distance by many who do us the honour to think we should be a pretty good match for France, even after the loss of America'.[12] Those Liston complained of were to be more accurate than Noailles. Britain was to be a

[12] AE. CP. Ang. 528 f. 54–5; BL. Add. 35517 f. 224.

good match for France when they next confronted each other in 1787, and France had already discovered that her continental influence was limited.

FROM IMPERIAL CONFLICT TO REVOLUTIONARY WAR, 1783–93

British Recovery, 1783–90

British attempts after the American war to gain continental allies were singularly unsuccessful. Both Joseph II and Frederick II rejected British approaches and, despite British efforts, a Franco-Dutch treaty was signed in 1785. Attempts to exploit continental crises in order to divide Austria from France also failed. In late 1784 Joseph nearly went to war with the Dutch as a result of his aggressive attempt to force the opening of the river Scheldt and thus increase the trade of the Austrian Netherlands in defiance of Dutch wishes and the terms of the Peace of Westphalia. The British hope that this would present France with an insuperable problem of choosing between two allies was, however, defeated by skilful French diplomacy and Joseph's unwillingness to push his scheme to the point of war. The following July George III, as elector of Hanover, formed with Frederick II and Saxony a *Fürstenbund* (League of Princes) intended to prevent Joseph from dominating the Empire. In particular it aimed to stop his Bavarian Exchange Scheme, a plan for the exchange of Bavaria and the Austrian Netherlands, which would have increased the homogeneity and contiguousness of Joseph's possessions. George's action, taken without consulting his British ministers, undermined their attempts to improve relations with Joseph and Catherine II, who both refused to discriminate between British and Hanoverian policy, but failed to tie Frederick to Britain.

The British failure to win allies was reflected in the low esteem Britain was held in and the extent to which French power and intentions were no longer seen as a threat by other continental monarchs, however much they might extend in the colonial world and despite the ability of France to inhibit Joseph's plans in the Low Countries and the Empire. In Britain the loss of America was exacerbated by successful Irish pressure for constitutional change in the relationship with London, the Yorkshire Association, a strong provincial movement for political reform, the Gordon Riots in London and the ministerial instability that lasted from the fall of North to Pitt's triumph in the 1784 general election. This turmoil led continental commentators, such as Joseph II and Frederick II, to place a low estimate on British strength and stability. Had a neutral observer been asked which European country would experience a revolution within a decade, he would probably have replied Britain, not France.

Diplomatic rivalry with France was matched by naval and colonial competition, particularly in India where concern about French intentions magnified France's interest in developing her position in the Indian Ocean which, with the Pacific, was the great area of imperial and commercial speculation in the last two decades of the century. Distrust was endemic, understandably so in light of the experience of the American war, which suggested that France would exploit any difficulties that Britain encountered. In this context the commercial negotiations that culminated in the Eden treaty of 26 September 1786 were of limited importance. The Peace of Versailles had stipulated such a treaty and Vergennes had been anxious for it, believing that it would help the French economy and bind the two nations together by economic links, rather as Shelburne hoped to do in the case of Britain and America. Shelburne supported the causes of freer trade and economic links between Britain and France, but after his fall in February 1783 the proposals received little support in the British ministry until threatened French reprisals led them to negotiate in earnest. The abolition of certain tariffs and the lowering of others in the treaty negotiated by William Eden were contentious steps in both countries and contemporaries were divided about their economic consequences, a difficult subject to assess not least because of the economic depression in France in the late 1780s and the varied and decentralized nature of the French economy. British manufactured exports certainly harmed certain French industries, although probably far less than complaints might suggest. The two commodities most noticeably affected were wines from France, and woollens from Britain. Since both had been smuggled in large quantities, the change to official trade did not at first mean growth. French colonial trade continued to grow, driving Britain from part of the prosperous trade in the re-export of colonial goods, such as sugar. Commercial links with France were defended with considerable enthusiasm by Pitt, who criticized the idea of natural enmities, but that notion was deeply entrenched in the British political nation, being expounded not only by opposition figures who criticized the treaty, such as Charles James Fox, but also by George III, the Marquis of Carmarthen, Foreign Secretary 1783–91, and most British diplomats. Carmarthen's view that the two powers were naturally in competition led to the dispatch of instructions to Sir Robert Ainslie, British envoy in Constantinople, that lent weight to French, Austrian and Russian complaints that he and the ministry encouraged the Turks to declare war on Russia in August 1787, thus activating the Austro-Russian defensive alliance of 1781. This meant that the two powers would be less able to intimidate Prussia from taking an anti-French stance in the Dutch crisis. This crisis had become a test of Anglo-French relations in large part because of the aggressive intervention of Sir James Harris, British envoy at The Hague, another diplomat who, supported by Carmarthen, was suspicious of France and sceptical of the Eden treaty.

The Dutch crisis fused British concern about French maritime and colonial intentions with her attempt to limit French influence in Europe. The fear that France would gain control of the Dutch navy and of Dutch colonies, particularly those on the route to India at Cape Town and in Ceylon, made the struggle between the British-supported Orangists and the French-backed Patriots more than simply a dispute for diplomatic dominance. As in America, France helped a movement seeking to create new political arrangements. Though not democrats, the Patriots were a movement of those in the middling orders traditionally excluded from the oligarchic world of Dutch politics and through their militia, the Free Corps, they were able to gain power in a number of areas, including the wealthiest province Holland. In late 1785 William V left The Hague. Harris's activity and British financial support helped the Orangist cause but they and Britain might not have succeeded but for the long-desired Prussian intervention of September 1787. This was provoked by the arrest and humiliating temporary detention of William's politically active wife Wilhelmina, the sister of Frederick William II, who had succeeded his uncle Frederick II in August 1786. This was an affront with results comparable to the return of the Infanta in 1725 and Frederick's attack on Louis XV's Saxon relations in 1756. It led to Prussian ultimatums to the Patriots and preparations for military intervention that were crucially encouraged by the outbreak of war in the Balkans, which tied the hands of France's ally Austria. French threats to act on behalf of their Dutch protégés were thwarted by a lack of money, a lack of diplomatic support and successful Anglo-Prussian brinkmanship. While Britain armed her fleet, Prussian forces invaded the United Provinces in September 1787 achieving a rapid and complete success. This victory prefigured the ability of the Austrians to restore order in the Austrian Netherlands and of Russian regulars to defeat Polish irregulars, but provided no precedent for Prussian action against the regular forces of revolutionary France.

The French failure to act led to their diplomatic nullity of the late 1780s. Arguably they could not have faced Britain and Prussia alone but they had been defeated and humiliated in a crisis of brinkmanship. Possibly the Balkan crisis was to blame, but the Austro-French alliance had been devoid of much meaning in terms of co-operation and shared views for a number of years and France's inability to influence her partner was if anything masked by the crisis. Had Louis XVI acted in 1787 and the Prussians not invaded then possibly he and the French monarchy would have achieved an aura of success and prestige that would have helped to counter the complex grievances of those years. As it was, the developing domestic, financial and constitutional crisis led to the Assembly of Notables in 1787, its failure and the decision in 1788 to summon an Estates General, a national representative body that had not met since 1614 and whose decisions it was impossible to predict. In foreign policy terms 1787 marked the beginning of the Revolution and of the first stage of revolutionary France's international position, one of nullity and inconsequential diplomatic gestures, that was to last until 1791.

French diplomatic impotence was underlined and exacerbated by the effects of the Dutch crisis. On the one side, Austria and Russia paid no heed to French attempts to mediate a Balkan peace that would both enable them to confront Prussia and also protect the interests of France's traditional ally Turkey. On the other side an Anglo-Dutch-Prussian alliance system was created that lent permanence to the consequences of the crisis. William V's authority was restored, many of the Patriots fleeing to France where during the Revolution they were to press for action against him, while moves for a Franco-Prussian *rapprochement* were blocked. Anglo-Dutch and Dutch-Prussian defensive treaties in April 1788 were followed on 13 August 1788 by an Anglo-Prussian defensive alliance, creating the so-called Triple Alliance of 1788.

This alliance was to lead Britain to take an active role in eastern European diplomacy and, in the Ochakov crisis of 1791, to confront Russia's Balkan plans. This interventionist policy was arguably only possible because of French weakness, just as previous episodes of confrontation with Russia in 1716–27 were, although due to Hanoverian commitments, made possible by alliance with France. Pitt, however, had to back down in 1791 in large part because opposition to Russia did not command the favourable resonances in the political nation that hostility to France enjoyed. In contrast, the previous year Pitt's aggressive attitude towards Spain in the Nootka Sound crisis had been in tune with political sentiment. Spanish determination to control the American Pacific coast south of Russian Alaska led to a clash with British fur-traders at Nootka Sound on the west coast of what is now Vancouver Island. Pitt demanded recompense for a destroyed trading post and seized ships, and used a substantial naval mobilization to press for a wide-ranging settlement of Anglo-Spanish colonial disputes. Seeking to resist, the Spaniards asked for French assistance under the Family Compact. This produced a confused response in Paris, where factional politics led the National Assembly to challenge the royal right to declare war, before in August it voted to arm a considerable fleet. Uncertainty over French intentions, justified scepticism about the ability of the French to prepare a large fleet, British pressure and the size of the British navy all led Spain to back down, though their concessions did not meet the demands of the British opposition. A settlement in October 1790 gave Britain access to the empty coastline north of Spanish California and secured Spanish consent to British whaling in the Pacific. Two years earlier a British penal colony had been established at New South Wales in the opposite corner of the Pacific. The French had been major Pacific explorers with state-sponsored expeditions under Pérouse and Bougainville, but it was Britain that was increasingly gaining ground around the ocean's rim. Her influence was to further increase during the following quarter-century as naval mastery in the wars of 1793–1815 allowed Britain to conquer the colonies of other powers and to dominate Europe's trans-oceanic trade.

Britain and the Revolution 1789–93

On 1 August 1791 the *Salisbury and Winchester Journal* reported, 'At a meeting of the gentlemen of the Hampshire club, established for the support of public liberty, held at the George Inn, in the city of Winchester, on the 22 ult. the following toasts were given [including] May all the nations of Europe renounce ambitious schemes of war and conquest . . . May Britons be as averse from invading the rights of others, as zealous in maintaining their own'. Initially there was considerable British enthusiasm for changes in France. Though the violence that accompanied episodes such as the storming of the Bastille in July 1789 was criticized, it was pointed out that violence had marked major episodes of constitutional change in Britain. France had been generally and inaccurately portrayed as a tyranny and the events of 1789 were commonly seen both as the overthrow of this tyranny and of the related power of the Catholic Church, and as the establishment of rights akin to those enjoyed by the British. Similarly Britain was widely praised in 'progressive' French political circles. There were more references to British than to American models in debates over the future shape of France and the British were generally seen as a free and prosperous nation benefiting from a constitutional monarchy and the rule of reasonable law. Initially there was little fear in France of war with Britain, as opposed to the continental monarchies, and in 1790 Robespierre argued that those who supported such a war were enemies of the Revolution. The possibility of a co-operative block of Britain, France and the United States was advanced by a number of groups, including the Jacobin merchants of Rouen.

However, there were also signs of tension from the outset, not least because of the unhelpful British response to French requests for help in the food crisis of 1789 and because of persistent rumours that Britain was secretly intervening in French politics by means of bribes. 'Pitt's gold', it was claimed, was meant to weaken France in order to allow Britain to seize her prosperous West Indian colonies. Bribery was certainly used during the Nootka Sound crisis, but policy towards Britain, as towards Austria, was in large part determined by unpredictable factional struggles within France, rather than by the policy of the British ministry. Initially, in late 1789, there had been concern that France would intervene in the Austrian Netherlands where the authority of Joseph II had been rejected, but France did not do so and Austrian control was reimposed in 1790. That year the hostile French position during the Nootka Sound crisis led to a new wave of xenophobia in much of the British press but, once the crisis had passed, the British ministry returned to their concern with events in eastern Europe, paying no heed to requests for action from French monarchical *émigrés* or to the attempt by Edmund Burke to link the Revolution to the danger of domestic subversion in his *Reflections on the Revolution in France*, with Swift's *Conduct of the Allies* (1711), arguably the most powerful commentary on foreign events to be offered to the British public that century. The ministry neither feared that France threatened British interests, nor were disposed to heed the declarations culminating in that of Pillnitz of 27 August 1791 by Frederick William II and Joseph II's successor, his brother Leopold II (1790–2), in which they called for united action to assist Louis XVI. Louis's flight to Varennes in June, an unsuccessful attempt to flee France in order to engineer the fall of the new political system, had led to a decisive abrogation of his powers. George III and the British ministry were opposed to intervening in France to secure a particular constitutional settlement, especially the reintroduction of a powerful monarchy, their relations with Austria and Prussia were cool following the reconciliation between those two powers and the collapse of the Anglo-Prussian alliance in the aftermath of the British back-down in the Ochakov crisis, and Pitt did not wish to jeopardize his attempts to improve Britain's overstretched finances by higher military expenditure or war.

Britain therefore adopted a neutral position when war broke out between Austria and France in April 1792. Initially there was governmental concern about the prospect of Austro-Prussian success, but their failure and the French overrunning of the Austrian Netherlands in November 1792 created a more worrying situation. The British ministry and many French politicians did not want war but the British felt bound to respond to the threat to the United Provinces and to a number of decress including the opening of the Scheldt and on 19 November 1792 the offer of French help to all subjects seeking to overthrow tyrannical governments. The autonomous French approach to diplomacy, their determination to reject the conventions and practices of *ancien régime* international relations and the absence of any strong government that could give a clear, firm direction to policy suggested that it would be impossible to fulfil hopes of a compromise settlement over the Low Countries, a crucial area of British interest. Tension was increased by mutual hostility towards domestic developments in the other country, moves in Britain against pro-French and apparently pro-French radical groups, and the radicalization of the French revolution, the September massacres, the abolition of the monarchy and the trial and, on 21 January 1793, execution of Louis XVI. This led to the expulsion of French diplomats in London. Suspicious of British intentions the French declared war on Britain and the United Provinces on 1 February 1793.

The British had already responded to the overthrow of Austrian control in the Austrian Netherlands by making approaches for co-operation to the continental monarchies. Britain now took a major role in creating the first Coalition (1793–7) against France but, as in their earlier wars with France, they found their allies unwilling both to subordinate their strategies to British wishes and, at least in British eyes, to forget traditional animosities and interests. Soon after revolutionary France declared war Eden, now Lord Auckland, expressed his wish that the world be restored 'to peace, or at least to that old state of disorder which was a paradise in comparison to the present "infernalité"'.[13] At least in so far as the war with France was concerned that

[13] Bodl. Bland Burges Deposit 31 f. 8.

state continued and Polish independence was soon to be its victim. British radicals had a point in contrasting the Pitt ministry's opposition to the French attempt to create a new political order in the Low Countries with its willingness to accept the second and third partitions of Poland in 1793 and 1795. However, the ministry's determination to influence the fate of eastern Europe had been victim of the Ochakov crisis and from 1792 the British concentrated on their traditional area of prime concern, the Low Countries. They should not have been surprised that other powers acted similarly.

IV

Practice and Theory in *Ancien Régime* International Relations

The academic study of international relations essentially dates from the late nineteenth century and it has tended to reflect the assumptions and methods of that period. All decisions were 'rational', factors of personality and prestige appear as aberrations and it is commonly assumed that national interests existed and both could and can be readily defined. This approach was lent weight by the understandable dominance in the study of international relations of diplomatic sources, which tend to rationalize decisions. They can be, however, a very misleading guide, not least because the foreign policies of rulers in this period were not the products of discrete semi-autonomous bureaucratic institutions, largely unrelated to domestic affairs. Instead, *ancien régime* institutions responsible for the conduct of foreign policy tended to be small, unspecialized and lacking in independence, and foreign policy was not an autonomous activity. Policy in most states was the product of court politics, and administrative institutions existed to carry out these policies and were themselves generally dominated by court factionalism. The personal views of monarchs were therefore central and the role of those who could influence them was crucial. Monarchs only had to be responsive to a limited extent, if at all, to the views of others and foreign policy was the field of government activity where royal power and authority tended to be greatest, precisely because there was little need for the co-operation between crowns and elites that was a characteristic feature of the governments of the period. It was not surprising then that the personal concentration of authority in the field of international relations led to a pronounced tendency towards volatility. The unpredictability of developments was a common theme of diplomatic correspondence. The French ambassador in Vienna wrote to a friend in December 1725 that; 'at a time when we are in a situation to give the law to Europe the smallest event could make us the weakest state in Europe'. The following July his Lorraine counterpart in Spain observed, 'this century is the century of major events.' The Sardinian envoy in London noted in October 1730 'anything is possible in a system as confused as that of today', a French diplomat suggested in January 1733 that the state of Europe was changeable to an unprecedented degree and that July a Palatine diplomat referred to the continual changes in the universe.[1] Central to the issue of monarchical interests was the question of dynasticism.

DYNASTICISM

The suggestion that monarchs should be, as Frederick II put it, 'first servants of the state' clashed with the conventional assessment of the relationship between rulers and their dynastic traditions, not least in assuming a clear concept of state interest that could serve as a guide. The customary view stressed the patrimonial nature of royal authority and the diplomatic documents of the period referred to sovereignty as property. In most monarchical states hereditary kingship was practised and rulers were conscious of their position as part of a family and of their responsibility to it. This encouraged a stress not only on dynastic and personal honour but also on the specific rights that were held to be the family's inheritance. These were a repeated theme not only of royal remarks but of the diplomacy of the period. They were employed by powerful rulers, such as Louis XIV in the War of Devolution and the Palatine inheritance dispute, but also by their weaker colleagues, discouraging them from compromising their claims by concessions. The Hohenzollerns of Brandenburg–Prussia maintained their claim to the Silesian duchy of Jägerndorf, confiscated from a Hohenzollern who had opposed the Habsburgs in the early 1620s, and it was raised by, among others, the Great Elector. In October 1725 the duke of Holstein-Gottorp told the French envoy in St Petersburg that he preferred to rely on providence and wait for helpful international developments rather than to take any step that would render him contemptible to his posterity.

Dynastic issues also ranged in size from the Spanish and Austrian successions or the Swedish succession in the 1740s, to the frequently as bitterly contested minor disputes that were so prominent in Germany and northern Italy, both areas of divided sovereignty. These disputes were generally legalistic in character and it is difficult to apply the notion of rulers as servants of their states to them, especially as, although some actions can be characterized as attempts to consolidate territories, others clearly were not. In 1715 Victor Amadeus II sought to prevent Imperial officials from heeding claims for immediate dependence on the Emperor from those whom he claimed were his vassals in the Langhes. Similarly in the 1720s the duke of Parma appealed for Anglo-French support against what he saw as Imperial support for disobedient vassals.

[1] Paris, Bibliothèque Victor Cousin, Fonds Richelieu 30 f. 134; Nancy, Archives de Meurthe-et-Moselle, Fonds de Vienne 202 No. 265; PRO. SP. 107/2, Ossorio to Gansinot, 3 Oct. 1730; AE. CP. Autriche sup. 11 f. 133; Munich, KB 88/1, Wachtendonck to von Schall, 21 July 1733.

The western regions of the Empire were another area of particular dispute. Aside from long-standing quarrels over French pretensions that in some cases, such as the Montbéliard and Saint-Hubert disputes, long survived Louis XIV, there were numerous other disagreements arising essentially from clashes over rights of property and sovereignty. In 1742 for example the duke of Zweibrücken complained about the seizure of the revenues of an abbey by the sovereign power, the duke of Lorraine, while in 1775 the rights of the elector Palatine, as ruler of Jülich and Berg, were involved in a complex quarrel created by Prussian opposition to the succession to a prebendary of Sittard. The attempt to reconcile interests by sharing authority could be successful, as in the alternating Protestant Hanoverian and Catholic prince-bishops of Osnabrück, but there were frequent problems elsewhere, for example in Maastricht, where the prince-bishops of Liège correctly felt that their privileges were being eroded by the Dutch, or in the Swiss region jointly ruled by the canton of Berne and the prince-bishop of Basle.

Such disputes commonly lasted for a long time with scant impact on broader diplomatic questions, and they could be referred to the interminable processes of generally imperial jurisdiction. When in 1716 the French envoy pressed Prince Eugene on a number of largely Italian issues in which the Emperor had used his power to, in French eyes, dispossess others, including the successions to Mantua, Mirandola and Castiglione, and the interests of a large number of individuals, Eugene retorted that the litigants should use judicial remedies. In 1726 the Dutch rejected an Austrian memorandum presented in response to complaints by the bishop of Liège concerning new Dutch fortifications at Maastricht. In 1752 the right of the princes of Hesse-Cassel to dispose of their possessions to their children became an issue in Austro-French discussions with a specific dispute over whether the right of primogeniture only applied to reigning princes. Concern was expressed that the landgrave of Hesse-Cassel was seeking to dispossess the cadet line of Hesse-Rottembourg and reference was made back to Hessian family conventions of 1627 and 1628. None of these issues were of great consequence but, in contrast complex disputes between Austria and the elector Palatine over feudal rights to not very substantial German fiefs such as Ortenau helped to block the Imperial Election Scheme in 1752–3.

Dynastic, especially succession claims, were an important means to the aggrandizement of both powerful and minor families, and they thus played a large role in the diplomacy of the period. The great disappointment of Frederick I of Prussia's reign was that he missed the bulk of the Orange inheritance, while his great triumph was the exaltation of himself and his dynasty by the acquisition of a royal title and its recognition. His son Frederick William I was unwilling to renounce the family's claims to the Orange inheritance for nearly two decades, while in 1732 he demonstrated his claim to the succession to East Friesland by adding it to his coat of arms, an important step in an age when titles were maintained, even if ridiculous, such as that of the kings of Britain to France and their Sardinian counterparts to

Cyprus and Jerusalem. At a more modest level the dukes of Baden-Durlach devoted their efforts in mid-century to gaining the succession to the duchy of Baden-Baden whose male line was dying out, and in 1771 negotiated an acceptable agreement.

Dynastic concerns were matched by the central role of monarchs in foreign policy; this combination ensured that tremendous attention was devoted to births, marriages and deaths in ruling houses. The health of rulers was a particular subject of concern as it was clear that monarchs did not always follow their predecessors' policies and even if they maintained existing alliances they might interpret them in a different fashion. The Bavarian envoy in Dresden pointed out correctly in March 1732 that Augustus II of Saxony was old and infirm and that whatever he agreed to would not be obligatory for his son, a view that was vindicated when Augustus III reversed his father's anti-Austrian policy the following year. Concern about the apparently imminent succession of Frederick II led diplomats to scrutinize his character, sexual orientation and love of fame in 1739, while in 1746 the French foreign minister expressed concern about Frederick's health as he felt that his successor might follow a different policy or be less capable. In practice the untrammelled authority of most hereditary monarchs in the field of foreign policy ensured that the situation in Europe was not too different to that described by a mid-century English consul in Algiers, 'Algiers being an arbitrary state, is apt like all others of that kind to change its views and politics with new princes . . . no peace made with an arbitrary prince can be depended on in the reign of his successor unless that successor ratify and renew it, because the peace depending upon the single will and faith of the prince who entered into it cannot bind the arbitrary will of his successor.'[2]

It was not invariably the case that new rulers changed policies. When Louis XV of France reached his majority and when George II of Britain succeeded they retained the Anglo-French alliance. However, fear or hope of change led to expectations developing around heirs. George II provided the young Frederick II with money and sought to arrange his marriage to one of George's daughters in the hope that when he succeeded he would reverse his father's policies in directions favourable to Hanover and Britain. Frederick did not do so but he himself based hopes on the pro-Prussian policies of Tsarina Elizabeth's successor Peter III and the latter's son, Catherine's successor, Paul I (1796–1801). Such hypothetical expectations increased international uncertainty with diplomats speculating on the policies of heirs as well as the health of monarchs, especially in countries perceived as particularly important or disruptive, like Prussia. In February 1772 one Bavarian diplomat commented on the reported ill-health of Frederick II, 'his death will cause without doubt one of the biggest revolutions in the political system', as a result of the likely influence of his brother.[3] Marital links, it was hoped or feared, would serve to

---

[2] Chelmsford, Essex CRO. D/D By 054.
[3] Munich, Bayr. Ges. Wien 698, Ritter to Beckers, 19 Feb. 1772.

influence the situation, as well as furthering dynastic interests and pretensions and dealing with the practical problem of securing successions. In 1751
the British expressed the hope that if his wife died, Ferdinand VI of Spain
would marry a Sardinian princess rather than a French one who would renew
the family alliance. The French minister Choiseul sought the marriage of the
future Louis XVI and an Austrian archduchess in order to strengthen the
Austro-French alliance. His scheme succeeded in 1770 finally defeating
proposals for a Saxon marriage for Louis.

Marital links could, however, be as ineffective in influencing policy as
appeals to supposed natural interests. The unpredictable policies of many
rulers led diplomatic commentators to stress the role of personal passions and
random factors. The French persistently overestimated the amount of leverage on Max Emmanuel of Bavaria which his sister's marriage to the dauphin
gave them, while the French soldier-diplomat Villars was convinced that Max
was influenced by his passion for his Austrian mistress and the desire for glory
in the war against the Turk which led him to fight at Mohacs. A Bavarian
diplomat wrote in 1726 of the Spanish diplomat Ripperda's folly and ambition, adding 'it is the men who display those characteristics who I fear will
cause trouble, because even if the world is wisely arranged and Europe is
tranquil it only takes a fool and an ambitious man to reverse all the measures
that the wisest heads could have devised'. The French lawyer D'Aube
reflected a decade later that the smallest court disputes could lead to war, so
that people were controlled by the passions of those who governed them, and
he claimed that 'most great events pompously transmitted by history had only
frivolous causes'. The French envoy in Berlin complained in 1732 that neither
Frederick William I nor his ministers had any fixed plan. In 1776 a British
diplomat, writing of the dispute between Spain and Portugal, noted 'as the
violent passions of individuals at both courts are supposed to have more share
in the quarrel; than any considerations of state, I will not pretend to guess at
the catastrophe'.[4] These two themes of the role of personality and trivial
events in history, were widely discussed whether by commentary upon the
deeds of great nations in the past or the personal 'histories' of contemporaries,
fictional or otherwise, presented in print or on stage: the contrast was usually
made between such causes and 'rational' system. Bishop Burnet, a prominent
late-seventeenth-century Whig apologist, wrote of the Dutch statesman De
Witt,

> he laid down this as a maxim, that all princes and states followed their own
> interests; so, by observing what their true interests were, he thought he could
> without great intelligence calculate what they were about. He did not enough
> consider, how far passions, amours, humours and opinions, wrought on the
> world, chiefly on princes.

---

[4] Munich KS 17087, Albert to Malknecht, 4 Feb. 1726; Paris, Bibliothèque Nationale, n.a.f. 9513 p. 166; AE. CP.
Prusse 93 f. 273; BL. Add. 35574 f. 2.

The accuracy of such judgements must be considered, especially as an obvious characteristic of the period was the attempt to systematize international relations, an attempt arguably encouraged by a greater willingness in negotiations to forego dynastic claims for other advantages. It is necessary to consider the theoretical bases of such systematization before asking how far the nature of international relations did change.

THE IDEA OF 'NATURAL INTERESTS'

The ways in which many rulers and ministers understood international relations in the period may appear rigid to the modern observer. The essentially static concept of the balance of power was employed frequently on both a European and a regional scale. However, the rulers, ministers and diplomats of the period were aware of the constant mutability of international affairs. They realized that the essentially personal nature of monarchical government, the generally autocratic direction of diplomacy in an age that regarded the conduct of foreign policy as one of the essential attributes of sovereignty and the dominance of dynastic concerns in such a system, tended to make diplomacy unpredictable, secretive and subject to rapid change. The theory of the balance of power could be reconciled with the often kaleidoscopic reality of international relations by means of the notion of 'natural interests', which was also of use if mechanistic ideas of the international system were to be more widely applied. The idea was crucial to the attempts both to find and encourage order in international relations and it drew on diverse sources including the widespread interest in mechanistic systems, especially in the post-Newtonian world, in a neo-platonic search for reality amidst the delusions of the world, and in a desire to discover the divinely created natural laws that governed or should govern the relations of human society. It was supposed that each state possessed a set of strategic, territorial and, to a lesser extent, commercial interests which, correctly assessed, pointed out the foreign policy it should follow, and it was assumed both that able rulers and ministers could interpret these interests and that there was only one correct foreign policy for each state, which would enable it both to serve its sole interests and to fulfil the essentially harmonious order of the international system.

This seemingly inflexible model was in fact very useful because it accepted that the international system was not static and that interests could alter, not least in relation to changes in other countries. It was assumed by contemporaries, both diplomats and publicists, that discrepancies between the slowly changing policies dictated by the relationships between natural interests and the balance of power, and the faster altering reality of international affairs, could be explained by suggesting that rulers were unaware of the true interests of the countries they ruled. This failing could take the form of foolish ignorance or of the perverse preference for particular interests. A good example of the latter was held to be Spanish policy in the second quarter of the century. Philip V (1700–46), after having sons by his first wife, had several more by his second, the Italian princess Elizabeth Farnese. A domineering individual, she helped to direct her husband's policy to the goal, eventually successful, of securing Italian dominions for her sons: Naples and Sicily in 1735, Parma and Piacenza in 1748. In the eyes of many contemporaries these extremely costly schemes were an aberration from the 'natural interest' of Spain, which was generally held to entail the reversal of those clauses of the Peace of Utrecht, by which Britain had gained Gibraltar, Minorca and commercial concessions in the Spanish empire, and possibly also those clauses by which the crown of Spain, as opposed to cadet princes, had lost Italian territories.

The idea of natural interest aided the attempt to devise systems that could or should explain international relations both as they were and as they ought to be. It therefore satisfied the desire to find a rational explanation of how foreign policies could be combined to produce an acceptable diplomatic system. Many diplomats employed this intellectual device to discuss negotiations, the need for particular alliances and, by arguing that such natural interests were being ignored, the reason why negotiations had failed or been crossed by contrary alliances. St Saphorin, the Swiss Protestant who represented George I in Vienna, reflected in 1722 that a government that acted on solid principles was likely to be constant and that the only diplomatic liaisons that could be counted on were those based on a conformity of mutual interests. Three years later the French foreign minister Morville complained that Philip V in his anger with the French decision to renounce a Spanish bride for Louis XV would listen neither to reason, nor to motives of conscience or of state interest. In 1726 Morville claimed that the nature of Austrian and Prussian interests would prevent them from ever having good relations, a view that did not prevent several years of relatively satisfactory alliance. Morville's successor Chauvelin was, however, more accurate in his view that the Austro-Spanish First Treaty of Vienna (1725), which he described as the result of caprice, would not last because it was contrary to their natural interests, though having collapsed in 1729, it was revived in 1731 as part of a tripartite system with Britain before collapsing again in 1733. That May the earl of Kinnoull, a British diplomat, wrote to a colleague, 'the natural politics of Europe must necessarily unite the interests of the Emperor and those of His Majesty for a vast number of years',[5] but in fact the Anglo-Austrian alliance of 1731 collapsed in 1733 with Britain's refusal to provide stipulated assistance, and relations remained poor until 1741. Soon after his accession in 1740 Frederick II stressed to the British envoy the need for mutually advantageous alliance based on the interests of rulers,

[5] BL. Add. 23788 f. 175.

> Princes were chiefly governed by their interests; That before he entered into engagements of any kind he would be sure of what he did, and see clear into what the powers he contracted with would do for him, as he was determined to stick to his engagements when once he had taken them . . . he said that he was sensible alliances and friendship between princes could not subsist long if the advantages were not reciprocal.[6]

In practice it soon became clear that Frederick was swayed chiefly by the pressures of being the ruler of a small state who sought gains and the opportunism both of Prussian policy and of that of other rulers. His view of reciprocal advantages was in contemporary eyes a partial one. Nevertheless that did not prevent Frederick from criticizing other countries, such as Russia in 1744, for lacking a firm system or from writing in 1745 that alliances should be founded on mutual interests. As a result he argued in 1748 that Anglo-French relations would be limited to meaningless compliments and would never extend to anything solid. Natural interest was so useful a concept precisely because it could be applied in all circumstances, but that did not mean that it was interpreted in a similar fashion. The firm Russian system that Frederick sought in August 1744 was different from the 'true and natural interests' that a British diplomat wished to convince her of in the same month.[7] In June 1742 the Dutch envoy in Stockholm spoke of the Russians beating their Swedish enemies 'into a way of thinking more suitable to their true interests', a view not shared by many Swedes. It was scarcely surprising that some commentators found the concept of little explanatory value. The duke of Newcastle might claim in 1745 'the great powers, like France will not act from pique, and resentment, but according to their interest', but British diplomats were less sure. The experienced envoy in Spain Benjamin Keene wrote in 1733, 'where passion and chance have so great a hand in matters, as they have in this country, it is as difficult to reduce their actions to system, as it is hazardous to say that the same situation will last for 24 hours'. He reported the explanation of Patino, the Spanish foreign minister, for Spain's abandonment of her Austrian alliance in 1733, 'that their declaring war was not the effect of any scheme laid with France *de longue main*, but the work of pique improved by the French', and when he returned to Spain after the Anglo-Spanish conflict of 1739–48 he noted 'I have found a country without any solid system'. Sir Cyril Wych, his counterpart in St Petersburg, wrote in 1743 of 'the pernicious designs of a set of wretches, who, to serve France, will neglect no opportunity to induce her Imperial Majesty to enter into schemes, which are directly opposite to the true interest of Russia, and understood as such, by the ministers'. Frederick II complained about Russia in 1781, 'I can't see any reflection or wisdom there. All her actions are arbitrary, without principle or plan, and Catherine only considers her passion to establish a Greek empire'.[8]

[6] PRO. SP. 90/48, Dickens to Harrington, 17 Aug. 1740.
[7] *Politische Correspondenz* III, 263, IV, 67, VI, 146–7, 151; PRO. SP. 84/406 f. 50.
[8] PRO. SP. 95/91 f. 19, 43/37, Newcastle to Harrington, 18 Aug. 1745, 94/116, Keene to Delafaye, 16 Feb. 1733, 94/119, Keene to Newcastle, 10 May 1734, 94/135 f. 59, 91/35, Wych to Carteret, 26 Nov. 1743; *Politische Correspondenz* XXXXVI, 322.

Others were more sceptical of theorizing. One British diplomat in 1722 criticized the Italians, whom he claimed were generally inaccurate in their extensive speculations, on the grounds that they were over-complex in their analyses which made too much of the idea of a system, and ignorant of the facts. Wych claimed in 1740 that it was in Denmark's interest to be pro-British but he added, 'yet, as it has been frequently observed, that nothing is so fallacious, as to reason upon the councils or conduct of princes and states from what one conceives to be the true interest of their countries, and that there is no better way of judging, what may be the measures that a court is like to fall into, than by the personal temper and understanding of the chief minister'.[9] Many found it worthwhile to stress the role of chance and divine intercession, which man could do little to influence. This was particularly the case with war-time diplomacy and speculation, when providence in the form of military success was emphasized. In October 1742 the Emperor Charles VII, (Charles Albert of Bavaria), informed Cardinal Fleury, the first minister of his French ally, that God had tested Charles and was responsible for the Austrian loss of his capital city of Munich. In the same month the earl of Stair, commander of the British army in the Austrian Netherlands, wrote to a fellow Scottish aristocrat, 'Everything makes it plain that providence governs this world absolutely, and makes wise men play the fool, when she wants that it should be so'.[10]

And yet however random, incomprehensible or perverse policies might seem it was clearly necessary for rulers and diplomats to have some guidelines other than the observation of chance and divine action. At home governments attempted to face an uncertain world by the increase of military strength and by domestic reforms. The diplomatic counterpart to this process was provided by the ideas of the balance of power and of collective security.

THE BALANCE OF POWER

The idea of comparing the strength of powers and their alliances to a balance had existed since at least the fifteenth century and in the period under study it was commonly applied to describe either the actual or the desired state of affairs. There was some uncertainty as to whether the balance constituted a natural system and force in the sense that it was the necessary consequence of international relations so that if any one power became too strong others would combine against it. It was more commonly argued that the balance was a desired goal that required positive action. As an equilibrium, however desirable, could not control the random factor of the personal policies of rulers it was not generally seen as an independent element within the international

[9] PRO. SP. 92/31 f. 163, 82/61 f. 81.
[10] AE. CP. Bavière 100 f. 217; San Marino California. Huntington Library (hereafter HO) LO 7656.

system that would act to prevent the hegemony of any one power. If the flexibility of the concept of the balance aided its application, difficulties were encountered in relating regional balances to the wider European one. In its regional sense the term was applied most commonly to the Baltic, the Empire (Germany) and Italy. While discussing the partition of the Spanish inheritance, a French envoy suggested to William III of England in 1698 that the Milanese be given to Victor Amadeus II of Savoy-Piedmont in order to create a power capable of balancing Habsburg power and able to prevent it from harming other Italian princes. In 1725 the French envoy in Turin also thought the Italian balance, which he saw as crucial to local peace and tranquillity, required stronger anti-Habsburg rulers and he proposed that the territories allocated to Philip V's son Don Carlos be increased.

If the Habsburgs were seen as the principal threat to the Italian balance, at least until 1733, the growth in Russian power appeared to threaten what was generally termed 'the balance of the north'. However, the extent to which this balance would be affected by Dano-Swedish co-operation or by developments in Polish or Russian policy was far from clear. Prusso-Swedish co-operation in confrontation with Russia in 1747–51 could possibly be held to preserve a regional balance by preventing Russian intervention in Swedish politics, but was that in turn challenged by Austrian backing for Russia against Prussia? Similarly the creation in 1744 of a German league to support Charles VII was seen both as a means to preserve the balance of the Empire against Austria and as a tool of French attempts to destroy the European balance. A Sardinian diplomat complained the following year that his Austrian and Saxon counterparts argued that the anti-Bourbon effort should be concentrated in the Empire, not Italy, because Germany was more important for the European balance. It was even more difficult to include any analysis of the maritime and colonial situation. French representatives argued that Britain's success in these spheres challenged any notion of balance, and envisaged, as in 1769, 'a plan for a general confederation which could re-establish the maritime balance',[11] but it was difficult to assess the strategic value of colonial possessions or the extent of naval preparedness, as opposed to the number of warships. Nonetheless Britain's ability to play an active role in the European balance was largely a reflection of her perceived disproportionate role in the maritime one. A similar case for European leverage could be and was made for the Russian position in the Baltic and eastern Europe and the Austrian one in Italy and the Empire.

It was fully appreciated that domestic developments had to be taken into account in discussing states' relations to the general and regional balances. The obvious criteria of population and territory were important, but though Poland was one of the largest and most populous states in Europe, exceeding Prussia in both categories, it was not a major active influence upon European relations after the Great Northern war (1700–21). The ability of rulers to

[11] AE. MD. Ang. 56 f. 22.

mobilize the resources of their territories was vital. Thus Spain, whose role in the 1690s and 1700s was one of intended victim of partition schemes, became, by the 1720s, a major European power as a result of the political energy and administrative changes of Philip V and his ministers. Diplomats and publicists commented on the revival of Spanish power, the growth of her military forces and Spain's greater active participation in international affairs: accordingly they adjusted their assessment of its role in European relations. The increase in Spain's strength and her alliances with Austria (1725) and France (1733) were seen as developments that threatened other European powers. Able to encompass the growth in Spanish strength, the theories of the balance of power were also capable of assimilating the rise of Russian power. Russia's long alliance with Austria, which began in 1726 and lasted, though with varying degrees of intensity, until 1762, led to the two powers being put on the same side of the balance and contrasted with France and its eastern European allies, Sweden and Turkey. This was changed by the new diplomacy of 1756 (the Austro-French alliance) and the subsequent Seven Years' War (1756–63), which pitted Britain and Prussia against Austria, France, Russia and Sweden (though Britain was only at war with France). This realignment destroyed the essential political balance analysis namely Habsburg versus Bourbon, Austria against France, and from 1700 Spain, an analysis that had been possible throughout the early-modern period.

In assessing Russian strength contemporaries considered not so much size and population, as the ability of its government to bring Russia into line with the rest of Europe, to modernize its institutions and to resist the pressure from within Russia to return to old ways. Thus, in the 1720s and 1730s, Russian politics were viewed from outside as a struggle between the westernizers and the 'Old Russ'. It was held that if the latter won, Russia would relapse into 'barbarism' and abandon both her role in international affairs and her commitments to other European powers, such as Austria or the troublesome dukes of Holstein-Gottorp and Mecklenburg. Thus the balance of power, both regionally among the Baltic states and in Europe as a whole, was held to depend on struggles within one country, illustrating the degree to which internal developments within the major states were seen as significant aspects of international relations. Other examples were the attention paid to political disputes in Britain, Sweden and the United Provinces. The struggles in the Swedish 'Age of Liberty' (1719–72) had a clear bearing upon the ability of Sweden to act in international affairs, were seen in this light and led to intervention by foreign powers. The very uncertainty as to how power could be measured ensured that differing developments, whether constitutional alterations, as in Sweden, improvements in governmental ability to mobilize resources, as in Spain, or far-reaching political changes, as in Russia, could be assimilated into the theory of the balance. In political circles there was no sense of a fixed set of theoretical guidelines. Issues such as the supposed Russian threat to the balance in the late 1710s, or the relationship in 1733–5 between the general balance and the Italian regional balance, were fiercely debated.

There was a lack of clarity as to whether powers could hold the balance, as Frederick II was described as doing in 1744 and as Newcastle claimed Britain was doing in 1753, and, if so, what that meant. There was also considerable disagreement as to who threatened the balance. Though they used the notion against the Habsburgs, for example in the 1700s, French diplomats were particularly critical of its application not least because it was clearly used as a device to encourage opposition to them, from Louis XIV's reign until the 1750s. It was thus used for instance in the Westminster Parliament, in the Lords' Address of 1701 and Queen Anne's speech of 1705. The duke of Manchester, British envoy in Venice, reported from Venice in 1707 that he had 'proposed their entering into such alliances as will restore the balance of power in Europe, and which has been the only view the Queen has had in engaging in this present war'. In 1739 the British envoy in Vienna, worried by Austrian defeats at the hands of the Turks, wrote of the need 'for a new weight, in the place of that which is lost, in the general balance of Europe against the House of Bourbon', while the Dutch foreign minister was worried by the weakness of the balance which he ascribed not only to Austrian defeats 'which turns the balance altogether on the side of France, which is dangerous for her neighbours, particularly, whilst the powers which should join in counterbalancing France, hang so little together, and that there is but small appearance that they will soon be reunited again, how much soever their common security may require it'.[12]

The linking of the balance with the preservation both of European and of British peace and liberties was not simply a public expression of British policy. The instructions Edward Finch received when he was appointed to St Petersburg in February 1740 informed him that French strength was a threat to Europe and offer an interesting guide to the manner in which affairs were understood,

> we had conceived the justest apprehensions of those dangers, which threatened the tranquillity of Europe, and the utter subversion of the balance of power necessary to be maintained therein for the public security, unless proper, and timely means were found, for obviating so great evils, and calamities; and as we could not but look upon the prosperity, liberties, and safety of our own kingdoms, and subjects to be entirely interwoven with, and dependent on the preservation of the said balance of power; we therefore immediately determined to exert our utmost endeavours towards the attainment of that desirable end, and reflected, that there was no other power in Europe, as affairs stood then constituted, whose assistance therein could be of so great use to us, and whose weight and strength, in conjunction with our own, could be, with equal efficacy, opposed to the dangerous machinations which appeared to be on foot, as that of our good sister the Czarina of Muscovy.

[12] Huntingdon, CRO. DD M36/8 p. 48; PRO. SP. 80/136 f. 101.

Stair was more succinct when he wrote in 1742 of 'his Majesty's measures, which are principally directed to preserve the liberties of Europe by a Balance of Power.'[13] The French understandably were unimpressed by such arguments, though their support for Jacobitism, the cause of the exiled Stuarts which could destabilize British politics, appeared to vindicate it. Louis XIV did not appreciate the argument in 1711–14 that Charles VI would not only be no threat to Europe if he ruled both Austria and Spain, but also that he would thus be less powerful than Louis. In 1733 the French envoy in Berlin told Frederick William I, who had fought Louis during the War of the Spanish Succession (1701–14), that he could recognize in him the revival of the ancient prejudice against the supported French intention to create a universal monarchy, but he denied that France would destroy the balance. Fifteen years later the duke of Richelieu referred to this fear as chimerical.

The notion was also criticized in Britain. In 1744 the popular London preacher 'Orator' Henley criticized British opposition to France as aggressive, adding 'The pretence is the Balance of Power. What this Balance of Power is no Parliament ever yet has explained nor one member ever yet once mentioned it in the House of Commons though it has cost the nation above 300 millions'.[14] Opposition newspapers exposed the contradiction between ministerial arguments in 1741 that the Habsburg inheritance had to be preserved entire in order to maintain the balance and governmental willingness to negotiate a peace by which territories were lost. And yet the idea was still used heavily in the early 1750s even if it was clearly understood in a diversity of ways. Count Kaunitz, the Austrian envoy in Paris, argued in 1752 that 'the security and existence of all the European powers who wanted to see a balance maintained, was dependent on no power becoming sufficiently strong to upset the balance; exposed as Austria is from all directions, she is the most concerned'.

The previous year Newcastle had thought the balance endangered by France and her allies, while his brother Henry Pelham noted, 'I have always wished for a strict union between Spain and Great Britain; which joined with the House of Austria, is in my mind a real balance of power against any the most aspiring governments'. However, an alliance of Spain, Britain, Austria and her ally Russia could scarcely be described as anything other than a stronger party which indeed appeared to be what the British and Austrians intended when they spoke of holding the balance or of a balance designed to discourage aggressors. They denounced potential threats to the balance, yet failed to consider themselves as a group causing just such a threat. They would not have appreciated the advice of the Sardinian envoy in London to his Spanish counterpart that the true system of Spain should be to conserve the balance by always joining the weakest party, if that had entailed Spain joining

[13] PRO. SP. 91/24, Instructions 29 Feb. 1740; HO LO 7669.
[14] BL. Add. 33052 f. 262.

their rivals.[15] Thus the balance was both ambiguous and yet a tangible image that could lead to references to throwing a weight into the scale or keeping the beam continually agitated.

After 1755 the idea of the balance was less invoked, or at least used with less certainty that it was something which could be assessed and altered; in particular the concept worked less well on a European scale. In the period 1763–91, with Britain, France and Spain competing for colonial and maritime supremacy, and Austria, Prussia and Russia vying for superiority in eastern Europe, the links between international affairs in the two halves of Europe became less close and the theory of balance less relevant. However the concept was still used, the Palatine foreign minister for example in January 1772 considering the Austro-Prussian concert, which was part of the diplomatic revolution that produced and was produced by the First Partition of Poland, as greatly surpassing the balance while in August 1781 Frederick II wrote of the need to counter-balance the loss of his Russian ally to Austria by finding a new ally, 'in order to be able to put the balance back in its correct equilibrium'. In 1779 an English politician William Eden suggested that 'though that balance in our times has had great changes, it is demonstrably the interest of all the leading empires to maintain it in its present position'.[16] Preventing other powers, including allies, from becoming more powerful unless an equivalent was obtained was a central feature of the diplomacy of the period, and it underlay in particular the partitions of Poland and the apparently imminent partition of the weakening Turkish Empire, just as earlier it had been important during the negotiations over the Spanish Succession. The notion of the balance had not been replaced before the conquests of revolutionary France caused a revival of older ideas of a single state threatening the European system.

COLLECTIVE SECURITY

The idea that rulers should co-operate to oppose any unwanted change in the European system caused by the foreign actions of a sovereign power (as opposed to domestic disturbances) was an attractive one though it clashed both with the widespread interest in territorial gain and, at times, with the exigencies of alliance politics. It was therefore most commonly entertained in periods of exhaustion after major wars, and in regional systems, such as Italy and much of the Empire, where there were a number of minor powers and concern about the possible intentions of more powerful rulers. In one respect the willingness of major powers to co-operate in the attack upon and partition of a weaker counterpart, as during the Great Northern War at the eventual

---

[15] H. Schlitter, *Correspondance secrète entre le Comte Kaunitz et . . . Koch* (Paris, 1899) p. 197; PRO. 30/29/1/11 f. 327–8; Turin, Archivio di Stato, Lettere Ministri Inghilterra 56, 19 Aug. 1751.
[16] *Politische Correspondenz* xxxxvi, 83; *Four Letters to the Earl of Carlisle* (1779) p. 60.

expense of Sweden and in the partitions of Poland, represented the antithesis of the idea of collective security. In so far though as it entailed agreement between all the relevant powers bar one and an attempt to settle a matter through collective actions there were common aspects.

In the negotiations between Louis XIV and William III in 1698–1700 concerning the partition of the inheritance of the kings of Spain there were provisions for common action against rulers who might defy the agreement, clauses which were an important attempt to further the practice of collective security, though they fell victim to circumstances and a division between the two monarchs. Similarly the attempt during negotiations in 1709 to end the War of the Spanish Succession to make Louis agree to help militarily in the expulsion from Spain of his grandson Philip V if he refused to accept the agreement of the other powers that he should abandon his claim was defeated by Louis's refusal. However, the efforts in the late 1710s and early 1720s to preserve the Utrecht settlement and to prevent any major change in international relations can be seen as an important attempt to use a system of collective security to maintain peace and a given international order. This has been linked to the congresses of Cambrai and Soissons, which first met in 1724 and 1728 respectively and were attempts to settle outstanding diplomatic problems by negotiations involving most of the major powers, though neither Russia nor many of the second-rank powers were invited. However, the congresses were both unsuccessful and rapidly overtaken by aggressive moves. The diplomacy of the late 1710s was more successful though it is important not to exaggerate either the success or the novelty of attitudes in this period. The principal achievement was the defeat of Philip V's attempt to reverse the Peace of Utrecht's exclusion of the crown of Spain from its former Italian possessions. The view of the British government was expressed in a London newspaper, sympathetic to it, the *Whitehall Evening Post*, on 29 November 1718.

> I am willing to put the sum of the argument upon this question, whether any particular nation arming itself for a war, and beginning that war by unjustly falling upon her weakest neighbours, who, if she conquers, will add to her power, and make her formidable to her other neighbouring princes, by her becoming exorbitantly great, does not give just cause to those other nations, though not otherwise concerned, to fall upon her and reduce her to such a state as may check her ambitious designs.

This action to confine Spanish ambition was based on shared Anglo-French interests that led to and in turn arose from their alliance of 1716. The French regent, the duke of Orléans, noted in June 1718 'peace is the system of England. It is also mine'.[17] Both were ready to resist Philip's attempt to achieve his ends by an Italian war, just as both had reasons of their own for opposing Philip. However, not only did the alliance fail to intimidate Philip into maintaining the peace but its third major partner, Charles VI, used the

---

[17] AE. CP. Ang. 312 f. 274.

conflict to further his expansionist aims by gaining Sicily in exchange for barren Sardinia. Indeed the manner in which during the Anglo-French alliance of 1716–31 both Charles and Philip, in the person of his son Carlos improved their position in Italy, despite the complaints of Italian princes, suggests that caution is required in praising the achievements of collective security. The Anglo-French alliance certainly failed in the Baltic to create a system that would balance Russia and thus integrate her into European diplomacy with less danger. The attempt in 1719–20 to intimidate Peter I into yielding conquered Swedish possessions in the eastern Balkans as part of a settlement of the Great Northern War failed.

The idea of shared interests between major powers that could serve as the basis of an international system maintained by collective security proved even harder to achieve in the 1720s. However, attempts were made to create alliances that would be strong enough to intimidate other powers and in that sense collective security was a constant feature, not least because it was believed correctly that it would be impossible to satisfy all rulers. In October 1727 the experienced Austrian diplomat Penterridter wrote to a colleague reflecting that delays

> arise from general systems which embrace too much at once, because to wish to put all the powers under the same flag is nearly impossible. I do not dispute that one can have at the same time peace with every one, if one wants it, but it is still necessary to choose those that can most contribute to and maintain it. Religion and the weight that the Emperor, France and Spain united can give to peace should determine the choice, because those three powers once united, it would be difficult for another to trouble them successfully.[18]

This attractive proposal was, however, intended to serve a diplomatic objective that was flawed by incompatible Austro-Spanish views in Italy and by French opposition to plans for the indivisible inheritance of the Habsburg lands. An obvious feature of the international relations of the late seventeenth and early eighteenth centuries was the unwillingness of major rulers to surrender dynastic and other territorial pretensions for the sake of diplomatic arrangements, other than at the end of a major war. Second-rank rulers, who anyway tended not to have such tempting dynastic prospects, were more willing in some cases to accept compromise in the form of equivalent gains, but even some of them were unyielding, such as the elector Palatine in the 1730s who refused to negotiate about the succession to Jülich and Berg.

If the idea of collective security received a boost from the end of the War of the Spanish Succession, it was revived again at the end of that of the Austrian Succession (1740–8). Towards the end of the war, when it was clear to both alliances that it had been particularly inconclusive, each began planning for a post-war Europe in which they would be powerful enough to dissuade the other from aggressive acts. In 1746 d'Argenson, the French foreign minister,

[18] HHStA. Nachlass Fonseca 21 f. 382–3.

stressed the need for France and Prussia to prevent their rivals from creating new troubles after peace was signed. The duke of Newcastle sought to achieve the same end by maintaining the wartime alliance. There were contrary suggestions of a general agreement. In 1748 the Spanish diplomat Macanas pressed for a mutual territorial guarantee as part of the peace. The following year Puysieulx, D'Argenson's successor, 'went even so far as to say, he thought that England and France should tell the rest of Europe, that they would unite their force, against whoever should attempt to disturb the peace'. That summer a British diplomat was told in Dresden 'that if the king of Prussia continued in his present way of proceeding, all the chief powers of Europe would find themselves obliged to fall upon him, and bring him to reason'. In 1750 Puysieulx informed his envoy in Vienna that if Austria and her allies wanted peace they could count on France who was, he claimed, always ready to act against any power that tries to trouble it.[19]

Distrust and differing interests, however, ensured that definitions of peaceful and aggressive intentions and actions varied, Anglo-French restraint helped to defuse a Baltic crisis in 1749–50 and Austria, Sardinia and Spain devised a mutually acceptable collective security system for Italy that was to last until the French Revolution, but in the Empire and eastern Europe tension appreciably increased in the early 1750s. The Italian settlement reflected a balance between Habsburg and Bourbon territories that left both reasonably satisfied while their interests were directed elsewhere. Such a situation was not possible in trans-Alpine Europe where France felt bound to her Prussian ally in opposition to Habsburg determination to regain Silesia, lost in the recent war, while Prussia justifiably feared Russian aggression.

Notions of collective security were also of interest to minor states, but in general they were unable to unite effectively to protect themselves from the major powers. In theory the Imperial constitution provided a system of collective security that could both punish German princes who breached it and unite the Empire against external aggressors, but this system was generally only of value in very minor disputes and was otherwise either substantially ineffective or manipulated by the major rulers. The diversity of interests among its members was simply too great, and the appeal of bribery or other advantage too powerful. As a result there were occasional calls, for example by the Bavarian foreign minister in 1769, for new collective systems that would ensure security. On various occasions there was talk of forming such leagues in Italy. Some Italian ministers and intellectuals dreamed of an alliance of independent Italian states, able to prevent the Habsburgs and the Bourbons from manipulating Italian rivalries for their own ends. These schemes were unsuccessful because of disputes between the Italian powers, a habit of dependence on extra-Italian alliances and reluctance to think in terms of Italy or Italian political interests. Talk in 1708 of a league of Venice, the Papal States, Parma, Savoy-Piedmont and Tuscany for the liberty of Italy

[19] BL. Add. 35355 f. 34; PRO. SP. 88/70. 2 July 1749; AE. CP. Autriche 248 f. 26.

and in opposition to foreign troops collapsed before the reality of rivalries, including those of Venice and Savoy-Piedmont, Savoy-Piedmont and the Papacy, and Venice and the Papacy. The independent Italian states failed to help Pope Clement XI in his frontier dispute with the Emperor Joseph I in 1708 and the projected Italian league became instead a plan for an Italian-French league, supported by French troops, to free Italy from the Austrian yoke, territorial gains in the Milanese being another prize. In the event the French were as unable as Venice and Savoy-Piedmont to provide assistance, but the events oi 1708 illustrated the extent to which minor powers could defend their position only by seeking assistance from major states, a process that drew them into great-power conflicts. In a similar fashion attempts to create an independent league of German powers in 1744 were dependent on French support, while the countries opposed to Britain's interpretations of her maritime rights in controlling neutral trade during the War of American Independence, such as Denmark, Prussia and Sweden, united in the Armed Neutrality of 1780 under Russian leadership. German anxiety about the schemes of the Emperor Joseph II led to a league of princes under Prussian leadership in 1785.

Maritime rights were an obvious subject for co-operation because of the role of a loosely agreed international law, but schemes for a league to defend them were flawed by political interests. The French proposal of July 1749 for a maritime union of France, Spain, Sweden and Denmark with a stipulated provision of warships for mutual defence was explicitly anti-British, while the divergent political interests of the members of the League of Armed Neutrality prevented it from having its desired impact. On sea, as on land, there was no agreement over a code of law, no court of international justice and no generally shared interests. Under these circumstances talk of mutual guarantees for collective security served partial ends, defining competing alliances rather than providing a means for sustaining a peaceful international order.

EXPANSIONISM AND EXCHANGES

If rulers sought dynastic aggrandizement, this did not prevent both a more general interest in territorial gains and a willingness to consider exchanges and equivalents. A number of rulers and ruling groups were content with the extent of their territories either because they believed that they were satisfactory as, for example, the Swedes appeared to feel was the case in the last four decades of the seventeenth century or because it was imprudent to take the risks of offending other powers. Republics, which anyway had no dynastic pretensions, tended simply to retain what they possessed. That was always the first priority for all rulers, and personal preferences and circumstances ensured that the views of many went no further. Defensive treaties were more common than offensive clauses therefore, though a desire to regain lost territories could give an offensive direction to diplomacy, as with the Austrian wish to recapture Silesia. If Maria Theresa strove to defend her inheritance rather than to acquire additional territories, the effect of the loss of Silesia was to make Austria a dissatisfied as well as powerful country, a category of state from which came the principal threat to peace. Kaunitz might suggest to Joseph II in August 1769 that Joseph inform Frederick II that Austrian policy had always been pacific and that they appreciated that wars were a misfortune, but such assurances were of little value in light of the inconstant nature of diplomacy and the large size of military forces. British assurances were more convincing, coming from a country in which interest in continental acquisition was rare. In October 1725 a British official told the Portuguese envoy that 'it was the interest of all mankind to be well with us; for we had no conquests or acquisitions to make; no view but to preserve peace and good neighbourhood, and consequently we might upon occasion be helpful but could never be burthensome to our friends'. In 1769 the British envoy in Paris told Choiseul, the French foreign minister, 'that we did not desire to see any change or alteration in the political system of Europe; that England had no views of aggrandizement, and it was to be wished that other powers would show the same moderation'.[20] Britain's position as the only major power without a substantial army lent credence to these claims, while her unwillingness in the late 1730s and in 1763–85 to take an active role in continental diplomacy made her of little value as an ally to powers that sought territorial change. Though the Bourbons opposed British colonial gains they were of little importance to the other major powers, and thus Britain played a less disruptive role, after the failure of her interventionist policies of 1742–53, than Russia, the other major power that was making substantial territorial gains at the margins of the European political system.

Other powers sought major gains, and rulers achieved much through diplomacy and war. Spain regained an Italian empire, Russia obtained a window on the Baltic. Prussia became a major power. Rulers were willing to consider substantial alterations in the international system. Austria, Prussia and Russia each seized a section of Poland in the First Partition (1772), but similar schemes had been considered on a number of occasions earlier in the century. The partition of the Habsburg inheritance was planned in 1741. Possession of significant territories, such as Silesia and the western Milanese, was gained and retained through conflict, though holding on to Silesia took a lot of Prussian effort. Far larger areas were fought for and war plans, if successful, would have entailed fundamental alterations in European relations. The most ambitious plans related to the Balkans where, on a number of occasions, the Austrians and Russians planned major conquests. Elsewhere in Europe ambitious plans for territorial redistribution were advanced, as in the Baltic during the Great Northern War or in 1784 when Gustavus III of Sweden

20 PRO. SP. 43/75, Delafaye to Tilson, 15 Oct. 1725, 78/277 f. 117.

was forced to drop his aggressive plans against Norway. During the wars of the Spanish and Austrian Successions the reversal of Louis XIV's gains along France's eastern frontier was a goal of his opponents while during the War of the Austrian Succession and the Seven Years' War the partition of Prussia was proposed. These schemes, though difficult to execute, were not obviously beyond the military capabilities of the powers of the period.

Aggressive plans were particularly serious for minor states. Frequently occupied by other powers or forced to provide supplies in wartime, they could suffer in subsequent peace treaties. Joseph Clément, archbishop-elector of Cologne and prince-bishop of Liège, found that the Dutch, having occupied his fortresses of Bonn, Huy and Liège during the War of the Spanish Succession, could only be removed with considerable difficulties. Genoa feared the rulers of Savoy-Piedmont, Venice the Austrians. The seizure of the inheritance of the Gonzaga dukes of Mantua by the Austrians, when the last duke died in 1708, revealed the ability of the powerful to disinherit heirs. In the same year Austrian troops who occupied the papal town of Comacchio easily defeated Clement XI in the subsequent war. If minor Italian states suffered most from Austria, their German counterparts had more varied persecutors. Louis XIV's successors were less difficult neighbours for the rulers in the west of the Empire, but the schemes of both Austria and Prussia were seen as threats elsewhere. Prussia bullied the surrounding princes by, in particular, forcible recruiting for her army, from which Mecklenburg suffered especially. Prussian treatment of her neighbours illustrated the degree to which strength bred strength, increasing the gap in relative power between states. In the north of the empire Sweden played a progressively more minor role, but the Danes gained control of ducal Schleswig. In eastern Europe weaker political units also suffered. Hungary, the Ukraine and Moldavia all failed in the first eleven years of the eighteenth century to break free from the embrace of Austria, Russia and Turkey respectively. Russia exercised an effective protectorate over Poland for most of the period from the 1710s and also controlled the Duchy of Courland whose eighteenth-century dukes were appointed in response to Russian wishes.

For many powers dynastic pretensions did not provide a framework for territorial expansion. This was especially true in eastern Europe and for Britain. In this respect a number of powers, such as Russia and Britain, sought territories without the sanction of a legitimate claim. Britain had no claim to Gibraltar and Minorca, both of which she was ceded in the Peace of Utrecht, other than her conquest of them during the War of the Spanish Succession. The acquisition of territories without benefit of a legitimate claim was scarcely novel but it could cause outrage, particularly in western Europe. However, the legitimist principle of basing pretensions on dynastic and other legal claims was also tempered by a more general stress on considerations of *raison d'état* (reason of state). This entailed an emphaiss not on the patrimonial imperatives of competing dynasties, but on the interests of autonomous political entities, especially defensible frontiers, contiguous territories, and military and economic strength. Dynastic objectives or at least claims could be advanced to forward these aims, though Frederick II was unusual in his willingness to admit that such claims were merely a matter of form. Such ideas could serve to accentuate the willingness to negotiate and the importance of compromise, especially by means of such devices as exchanges and equivalents, but it is difficult to demonstrate that *raison d'état* helped to defuse crises whereas dynasticism accentuated them. In addition it is by no means clear that it is helpful to distinguish the categories to which it is anyway difficult to allocate particular rulers or countries. The objectives and views summarized by the term *raison d'état* were scarcely novel and it was quite possible for rulers such as Louis XIV to pursue such views, not least in colonial expansion, while at the same time defending dynastic pretensions. The greater territorial stability of Mediterranean and western Europe after 1748 has led to an under-estimate of the continued importance of dynastic themes in these regions. If the dissection of Poland in accordance with cold-blooded notions of *raison d'état* might appear to exemplify a different diplomatic idiom and rationale, it is difficult to see it as substantially different in effect to the Russian gains of the eastern Ukraine and the Baltic provinces in 1667 and 1721 respectively.

Exchange plans paid as little attention to the views of the inhabitants concerned as dynastic schemes did. Some were far-ranging, such as the proposal in 1669, revived in 1688, for France to gain the Spanish Netherlands in return for Roussillon and acceptance of a Spanish conquest of Portugal. The possible exchange by the dukes of Bavaria and Lorraine of their territories for gains elsewhere, principally in Italy, was a persistent theme in the diplomacy of the period 1698–1713. So also was the idea that the ruler of Savoy-Piedmont should yield Savoy to France in return for Italian gains, an idea that recurred during the first half of the century, for example in 1725 and in the 1740s. Another long-standing proposal was that of the exchange of Bavaria for the Austrian Netherlands which was discussed in the period and supported actively by Joseph II. It was also advocated in 1743 by a Göttingen professor as a 'patriotic project' that would bring peace to the Empire and create a stronger barrier against France by providing the Austrian Netherlands with a resident ruler. Many exchange schemes were smaller in scale. Frederick William of Brandenburg-Prussia sought as part of the price for providing troops against the Turks in 1683 the satisfaction of Hohenzollern claims in Silesia, but he was willing to accept as an equivalent the Swedish cession of Stettin. In 1698 Augustus II proposed an exchange in order to obtain a direct territorial link between Saxony and Poland through Silesia. In 1744 the elector palatine pressed for the cession of the distant Duchy of Neuburg in order to get an equivalent in the Austrian Netherlands that would be contiguous with his Jülich–Berg territories. None of these took place, any more than a rumoured Dutch scheme of 1769 to acquire Cleves and Prussian Guelders in exchange for lands that were to be purchased from Denmark, or the proposal of 1774 for an exchange between Mecklenburg, which was contiguous with Prussia, and the central German territories of Ansbach and Bayreuth which were held by another branch of the Hohenzollerns to which those of Berlin hoped to succeed. The exchange in 1773 by the king of Denmark of the non-contiguous German duchies of Oldenburg and Delmenhorst for the contiguous ducal parts of Holstein and Russian recognition of his position in Schleswig was achieved only after years of negotiation.

The difficulties that exchange schemes encountered suggest that there was considerable reluctance to surrender dynastic claims and to envisage new arrangements. A related aspect of the grip of traditional ideas was the continued importance of diplomatic ceremonial as an expression of monarchical glory and reputation, and the reluctance to accept compromises and new suggestions in this sphere. For rulers to lose either lands or honours which had formerly been theirs was to some extent to lose face. Louis XIV was by no means the last monarch to have a keen sense of *gloire*, his personal and dynastic honour. Charles VI was similarly conscious, not least in his dealing with the princes of the Empire. In 1745 the Swedish envoy in Paris pressed for expenses to accompany Louis XV in his campaign. Advised by French ministers to make the journey he reported '*Gloire* being the first interest of rulers and a young monarch, who wishes to acquire it, naturally desiring that his glory should receive the homage that he believes due to it, I think it essential for the service of the king to avoid the consequences that might arise from my absence at a moment which all of France places among the most glorious of the monarchy'. The following January the French envoy in Spain wrote of Louis's uncle Philip's concern for his son Don Philip, 'I would not be at all surprised that the king, once convinced that his honour was involved, should take the most extreme steps . . . he is capable, when he is struck by an idea, especially if it concerns his dignity, to carry his opinion to an invincible stubbornness'.[21] It was not surprising that rulers should use considerations of glory and honour in their diplomatic correspondence, Charles VII appealing to Louis XV for assistance on that basis in 1743, nor that they should sponsor the customary presentation of the royal hero as victor as a major artistic theme: Louis XV being presented as Jupiter by Nicholas Coustou and Charles III in an equestrian statue by Bouchardon; when George II took the field successfully in 1743 at the battle of Dettingen, Handel composed a magnificent *Te Deum* and Anthem.

Considerations of *gloire* and honour appear less frequently in the correspondence of the partitioning monarchs, Catherine II, Frederick II and Joseph II, of the contemporaries competing for maritime hegemony, Charles III, George III and Louis XVI, than earlier in the century. However, the extent and nature of the shift has not been systematically studied and it is by no means clear what significance should be attached to what may be shifts in style as much as in substance. *Gloire* and honour did not disappear from correspondence. Discussing Anglo-Prussian differences in 1753, Frederick II informed his

[21] J. Heidner (ed.), *Carl Fredrik Scheffer* (Stockholm, 1982) pp. 87–8; AE. CP. Espagne 488 f. 144.

envoy in London that he should not propose things 'incompatible with my dignity and *gloire*, and which would lead to me yielding to the pride of George II', who was his uncle. Twenty years later D'Aiguillon, the French foreign minister, told the British envoy, 'A great nation never must lose sight of its honour, never must sacrifice *that* to any prudential consideration whatever',[22] while in 1781 Kaunitz stressed to Joseph II the importance of not compromising the Imperial position of prominence in negotiations with Catherine. Kaunitz's concern reflected the benefits that were believed to flow from diplomatic eminence which were fostered and defended by a stress on precedence and magnificence. International relations were a major sphere for the display of monarchical power and an important source of prestige. The extraordinary sumptuousness of the public entries of Portuguese envoys in Vienna (1707), Rome (1709, 1716, 1718) and Paris (1715) might suggest a Baroque fashion but concern for magnificence and ceremonial was still marked later in the century. Reporting his public entry into Vienna in 1752 the French envoy hoped that it passed with all the magnificence appropriate to royal dignity. The following year his counterpart at The Hague aroused the opposition of other diplomats, but won favour at Paris, by advancing new pretensions concerning the formal visits of these diplomats after his public entry. Disputes over precedence involved a significant amount of diplomatic activity, such as that in Turin in 1755 between the Spanish envoy and a cardinal. In July 1763 the French were worried both that the British envoy at Vienna might seek equality or precedence and because of a dispute of precedence between the carriages of the duke of Bourbon and of the wife of the Austrian envoy. Such concerns, as well as the weight placed upon royal marriages as symbols and supports of alliances, were indicative of attitudes that were remarkably conservative. Indeed, the whole structure of diplomatic representation in Europe followed similarly conservative and hierarchical lines, with the rank of accredited diplomat and degree of ceremonial appropriate to each capital carefully graded and jealously watched.

LAW AND IDEOLOGY

Notions of natural law and Christian behaviour played a central role in late-seventeenth-century theoretical writing about international relations. If the Old Testament warrior kings of Israel provided the models put forward by court preachers, other writers such as Grotius (1583–1645). Pufendorf (1632–94) and Leibniz (1646–1716) were more concerned to employ natural law as a guide to the conduct of international relations. A major challenge came from Hobbes (1588–1679) and Spinoza (1632–77) who stressed the

---

[22] *Politische Correspondenz* X, 166; PRO. SP. 78/287 f. 147.

role of power and were sceptical about traditional notions of international law. In his *De Cive* and *Leviathan* Hobbes interpreted natural law as self-preservation and argued that states, like individuals, were naturally competitive. Hobbes rejected the notion of an innate natural law in favour of a simple imperative of self-preservation. Grotius, Pufendorf and Leibniz had a more idealistic conception of the natural order and saw international law as an aspect of natural law, a permanent code of moral values implanted by God and accessible to reason, and a necessary guide to state behaviour. In his *De Jure Naturae et Gentium* (1688) Pufendorf argued, however, that a ruler was bound by a treaty only if it did not conflict with the interests of his state, as his obligation to that was stronger. Leibniz responded to a continual theme in Christian thought, the urge for political unity in order to create harmony, but most thinkers accepted that the solution to international problems had to be found in creating a code of conduct for relations between states, rather than in joining them together in a federation or a unitary state. Similarly projects of universal peace, such as that of the French writer Saint-Pierre, had little effect. Natural law theories bolstered by the authority of Locke remained important in the eighteenth century, influencing for example the thought of Christian Wolff (1676–1756); and Grotius was reprinted or translated about fifty times between 1625 and 1758. In 1758 Emmerich de Vattel's *Le Droit des Gens* appeared, an influential work that was translated into English in 1759 and German in 1760. Vattel stressed the natural law basis of international law and emphasized the liberty of nations as a feature of natural law relating to sovereign states. This entailed not the liberty to oppress others but the peaceful enjoyment of rights.

Vattel's optimistic legal framework was matched by the attempts of certain prominent French intellectuals to advocate an international order based on morality and reason. They were suspicious of the intentions and conduct both of international diplomacy and of French foreign policy, believing them to be manipulative, dishonest and aggressive. In common with natural law theorists they had little understanding of dynamic elements in international relations, the scope of change and the attempt by certain powerful rulers to match diplomatic developments to their growing power. It may be no coincidence that just as many natural law theorists came from the federal states of the Empire and the United Provinces with their stress on legal relationships and their, in most cases, only limited interest in aggression, so the French *philosophes* came from a power that had largely ceased to seek European territorial gains and that after 1763 played only a limited role in continental diplomacy.

The *philosophes* argued that all people essentially sought peace, that national interests, if correctly understood, were naturally compatible, and that war arose from irrational causes such as religion, and from the nature of diplomacy. They therefore pressed for open diplomacy much as they deplored the harmful effects to trade of guild secrets, monopolies and tariff barriers. Some radicals, such as Rousseau and Condorcet, argued that reform necessitated the transer of control over foreign policy from essentially bellicose, irrational and selfish monarchs to the people who would be led by reason and would love peace. In line with most thought of the period, the *philosophes* held that each nation had its true and rational interest.

Attractive as these ideas were, the *philosophes* were often inconsistent and somewhat confused when it came to having to discuss the real world. The French conquest of Corsica in 1768–9 was criticized by, among others, Voltaire and Rousseau, who felt that the government should concentrate on domestic problems rather than foreign adventurism, and romanticized the Corsicans. In contrast the Poles generally received a less sympathetic treatment as the partitioning monarchs appeared more progressive and receptive to current intellectual fashions while the Poles could be dismissed as feudal Catholic bigots. Voltaire and Diderot praised Catherine II's war against the Turks which rapidly became one of Russian conquest.

Monarchs and ministers referred to legal and philosophical concepts but it is unclear whether these were sufficiently coherent or readily applicable to provide any guidance. In the late 1730s British ministers were convinced that the law of nations gave British vessels extensive rights of navigation in all but coastal waters such as those of Spain in the Caribbean; Spanish ministers on the other hand believed that British ships had only those narrow privileges conceded in past treaties. Neither side had any court or legal decision to which to appeal, and arbitration was ultimately left to the event of war. The duke of Newcastle wrote in February 1752 of discouraging a Prussian East Indies trading company 'as far as the Law of Nations will justify us in so doing' adding the following January that Frederick had acted 'without any regard, either to particular treaties, or to the general law of nations'.[23] References to law were generally made when criticizing the conduct of others rather than when discussing one's own policy. By the second half of the century it was increasingly fashionable to explain policy with reference to non-national rational goals but that no more precluded the pursuit of selfish interests than the universal goals expounded in earlier wars against Louis XIV and the Turks had done. Frederick II, described in 1742 as a man whom 'no laws human or divine' could bind, wrote of himself in November 1756 as a 'citizen of Europe who has most at heart the good of his allies and the independence of his country, who hates tyranny and only seeks the good of Europe'. Six years later the Dutch warned Spain not to attack Portugal, 'the making war upon a principle of superiority or motive of convenience, being a sort of challenge to every neutral power', while in 1774 d'Aiguillon and the British envoy talked 'upon the advantage that must accrue to both Nations, from persisting in the same pacific sentiments, the same wise plan of policy, which they had pursued of late, and which nothing but narrow national prejudice, could ever wish to change'.[24]

[23] PRO. SP. 84/458, 462, 4 Feb. 1752, 19 Jan. 1753.
[24] BL. Add. 23810 f. 211, 6843 f. 38; *London Chronicle* 30 Jan. 1762; PRO. SP. 78/299 f. 104.

It is difficult to assess how far views were influenced by new thoughts. As foreign policy was largely a matter of monarchs and aristocratic ministers and diplomats, it is likely that the influence of new attitudes would have depended on their receptiveness, and this would have varied. More to the point the diffuse and unspecific character of new views would probably have ensured that they were more influential in the retrospective explanation of policy than in the determination of particular moves. It was not until the French Revolution that an attempt was made to put into practice the radical conception of foreign policy and to create a new international order. It certainly did not produce peace and though the monarch was deposed and apparently irrational agreements such as the closure of the Scheldt river swept aside it is difficult to accept that revolutionary foreign policy was any more in the interests of the people, however defined, than its *ancien régime* predecessor.

INTERVENTION IN DOMESTIC POLITICS

The determination of major powers to dominate their weaker neighbours was intertwined with the intervention of states in the domestic politics of other countries. This was particularly apparent in the case of countries with powerful representative assemblies: Britain, Poland, Sweden and the United Provinces. Politicians developed links with envoys, information was exchanged and bribes received. The connections between foreign policy and domestic politics lent urgency to these links and encouraged the intervention of foreign powers: Russian in Poland and Sweden; Austrian support of the Whigs in Britain under Queen Anne, which led to their envoy being forbidden the court in 1711; French financial support for the Hat party which came to power in Sweden in 1738, French opposition to the previous dominant minister Count Horn springing from his refusal to support anti-Russian policies. In states with representative assemblies and traditions of foreign intervention it was easy to turn to foreign support. In 1702 the Estates of Liège refused to vote money for the Prince-Bishop Joseph Clément, regarding him as pro-French. Joseph Clément was furious in 1714 when the chapter of Liège sought to send an envoy to the peace conference at Baden.

Seeking foreign aid was simpler when the government was regarded as illegitimate, politics sliding into conspiracy in response to opportunity abroad, an absence of hope for peaceful domestic change and traditions of political action that comprehended resistance even if the legal position of resistance theory was often weak. The French envoy at the Imperial Diet suggested in December 1688 that the manifesto of William III of Orange justifying his invasion of England could just as easily be used to justify the Hungarian rebels against Leopold I. During their rebellion of 1703–11 the Hungarians sought French assistance and planned with Bavaria a joint attack on Austria, though by no means all conspiracies led to rebellion or received the foreign support they sought. In 1689 the French envoy in Madrid received a Neapolitan approach for military support for a rebellion that would transfer the kingdom from Spanish rule to French protection, but little came of it. In 1719 the British, then at war with Spain, turned down a vague approach for support for Andalusian dissidents. However, elsewhere conspiracy was a central aspect of politics. Polish politicians of all descriptions appealed for foreign support under the ostensible guise of defending Polish liberties. Prussian and Russian rulers, such as Frederick William of Brandenburg-Prussia, provided such support, in order to keep the country weak. In 1701 James Sobieski pressed Charles XII of Sweden to invade Poland to prevent Augustus II from suppressing Polish liberties. Opponents of the Stuarts obtained Dutch aid in 1688; the Stuarts themselves received Bourbon assistance for much of the next 71 years. France provided assistance to the American opponents of British rule, a step that led to war in 1778. The financial consequences were serious for France, although had Britain crushed the rebellion and France not intervened, she would probably have been unable to defend her maritime and colonial position from British hegemony. In imperial matters particularly, the link between domestic and international policies and actions was strong.

Intervention was not restricted to states with representative assemblies. An essential feature of the diplomacy of the period was the attempt to influence the policies of powers by manipulating the factional and personal politics of courts and royal families. This was generally peaceful, an established and accepted diplomatic practice, but it was frequently conspiratorial and at times could slide into hostile intervention. In 1715 the British envoy in Madrid complained that

> there is nobody here capable of governing, for if there were, I am sure the protection of the king would support him against all the feeble opposition he would meet with. This must be the measure we must endeavour to pursue here, and if there ever be a man of spirit, and sense at the head of affairs, I believe it will be no difficult matter to engage him in the interests of His Majesty, they are so apparently those of Spain; and indeed he will find his security in it.

The French envoy in London was more sweeping in 1733, writing 'all powers are divided and in each we can have a party disposed to support us.'[25]

Intervention was most marked in wartime with governments seeking to overthrow hostile regimes. In 1719 Philip V both issued a manifesto against the duke of Orléans, encouraging the French to revolt and their troops to desert, and also supported a Jacobite invasion of Scotland, while the Anglo-French alliance sought to have Alberoni dismissed as his chief minister. The French supported Jacobite schemes in 1744–6, while the British were urged

---

[25] SRO. GD. 135/141/3A, 4 Oct. 1715; AE. CP. Ang. 379 f. 158.

by the Dutch politician William Bentinck to respond in kind by supporting the Protestants in the Cévennes, as they had done in the War of the Spanish Succession. The Jacobite rising exposed the contradictory nature of British policy for at the same time as she received foreign support to suppress it she was encouraging rebellion in Corsica. On the other hand British diplomats felt that the French support of rebels meant that, as one put it, France had no 'principles they will allow to be the immovable foundation of public or private society.'[26] The French responded to Anglo-Sardinian intrigues in Corsica by attempting in 1748 to foment a rebellion on the island of Sardinia. At this level of involvement, destabilization was being used almost as a routine diplomatic weapon. Intervention could be intended to help allies resist hostile domestic acts, such as the assistance provided to Britain to assist against Jacobite conspiracies or French military support of the bishop of Liège in 1684. This last was repeated in 1702 while the Emperor freed Joseph Clément's subjects from their oath of obedience unless he heeded an edict to break his French alliance and expel French troops, which led Joseph Clément to accuse Leopold of limiting princely sovereignty.

States could also intervene to influence political developments. In 1711 the nobility of the prince-bishopric of Hildesheim thanked neighbouring Hanover for protecting them in their privileges and religion. Until it became a Prussian territory in 1744 the Dutch frequently intervened in neighbouring East Friesland in support of the town of Emden in its opposition to princely demands. In 1747 the British proposed a Russian invasion of Finland in order to overturn the pro-French party in Sweden. Guidelines to acceptable behaviour were lacking, so that nations tended to pursue their own perceived interests, at the risk of threats and brinkmanship leading to an exacerbation of distrust and tension. When in 1769 Choiseul threatened to provide financial assistance for dissident Americans in reprisal for a private British subscription in favour of the Corsicans, the British envoy denied that there could be any comparison. Religion was another cause of interference but it was most important in the case of relations between powerful and weak states, such as Russia and Poland in the 1760s. When strength was more finely balanced, as between Britain and both Austria and France, complaints such as those of the 1720s about the treatment of co-religionists could lead to replies in kind.

In 1781 Frederick II responded to an appeal for help from his niece, the princess of Orange, with the statement, 'it is not appropriate for a foreign power to meddle in the domestic affairs of all other powers; I respect the limits that public law prescribes'. However, the nature of such limits was far from clear and in 1787 Frederick's successor was prepared to invade the United Provinces in response to a plea from the same woman, his sister. It was natural to seek to influence domestic affairs when they could have such an important bearing on national strength and foreign policy.

---

[26] Farmington Connecticut, Weston Papers 18, Titley to Weston 26 July 1746.

RELIGION

The role of religious considerations in international relations from the begin-ning of the Reformation to the Peace of Westphalia (1648) is a much debated subject but less attention has been devoted to the topic for the succeeding 150 years. This is surprising as religion was not only a source of moral views, but also a powerful ideological force that could play a major role in creating tensions between and within states. Furthermore, in the absence of strong nationalistic traditions, it was religious loyalties that served to articulate political loyalties and thus provide an additional reason for hostility to religious minorities. The most important religious divide was that between Christendom and Islam. Tension along it was not constant and was stronger in the Balkans and around the Black Sea than in the western Mediterranean or the Adriatic but it was always a factor. In North Africa the English in 1684 abandoned Tangier to the Moroccans, who attacked Ceuta, Melilla and Penon in 1770s while the Spaniards attacked Oran in 1732 and Algiers in 1775. Divisions between the Islamic powers limited their impact on Christendom. Sultan Muley Ismael, the aggressive ruler of Morocco from 1672 to 1727, captured La Mamora (1681), Larche (1689) and Arzila (1691) from Spain and Tangier, and besieged Ceuta (1694–1720) but he also invaded the Turkish tributary territory of Algiers in 1701. Concern about the Islamic powers affected their neighbours and, because of that, other states that were con-cerned about their strength and policies. It also influenced much of the population of the neighbouring lands, whether Italian or Hungarian peasants fearing Turkish raids, merchants worried about privateers or German, Polish and Russian aristocrats and clerics who sought the defeat of what Catherine II was to call 'the common enemy of the Christian name', when she appealed for support in face of a Turkish declaration of war in 1768. That however did not prevent alliances or agreement between Christian powers and the Turks and these became more frequent. Similarly gains at the expense of the Turks were not viewed by rival powers with delight.

The situation within Christendom was comparable. International tension arising from religious differences was common, though it did not dictate the diplomatic agenda. Religion was most important as a cause and subject of dispute in the Empire, Poland and Hungary but in the last two it was essentially a domestic matter. That did not prevent Protestant diplomatic pressure on behalf of their co-religionists, for example the Dutch rescue of Hungarian clergy from the galleys in the 1670s, Anglo-Prussian complaints after the so-called Thorn massacre in Poland in 1724 and Prussian pressure over the treatment of Bohemian Protestants in 1735. The effectiveness of such action varied. Episodic direct impact could not compensate for the general social, legal and political pressure that had by 1717 led to a ban on the construction of Protestant churches in Poland. Complaints on behalf of co-religionists were not restricted to these areas. British intercession on behalf of the Piedmontese Waldensians, Swedish pressure in 1686 on behalf of Alsatian Lutherans whose religious rights were guaranteed by the Peace of Westphalia and papal complaints about treatment of priests in the United Provinces in 1687 were but three examples of what was a major topic of diplomatic activity and a prime source for creating images about other countries. Pages of diplomatic correspondence were taken up with the cases of girls supposedly inveigled into nunneries and the burial problems of merchants dying abroad.

It is unclear how far such tensions influenced governmental policies, though there was no shortage of talk about religious leagues. This could serve as a diplomatic tool, as when Louis XIV unsuccessfully sought Bavarian and Spanish support against William III in late 1688. In early 1689 court preachers told Pedro II of Portugal to attack the Dutch in the Indian Ocean in order to retake ancient losses to the Protestants at the same time that the Dutch envoy was citing the Austrian and Bavarian support for William as proof that his policy was not a confessional one. Pedro did nothing. The Bavarians criticized the Austrians during the War of the Spanish Succession for allying with Protestants and destroying Catholic solidarity but that had no more effect than Protestant pressure on behalf of the Hungarian Protestants. There was talk of Protestant leagues in 1719–22, the late 1730s and during the Seven Years' War, but there is little sign that shared religion created a strong disposition to negotiate. Just as monarchs and ministers might seek to benefit from shared sympathies, they could also be worried, as Louis XIV was in late 1714, that their apparent policies might serve to create a contrary league. Once wars began they were often conceived of as in part religious struggles, and this was certainly the case in Britain and the United Provinces during the conflicts with Louis XIV and in Britain and Prussia during the Seven Years' War. However, that did not prevent active wartime peace negotiations, alliances with powers of a different confession and interwar diplomacy in which religion played a much smaller role.

Church affairs provided a further topic of negotiation particularly among Catholic powers at Rome and in the Empire as the choice of Popes and of ecclesiastical rulers could be of great importance. The influence of the Wittelsbach family owed much to ecclesiastical pluralism. Before he was elected at Cologne and a number of other states, Joseph Clément, born in 1671, had already become prince-bishop of Freising in 1684 and of Regensburg in 1685, both principalities that increased the power of Bavaria. The Saxons and Habsburgs were generally less successful, but Clément of Saxony was prince-bishop of Freising before becoming archbishop-elector of Trier in 1769, while Frederick II resisted without success the succession of Joseph II's brother Maximilian in Cologne and Münster. Such elections led to a considerable amount of activity on the part of Catholic and, to a far lesser extent, Protestant powers as rulers competed to use and increase their influence. In general the major sees went to the men chosen by the powerful rulers. In

1725 when the prince of Saxe-Neustadt was a candidate in moves over the succession to the prince-bishopric of Eichstadt, the Saxon envoy in Munich argued that the Wittelsbachs already held numerous bishoprics and that in justice and reason the Saxons should have their turn. The dominance of the major dynasties increased the gap between their influence and that of minor rulers. The latter were generally forced into the role of interceders for favour, Duke Leopold of Lorraine for example seeking Imperial aid for his brother in 1711. Another subject that involved a lot of activity on the part of the Catholic envoys of the major powers was the support of religious foundations that their monarchs protected. The kings of France protected the Carthusian order and this led to action on the part of their envoys, for example their envoy in Spain, himself a bishop, in 1746 against apparent injustices. This posed greater problems in the second half of the century as in a partial 'nationalization' of the Catholic church rulers showed more determination to control the ecclesiastical system in their territories and often considerable hostility to those owing extra-territorial loyalties. The order which suffered most was the Society of Jesus (the Jesuits) which had few protectors. Their suppression represented the culmination of intensive diplomatic activity by many Catholic powers, including France, Portugal and Spain, in the 1760s and early 1770s. Conversely the French found they had to help the Carthusians in, for example, Naples where the French envoy, the Marquis de Clermont d'Amboise, devoted a lot of time to the subject in the late 1770s. He also repeatedly pressed the Neapolitan ministers on an inheritance due to the Bourbon family, a customary use of diplomatic representation in order to advance personal interests that reflected the role of the diplomat as the personal representative of the sovereign, rather than the bureaucratic delegate of a state. The importance of religion certainly varied but there is no doubt that it added to the complexity and unpredictability of diplomatic relations.

NATIONALISM

The extent and impact of nationalist feeling were limited. They were strongest in countries with clearly defined territorial extents, representative institutions and a sense of common history, such as Britain and Sweden. Policies such as British opposition to France and Swedish to Russia evoked a popular resonance within the political nation, the groups accustomed to discuss politics, that could influence policy and that certainly influenced the debate over it. In territories lacking such unifying and distinguishing features the situation was more complex. In much of Europe monarchs ruled what were often legally distinct territories and their possessions lacked either a shared sense of the past or often one of present interests. Many territories were divided ethnically, linguistically and religiously. Within the Empire the political system opposed an overarching constitutional and cultural sense of common German identity to a reality of conflicting territorial policies. Frederick II might, when stressing the need for good relations to an Austrian envoy in November 1768, say 'we are Germans', but he also encouraged his nobles and his army to think and talk in terms of a Prussian 'fatherland'. The sense of common German identity was more important in arousing and sustaining a degree of popular animosity against outsiders, for example Louis XIV from the 1670s, than in influencing policy. Animosities could also be strongly developed within the German and Italian nations, for example between Bavaria and the Tyrol. Contrasts between governmental policies and more widely diffused popular views were frequent and they indicate the limited role of the ordinary people in foreign policies that were essentially an aspect of sovereign authority and therefore non-consultative. These views were more important at times of war when the ability to mobilize resources was of great consequence. However popular views could then be sharply divided, as was often the case in the United Provinces. Even if 'nationalist' sentiment could define a common threat it was often the case that there were significant differences over the policies that should be adopted, especially in the context of alliance politics. During the period as a whole, and especially in the second half of the eighteenth century, the voice of political opinion became more clearly defined and heard over much of Europe but although, for example, it was generally agreed that the Austro-French alliance of 1756–91 was unpopular in France, this had scant impact on policy. Nationalist opinion only became really important with the revolutionary wars which both lessened disagreements between most of the powers in face of the onslaught of revolutionary France and politicized groups who responded to developments along national cum ideological lines.

TRADE

Commercial issues were a common topic of diplomatic activity. European states followed protectionist rather than free trade policies, establishing tariffs on manufactured imports in order to encourage domestic production and sponsoring trading companies. Their policies, described as mercantilist, reflected a sense that there was only a finite amount of demand, and thus that domestic production and foreign trade could only be boosted at the expense of those of other states and therefore led to a belief in the need for and efficacy of regulation.

As the economy was seen as a source of political and especially military, strength a competitive commercial policy was regarded as necessary. It was extended to the trans-oceanic world as a result of the belief that the mercantilist analysis was equally, indeed particularly valid, for trans-oceanic trade and colonial activity. Tea prices fell in 1753 because of the growing trade of countries such as Prussia, Denmark and Sweden that had hitherto played only a minor role. The prevalence of regulation ensured that a major topic of diplomatic activity was the attempts to win favourable terms and to prevent the deterioration in those already enjoyed by a state's merchants. Though collaborative initiatives were occasionally made, for example in response to Britain's wartime treatment of neutral trade, most commercial diplomacy took place in a competitive atmosphere. Thus even during the Anglo-French alliance of 1716–31 both powers anxiously watched the position of the other in Spanish trade, while in 1724 Lorraine pressed for the same duties on its salt imports into the Duchy of Luxemburg as the salt from the United Provinces enjoyed. Two years earlier the United Provinces was alarmed by new Prussian duties on cattle driven there from Jutland.

The idea that for every gain there must somewhere be a loss led to considerable concern over the effects of new trade routes. The Genoese were concerned about the development of Sardinian and Modenese ports on the Mediterranean, the Dutch were opposed to Prussian attempts to develop the trade of Emden, including plans to improve the navigation of the river Lippe, while in 1763 the Austrians feared that the trade of the Austrian Netherlands would be harmed by a possible road between Liège and the United Provinces.

Trade regulations could serve as weapons of political and commercial policy. Louis XIV stopped the Liège customs from charging French goods in 1688, and there was a trade war between France and Avignon in 1730–4. In the 1760s Frederick II employed hostile tariff policies towards Austria and Poland and thwarted Austrian attempts to divert Saxon trade from Silesia. Baden competed with neighbouring Württemberg in wine and cloth production and tariffs were organized accordingly. In 1783 the ruler of Baden interceded personally to have some restrictions abolished. In 1788–9 the alleged mistreatment of Bavarian merchants by the imperial free city of Augsburg led to a partial embargo. Trade played a relatively substantial diplomatic role in relations between countries that traded with each other but had only modest political links, such as Denmark and Spain and in the late eighteenth century France and Naples. Clermont d'Amboise devoted many pages of his despatches to the subject. In July 1776 he complained that, whereas the British were allowed to sell prohibited goods, the French were not and their ships were searched despite their privilege to the contrary. He added that French vice-consuls were alone threatened with the loss of the privilege of putting up their ruler's arms. The following month he complained about the more favourable treatment of the Genoese in the Calabrian oil trade, while in September the Neapolitans protested that a French ship had given a murderer refuge, episodes which reflected the fact that commerce and national rights and sensibilities were never truly separate. In 1776 disputes over the conduct of customs officers multiplied, though Clermont d'Amboise admitted in November that French traders were guilty of smuggling. Nevertheless, he complained of preferential treatment for the British. The Neapolitans alleged in December that their trade was restricted at Marseille. 1777 brought renewed disputes over the customs, the respect not paid to the French flag and the debts owed to Marseille grain merchants. The French were concerned about the willingness of Neapolitan consuls to allow Genoese and Tuscan smugglers to use their flag, while Clermont d'Amboise suggested that if the instructions to visit Neapolitan ships in Marseille were revoked this would help the French traders in Naples. In 1778 he pressed the Neapolitan government to allow grain exports to France and to stop the imprisonment of French sailors seized for smuggling.

Such complaints could be mirrored elsewhere but, though they could be a considerable diplomatic irritant, they were generally ineffective. The British envoy in Copenhagen complained in 1715, 'I should only have prostituted myself and the service I am employed in by continuing to threaten to no purpose. I have never neglected to solicit in favour of British subjects to the utmost of my power; had I been less zealous in this respect, I might perhaps have met with more kindness . . . but I can only solicit and not force; and these people are not to be won by reason and persuasion'.[27] French complaints about Spain were similar, even when the two powers were allied in war. The major trading powers were faced by the determination of other states to improve their economy and derive greater benefit from foreign trade. Thus Denmark, Sweden, Russia, Prussia, Austria, Naples, Sardinia and Portugal, to name only the most prominent examples, developed policies that the major trading countries of the late seventeenth century, England, France and the United Provinces, regarded as hostile.

The political consequences of this varied. It is readily possible to find examples of the personal commitment of rulers to commercial projects in the face of international hostility. Charles VI founded and fostered long-distance trading companies based at Ostend and Trieste despite marked Anglo-Dutch hostility to the former. Between its foundation in 1722 and its suspension in 1727 the Ostend Company was generally the major contentious item in Austro-Dutch relations. However, it was also the case that the enthusiasm of most monarchs for commercial projects did not extend to the point of compromising diplomatic relations for them, and one must not exaggerate the influence of commercial lobbies or governmental determination to foster trade. Economic advantage played only a modest role in the competing currents of alliance diplomacy. Trade played only a minor role in French foreign policy, despite the strong interest in commerce, particularly that of Spain and her empire. Adam Smith saw the French attack on the Dutch in 1672 as an economic war, but any stress on economic considerations exaggerates the influence of the finance minister, Colbert, underrates the personal direction of Louis, ignores the infrequency of economic considerations in his

---

[27] PRO. SP. 75/35 f. 29–30.

correspondence and fails to appreciate the extent to which he regarded mercenary considerations as incompatible with his *gloire*. When in 1745 the Swedish envoy tried to convince the French finance minister of the advantages of purchasing the iron of Sweden he was told that Louis XV was not an iron merchant. In 1749 the French envoy in Spain, denying charges of Franco-Spanish contraband trade, stated that Louis was no merchant.

In Britain and the United Provinces trade was more important, domestic pressure from mercantile lobbies stronger and governmental determination to support commerce greater. In the United Provinces the political influence of the Orangist stadtholders, whose views on foreign policy accorded with the dynastic and territorial interests of the British monarchs, in that from the late seventeenth century they were concerned with a balance of power not territorial aggrandizement, clashed with those of the major towns. There republicanism was strongest and commercial interests played a large role in affecting views on foreign policy. However, these varied. Thus in the War of the Spanish Succession Amsterdam with its strong interests in the East Indies trade was readier to come to a compromise peace than the province of Zeeland where privateering was important and the role of trade to the Caribbean ensured greater concern over French influence in the Spanish empire. Trade was clearly a force in Anglo-Bourbon enmity and British ministers frequently referred to the domestic pressures they were under in international commercial disputes. In 1749 a complaint about a Spanish ship searching a British merchantmen at sea in the Caribbean for contraband led to the Secretary of State writing to Sir Benjamin Keene, the envoy in Madrid, 'you know how extremely jealous this nation is of the least encroachments of this nature, and the Spaniards know it too; The least spark of this sort must, if not timely prevented, kindle a flame'.[28] Yet though commercial and colonial disputes were the occasion for confrontations or wars between Britain and the Bourbons, such as the Anglo-Spanish War of Jenkins' Ear which broke out in 1739, the outbreak of Anglo-French hostilities in North America in 1754 and the Anglo-Spanish confrontation over trade on the north-west American coast in 1790, similar disputes, such as between Britain and Spain in 1728–9 or between Britain and France over St Lucia in 1721–30, did not lead to conflict. The political context was crucial, because a united and powerful ministry in Britain could be as insensitive to domestic criticisms as any continental counterpart.

[28] PRO. SP. 94/136 f. 1.

CONCLUSION

Assessing the impact of different factors is made more difficult by the nature of foreign policy. As studies increasingly stress the wider political context of diplomacy, in particular the nature of court politics, so the misleading nature of the abstraction foreign policy becomes more clear and the substantial diplomatic records that remain seem more satisfactory as evidence of the attempted execution of policy than as a guide to its formation. In many countries it is not possible to follow what happened in conciliar discussions, let alone those outside the council. Diplomats did not always enjoy the confidence of ministers and rulers to whom they reported, let alone those to whom they were accredited. In writing their reports diplomats sought, consciously or unconsciously, to please their master, enhance their own importance and save face. Diplomatic exchanges and correspondence were as much intended to persuade as to explain. Sometimes the relative precision of negotiating by the exchange of memoranda, rather than verbally, was preferred. The British envoy in Venice reported in 1707, 'The method here is very extraordinary, and it is in effect treating with dumb people: for whatever is said is put down in writing; it is, true, a safe way, but tedious'.[29] Frederick II instructed his envoy in Paris to follow the same method in 1752 in order to obtain more precise answers. However, it was a method more suited to allies, such as France and Prussia in 1752, than to the characteristic ambiguities of diplomatic exchange, and rulers who were concerned about committing and compromising themselves instructed their envoys, for example Keene in 1749, to be cautious about committing themselves on paper. In seeking to create a good impression, diplomats stressed the good intentions of their masters and presented their moves as defensive. Chavigny, the French envoy at the Imperial Diet, argued in January 1727 that France should stress the disinterestedness and innocence of her views and her concern for the public good, but his views of the possibility of re-establishing 'good order' in the world and of a French policy based on Louis XV's *gloire* and prosperity were not readily compatible with those of others who proclaimed their concern for the public order. 'General unmeaning answers', such as those the British envoy in Paris promised to give his Swedish counterpart in January 1773, can be found throughout the diplomatic correspondence but they are not always easy to pick out and the question of the importance of the language used as a guide to the thinking of contemporaries is complicated by the role of deceit and dissimulation.

The role of the past was clearly important. Urging an Austro-French alliance, the Jacobite agent in Vienna said in 1727 'there was no sort of obstacle, but mere shadows, ancient impressions, and groundless prejudices

---

[29] Huntingdon CRO. DD M36/8 p. 48.

which ought to vanish before the eyes of sound statesmen.[30] In 1781 Frederick II complained that the Dutch acted as though Europe had not changed since 1688. Clearly continuity was important in a political culture that stressed hereditary rights and was heavily influenced by legalistic conceptions. The unstable nature of international affairs probably also encouraged in many an attempt to retain fixed points of reference. However, there was also a widespread willingness to negotiate new alignments and to develop bold schemes. These were often unsuccessful, and Frederick II consoled himself in August 1748 that hostile Austrian schemes were likely to fail, 'grand projects are easier to conceive than to execute because the vaster they are, the less the different interests of those who participate will allow them to succeed'. In 1763 the Russian vice chancellor attributed the failure of Kaunitz's anti-Prussian strategy to 'unexpected misfortunes, particularly the death of the Empress Elizabeth'.[31] The uncertainty of events and the instability of alliances seem to have encouraged rulers to simply negotiate more widely and to develop several plans, often contradictory, at once. This in turn helped to sustain a sense of instability and fluidity, of the unexpected becoming plausible, that is such a feature of the diplomatic correspondence of the period.

Thus the relatively fixed nature of the language employed in diplomacy did not betoken a rigid approach to international relations. Aspirations changed little but, as has generally been the case in periods when ideology has only played a relatively minor role in foreign policy, there was a continual willingness to manoeuvre diplomatically in order to further them.

---

[30] HHStA. England Varia 8, 29 June 1727.
[31] *Politische Correspondenz* VI, 197; PRO. SP. 91/72 f. 102.

V

The Mechanics of International Relations

In peacetime diplomacy served a variety of goals, including commercial objectives and the interests of courtiers and institutions whom the monarch chose to favour. Principal goals were furthered by negotiations either through diplomats at foreign courts or between ministers and foreign diplomats. In wartime military might and strategy were of central importance but so also were negotiations that sought to influence the conduct of allies, enemies and neutrals.

DIPLOMACY

By the second half of the seventeenth century most important states reciprocally maintained permanent embassies in peacetime. The three major exceptions were Russia, which only established its first permanent embassy, in Poland, in 1688, the Turkish empire, which did not decide to establish permanent embassies in Christian Europe until 1793, and the Papacy, whose representation was restricted to Catholic Europe. Diplomatic relations with Protestant courts were only established slowly and in the case of Britain the papal acknowledgement of the Stuart claim to the throne was a further bar. The major Christian states maintained embassies in Constantinople but the Turks preferred to send individual missions for particular negotiations. Other powers, even when they maintained permanent embassies, often used the same method to deal with important negotiations and to fulfil ceremonial functions, such as congratulations on accessions, marriages and births or installations with chivalric orders. The majority of rulers did not, however, maintain permanent embassies in more than a few capitals, if that. This was due to the cost, the difficulty of finding suitable diplomats and the absence of matters requiring negotiations. The idea of an integrated diplomatic network ignores the minor princes who in some cases had no permanent embassies. Instead they might use their courtiers for special missions, share an agent or rely on confidential newsletters. Frederick prince-bishop of Osnabrück, a brother of George I, received confidential newsletters from a number of capitals. The Italian Zamboni acted in the 1740s as London agent for the duke of Modena, the landgrave of Hesse-Darmstadt and the government of the Austrian Netherlands, among others, and he had earlier performed that function for Augustus II of Saxony-Poland. Aside from pay agents could benefit from diplomatic privilege to circumvent commercial regulations and to sell posts that conferred immunity from arrest, which were particularly useful to indebted tradesmen. An entire diplomatic subworld flourished in many capitals. In London Italian diplomats were notorious for helping traders to evade import duties and prohibitions.

Minor powers tended to maintain envoys, if at all, at Vienna, whose Imperial position and law court attracted German and north Italian envoys, Paris, The Hague, Rome, if they were Catholic, Madrid, for the Italians, and London increasingly after 1688. These courts, especially Paris, were important not only as political centres but as production and marketing centres for luxury industries that provided opulent and high-quality goods, such as mirrors, furniture, watches, clothes, paintings, mathematical instruments and books. The Bavarian envoy in Paris sent substantial quantities of furniture and clothes to Munich in the 1720s and 1730s. His Hesse-Cassel counterpart in London purchased paintings in mid-century, while the British envoy in Paris in the 1730s obtained truffles and truffled pies for the duke of Newcastle. The capitals to which minor powers sent envoys became the general places of negotiation with them, as, however widely spread their embassies might be, major states generally did not retain permanent envoys to these powers and lacked business sufficient to justify special embassies. No British envoy was accredited to Munich between 1726 and 1746 and the French maintained permanent embassies at only a few German courts. Thus important Anglo-Wittelsbach discussions in the winter of 1728–9 had to be handled at Paris, where Britain, Bavaria and the Palatinate were represented, and in the summer of 1729 were conducted on a temporary basis between a British Secretary of State who had accompanied George II to Hanover and the foreign minister of the elector of Cologne, who was in correspondence with Munich. The following winter the Wittelsbachs had to conduct them in Paris and via the envoy of their French ally in London. Such a system did not encourage the clear transmission of opinions, though it did enhance the diplomatic importance of particular capitals. Paris was probably the most important, certainly in the late seventeenth and first half of the eighteenth centuries, while The Hague was termed the 'whispering gallery of Europe' for its ability to register and repeat reports from throughout Europe. At the second-rank level, in terms of accredited diplomats, St Petersburg, Berlin and Turin became more important, though Turin's importance diminished with post-1748 Italian stability. The ending of Dutch representation led Charles Emmanuel III to threaten to withdraw his envoy from The Hague.

As diplomats represented their sovereigns, who were themselves conscious both of their own rank within a monarchical hierarchy and of the need to grade representation carefully, the senior diplomatic ranks were dominated by aristocrats and reflected this hierarchy. The most senior grade, that of ambassador, was generally allocated only to a small number of courts. Similarly monarchs devoted great care to the forms of address with which they honoured other rulers and to those they expected to receive. New pretensions were treated with great hostility. Ambassadors tended to be found most commonly at Paris, Madrid, Vienna and Rome, though the situation was not unchanging. The rest of the diplomatic hierarchy, from Envoys Extraordinary through a number of grades including Ministers Resident down to Secretaries of Embassy and unaccredited agents and secretaries, provided a large number of ranks that allowed distinctions in relations to be made and reciprocated. Most of the senior grades were occupied by aristocrats. The employment of clerics, very rare in Protestant Europe, was increasingly uncommon among Catholic states, with the prominent exception of the papal nuncios. Many aristocratic envoys held military posts in wartime and were thus in fairly continual service to their monarchs. Others took one or two missions and then returned to less onerous honorific service, often in ceremonial court posts, or left direct royal service. A few were permanent or semi-permanent diplomats though that was much more common at the more junior ranks, and in Spain a permanent diplomatic service developed only late in the eighteenth century. Consular posts were dominated by merchants. Senior diplomatic posts were expensive, in large part because of the importance of lavish hospitality and court ceremonial in the establishment of royal *gloire*, and, as the cost was not generally fully paid by the monarch, there was a further reason to appoint aristocrats.

The calibre of the diplomats is difficult to assess, especially if their necessary social skills are considered. Frederick II complained in June 1753 that a French diplomat lacked '*politesse*', and that was a quality much in demand. Influence often reflected the ability to make the right impression at court, whether hunting or taking part in the evening smoking and drinking sessions of Frederick William I or paying court to the Queen's chamber woman who Clermont d'Amboise believed was influential at Naples in 1777. The following year both he and the Austrian envoy sought to have compatriots appointed to teach the heir to the throne. Thus their training in certain skills, such as riding, as well as their general demeanour made aristocrats the most suitable choices as senior diplomats. Some disgraced themselves, the duke of Richelieu having to leave Vienna for his supposed involvement in black magic rites, but most represented their monarchs in the manner that they were supposed to do. Their ability in negotiation was tested less continually than their court skills and could anyway be compensated for in part by accentuating the role of the respective ministers and treating the diplomats more as gilded messengers.

The ability and experience of ministers responsible for negotiations varied greatly. Many were experienced diplomats, such as Bestuzhev, Choiseul, Kaunitz, Pombal, Vergennes, the Spanish foreign minister Richard Wall and many British Secretaries of State, including Stanhope, Sunderland, Carteret, Townshend, Harrington, Holderness, Grantham, Rochford and Stormont. Between 1688 and 1713 both the Portuguese Secretaries of State had been diplomats as indeed was the case of later Secretaries such as Mello. Others were not, such as Chauvelin, French foreign minister 1727–37, and the duke of Newcastle, a British Secretary of State 1724–54. Some diplomats complained about the courts to which they were accredited, Keene writing in 1749 from Spain, 'as the ministers here have no great experience in foreign affairs, and there being no council to digest and assist in their political transactions, this court must principally govern itself by the relations of their ministers abroad and consequently much depends upon the cast of their views and dispositions'.[1] In general however, diplomats complained not about the competence of the ministers they had to deal with abroad but about their lack of power or consistency in the face of court politics and monarchical views. In 1734 Walter Titley, who was to serve as British envoy in Copenhagen for over thirty years, reported success in a negotiation 'though with more difficulty than any one from the nature of it would be apt to imagine. Such an effect court intrigues and private interests can produce in the plainest and most natural affairs'.[2] Certain monarchs, such as Philip V and Frederick William I, acquired justified reputations for being difficult to deal with and in those circumstances it was not sufficient to reach an understanding with their ministers. In states with powerful representative institutions there was the additional hazard that policies might be overturned or qualified in light of unexpected domestic pressures. Rulers and ministers frequently complained that envoys exceeded instructions but it was difficult to provide orders that would comprehend all eventualities and impossible, in light of the available communications, readily to respond to developments by sending new instructions, so a lot of responsibility lay in the hands of the diplomats. Communications were uncertain as well as slow. Couriers could travel from The Hague and Paris to London in three days but adverse winds would prevent the packet boats from sailing and persistent westerlies could leave the ministry in London waiting for several posts from each of the capitals of northern Europe all of which would be waiting at The Hague. The ordinary post from St Petersburg to Hamburg took 17 days in 1745, though letters of the 7th nevertheless arrived on the 21st, but later in that month however a French agent in Hamburg complained that floods and bad roads made the posts very irregular. Rainfall affected the roads especially badly in the Empire, Poland and Russia, and there were often insufficient post horses. Many rivers were crossed, as in northern Italy, by ferries rather than bridges and heavy rains could make their passage impossible. Rivers were affected by drought, freezing and weirs, mountain crossings by ice and snow and sea routes by ice, heavy winds and, in the case of the Baltic, poor charts. Diplomats were

[1] PRO. SP. 94/135 f. 302.
[2] PRO. SP. 75/65 f. 47.

delayed as well as messengers. William Stanhope travelling on a vital mission from Paris to Seville in 1729, encountered difficulties in finding mules. It is not surprising that details of the movements of letters and couriers and their mishaps occurred frequently in the diplomatic correspondence nor that diplomats posted at any distance often felt forced to respond to developments in accordance with what they understood to be the intentions of their rulers. In November 1716 the British envoy in Copenhagen had to report failure, 'what sudden and unexpected turns matters betwixt the Muscovites and Danes took here, and what they are come to, in spite of all that could be done to prevent their taking that course. It was not possible, to be so lucky, to have directions upon every particular, either from England or Hanover in time, but keeping the main point in view of bringing about a good peace, as incidents fell in, what I thought might advance that in time, I did all I could to help them on'.[3]

Moves towards training diplomats were episodic in keeping with the nature of administrative reform in this period. The *Académie politique*, founded in 1712 by the French foreign minister Torcy to train diplomats, was affected by his fall in 1715 and disappeared in 1720. Regius Chairs of Modern History were founded at Oxford and Cambridge in 1724 to help in the training of possible recruits but few diplomats were thus obtained. Peter I sent Russian nobles abroad to increase their knowledge, especially of foreign languages, but the composition of the Russian diplomatic service was eclectic, and included a number of foreigners. That was a common, though decreasing, feature of many diplomatic services, reflecting the ability of rulers to pick whom they wished which also manifested itself in the large number of foreign military officers. Many Italians and Germans found employment in the service of major rulers. Italians were employed by, among others, Augustus II of Saxony-Poland, while La Chétardie and Saint-Séverin both served Louis XV. *Émigrés* could be appointed. The Jacobite Lord Marshal of Scotland was appointed envoy in Paris by Frederick II, while the Earl of Tyrconnel was his opposite number in Berlin, both choices that angered George II. The duke of Liria was appointed Spanish envoy to Russia in 1727, while his father, the duke of Berwick, an illegitimate son of James II, was a French Marshal, and his cousin, Lord Waldegrave was successively British envoy in Vienna and Paris.

Hiring foreigners, some of whom had already acquired experience, was one way to acquire talent and, like the use of military officers, it was employed more persistently than training establishments all of which, with the exception of the Pontifical Ecclesiastical Academy, founded in Rome in 1701, were short-lived. Aristocrats were disinclined to accept formal training and the prevalence of French as a diplomatic language helped to reduce the need for linguistic training. In the seventeenth century French had only been one of the leading diplomatic languages, and German, Italian, Latin and Spanish had all been important. However, the weakness of Spain in the late seventeenth

[3] PRO. SP. 75/36 f. 209.

century, followed by the accession of a Bourbon in 1700, the prestige that Louis XIV brought France, the greater role of Paris as a diplomatic centre, the decline in papal prestige and importance and the importance of German dialects helped to ensure that by the Utrecht negotiations French was the principal diplomatic language in western Europe. The Franco-Spanish treaty at Nijmegen was drawn up in French and Spanish, though the Austro-French treaty was in Latin. At Utrecht the Austrians used French. In eastern Europe German and Latin and, in Constantinople, Italian remained important, but in Europe as a whole French became the first language of most diplomats, used in international negotiations and treaties, between diplomats and sometimes as the language of diplomatic correspondence between rulers and ministers and their envoys. It was thus used extensively in the British diplomatic service under George I, and generally in Sardinian, Saxon and Wittelsbach diplomatic correspondence. Austria under Charles VI used largely German and Italian, though some French was also employed in confidential correspondence. With the accession of Frederick II French largely replaced German for Prussian diplomacy and under Maria Theresa it became more commonly used by Austrian diplomats.

The prominence of French reflected the international character of diplomacy and its interrelationship with monarchical and aristocratic society. The development of accepted conventions of diplomatic immunity and the increased ability to overcome confessional and precedence barriers further helped to create a united diplomatic world. This had an uneasy relationship with the growth in specialized national departments for the conduct of foreign affairs. In many countries these became more distinct and sophisticated, with greater care being taken to ensure that were permanent specialized staff, translators, maps and archives. In 1698 the authority of the French Secretary of State for the Marine over diplomats was defined and limited. In 1719 the old Russian Department of Embassies was replaced by the College of Foreign Affairs and in France a more systematic organization was created. In Portugal a separate office for foreign affairs was created only in 1736, though it had been considered desirable earlier. The office of Foreign Secretary was founded in Britain only in 1782 and a distinct staff established, replacing the previous system by which two, sometimes competing, Secretaries of State had been responsible for foreign affairs and a host of domestic matters, including public order. However, it would be wrong to exaggerate the scope or extent of these administrative changes. Many territories lacked specialized institutions and, where they existed, their staff was generally small and only trained on the job. The influence of such institutions was limited by the continued direct intervention of monarchs and other ministers. The comment in the instructions drawn up in 1725 for a Saxon envoy to Spain that without an appreciation of the internal state of a court it was impossible to understand its foreign policy was equally true at the end of the century. The frequency of correspondence with many diplomats was low and, especially in distant postings such as Constantinople, they were often left essentially to their own devices. It would be inappropriate to think of an administrative revolution in diplomacy or its oversight in this period.

FRONTIERS AND MAPS

One area in which the mechanics of diplomacy improved was mapping. This was linked to what has been seen as a more defined notion of frontiers, a move from the idea of a frontier as a zone to the idea of a distinct border that could be reproduced and charted on a map as a line. This change reflected a greater stress on undivided sovereignty that made ambiguous relationships, such as that between France and ten Alsatian cities established by the Peace of Westphalia, unacceptable to some rulers. However, traditional ideas proved to be very persistent and mapping often served simply to clarify incompatible notions and disputed territories.

Sovereignty caused particular problems when relatively coherent states expanded into or acquired territories whose control was divided, which was particularly the case in Germany and northern Italy. Difficulties can be better appreciated if it is stressed that abstractions such as France in fact described the patrimonies of ruling dynasties whose possessions and pretensions extended as a result of and in the context of feudal overlordships rather than one of 'natural' linear frontiers, such as rivers. In wartime control on the ground was asserted by powerful rulers but with peace the process of legal and diplomatic definition and contention was revived, especially as general peace settlements commonly ignored such specific minor points. In the conferences held at The Hague in December 1734 to try to settle the War of the Polish Succession it was agreed that the limits of French royal authority in Alsace and Flanders were hard to adjust but would be part of the general peace ending the war. In fact the issues continued to be agitated for decades. Typical of the points in dispute were those described in a memorandum to the Imperial Diet presented by the Palatine envoy on 4 July 1715 complaining of contraventions of the Peace of Baden of 1714, which had on the Upper Rhine substantially confirmed the Peace of Ryswick of 1697. The first complaint was that on 13 January 1715 the French had forcibly dislodged Palatine troops and taken possession of Seltz, an under-baillage of Germersheim, on the pretence that it formerly belonged to the district of Hagenau and was situated in Alsace, the sovereignty of which had been yielded to France by the Emperor and the Empire. That was the old basis of Louis XIV's forcible *réunion* policy of the years from 1679, and the Palatine envoy claimed that Seltz was held by the Elector Palatine until 1680, when it had been thus seized, but that Ryswick had determined that it should be restored to Germersheim. The second complaint arose from a provostship at Seltz which Louis XIV had given as part of the foundation to the Jesuit college at Strasbourg. The French argued that the college should keep it as Ryswick had stated that ecclesiastical benefices collated during the Nine Years' War (1688–97) were to remain with their present possessors. The Palatinate countered that collation was only personal, that it was to fall to its rightful owner on the death of an incumbent, that the French incorporation would defraud the owner of his right for ever and, that the provostship had been secularized at the time of the Reformation and then incorporated by the elector palatine into his territories. Thirdly the memorandum charged that the *intendant* of Alsace had forbidden French ships to pay tolls on the Rhine by Seltz, though that right had been confirmed to the elector Palatine at Ryswick and the tolls had been paid by the French until the start of the War of the Spanish Succession. In addition it was claimed that the French had seized two castles, both part of the succession of Veldent, on pretence of their being situated within the sovereignty of Alsace, turning out the elector's officials and disposing of the revenues, by virtue of a sentence of the Sovereign Council of Alsace to the princes of Birkenfeld and Sülzbach, who were disputing the succession with the elector palatine, whereas the elector had been put in possession by the Emperor in accordance with a decision of the Aulic Council, an Imperial court that met in Vienna, where the cause was still in process. Such localized disputes, small though they were, enmeshed diplomats sometimes for decades, and touched the interests of greater powers.

In 1715 the archbishop-electors of Trier, Mainz and Cologne, the prince-bishop of Speyer and the duke of Württemberg-Montbéliard all had grievances of the same nature with respect to fiefs and benefices lying in Alsace, all of which would have been as difficult to represent on a map. In 1721 the prince of Öttingen complained to the sovereign court of Colmar about the overlordship of 11 villages in Lower Alsace which his family had possessed for over three centuries, which the prince of Rohan had disputed with him and which the French court had allocated to Rohan. Five years later the duke of Württemberg pressed for the restoration of nine seigneuries belonging to the county of Montbéliard, complaining that due to illegal French exactions he had lost more than two thirds of the revenues of the territory. In 1742 the duke of Zweibrücken pressed the French against unilateral action in delimiting the borders of Alsace.

French strength had kept frontiers fluid and her territories growing under Louis XIV, but his successors showed more restraint, though continuing French strength ensured that she was essentially able to define acceptable frontiers and that other rulers found it difficult to achieve their objectives. In 1749 a frontier treaty was signed with the republic of Geneva. Interest in a 'rational' linear frontier only developed slowly. In 1745 Louis XV expressed his wish to conserve his enclaves in Hainault and the Austrian Netherlands, but in 1769, 1770, 1772 and 1779 treaties between France and the Austrian Netherlands removed enclaves by a process of exchange. In 1763 a similar exchange was agreed between France and the prince of Nassau. Along France's other frontiers progress was also slow. In 1688 the Spaniards proposed that a stretch of the Pyrenees border, currently undivided and common to both nations be partitioned, but as late as 1775 negotiations over the Pyrenees were still encountering difficulties. In 1715 Victor Amadeus II of Savoy-Piedmont pressing for the literal observation of the Peace of Utrecht, complained that the *intendant* of Dauphiné was falsely defining both the extent of the valley of Barcelonnette and the alpine watershed. The following year he called for a mutually acceptable agreement on the basis of the treaty made between the two rulers rather than a settlement dictated by one of them, and pointed out that neither had any jurisdiction over the other. A violent territorial struggle between two frontier communities led Victor Amadeus to stress the need for an agreement. In 1716 he also exchanged a barony in Poitiers for an estate which a Frenchman had in Piedmont. However it was not until the Treaty of Turin of 24 March 1760, a treaty that followed extensive negotiations, incorporated eight maps and thus delimited the watershed frontier, that an agreement was obtained.

Disputes between local communities did not only accentuate the problem of frontiers in the Savoy Alps. The longstanding conflict between two Apennine communities, Mioglia and Sassello, exacerbated and was in turn exacerbated by frontier disputes between Sardinia, Genoa and the Austrian Duchy of Milan in the first half of the eighteenth century. In Italy problems of overlordship and disputed frontiers were complicated by rivers that shifted in their course, creating islands that inspired disputes between Milan and Parma in the 1730s and Milan and Sardinia in the 1760s. Disagreements over overlordship were a particular problem in the Langhes region between Milan and Sardinia and between Milan and Parma and the two latter were disputing their frontiers in the 1760s as in the 1720s. Negotiations between Geneva and Sardinia, begun in 1738, produced a frontier treaty in 1754. In 1743 the Austrians demanded to see old maps and that Venice name an experienced mathematician to work in concert with theirs in the regulation of the frontier, disputes over which had lasted for 200 years. The same year Venice accused the Papal States of breaking the frontier in establishing a chain of posts to enforce quarantine regulations against the plague. Venetian forces drove their papal counterparts back. By 1752 the Austro-Venetian frontier was accurately delimited. German frontiers and overlordships created numerous difficulties, both in the case of the minor rulers and for the major princes. Prussia and Saxony had frontier disputes, for example in 1725, as did Prussia and Hanover. In 1719 alterations caused by works on the river Elbe led to a major dispute between the latter two. Peace treaties often allocated frontier disputes to subsequent negotiations but these could take years and still be unsuccessful. The boundary settlement following the Austro-Turkish peace of 1739 was not finalized until 1744, because of disagreements over the Bosnian frontier. That of Finland was still unsettled in 1756 despite the fact that Russia and Sweden had been at peace since 1743.

Maps played an important role in the increasing definition of frontiers and were increasingly referred to in negotiations, Torcy telling his British counterpart in 1712 to look at a map in order to see the strategic threat posed by Victor Amadeus's alpine demands. In 1750 Puysieulx, a successor of Torcy, remarked that a simple examination of a map would show that it was in the interest of the elector Palatine to be always united with France. However, in many of the negotiations diplomats invoked not such simple realism but a range of what might seem to be anachronistic criteria. In the extensive negotiations between France and the prince-bishop of Liège over Bouillon between 1697 and the mid eighteenth century, references were made as far back as the eleventh century, and fantastic genealogies, legendary medieval tales and ancient authors who based their comments on hearsay played a major role. In 1699–1701 Austrian and Turkish commissioners were forced to deal with the ambiguous and contradictory wording of the Peace of Karlowitz (1699) on such matters as the 'ancient' frontiers and Transylvania, the status of islands where the rivers Sava and Maros formed the new border and the nature of the frontier where it was defined as a straight line. The treaty stipulated that the commissioners were to survey and agree the new frontier and the Austrian commissioner was instructed to draw a definitive map by his government. Maps were also increasingly important for military reasons as a tool in military planning. In 1753 Frederick II was obliged to assure the Polish government that his mapping of Silesia was not intended to regulate the Silesia-Polish frontiers. He claimed that it was not up to one ruler to thus define a border, though that was precisely what he was to do for several years after the First Partition of Poland, taking advantage of all sorts of claims and bases for frontiers to make successive advances beyond what were understood to be his gains. A major military survey of Bohemia was begun in the 1760s and completed under Joseph II.

As rulers were increasingly interested in having maps of their territories, part of the greater concern to have reliable information that led also to censuses, land surveys and more extensive economic statistics, it was not surprising that they also sought more accurate maps of frontier territories. The larger role of geographical features in diplomacy was also important. Rivers were used to delimit frontiers at Nijmegen (1678/9) and the practice was continued at Ryswick. In 1718 a map formed part of an Austro-Dutch treaty delimiting the frontier. Maps may indeed have brought a new geographical precision to territorial demands and it is understandable that embryonic foreign offices began to collect and store them in a systematic basis. In the 1770s the French foreign office created its own geographical section and acquired a large collection of maps. However, maps were not without their problems. They could of course accentuate and make more readily apparent conflicting territorial views. This was particularly the case in colonial disputes, such as that between Britain and France in the 1750s over their North American frontier. In addition the devices of printed linear boundaries, different coloration and textual specification were only introduced slowly and were sometimes of limited applicability. The political symbolism of maps was inconsistent. The French 1695 and the Dutch 1696 and 1700 editions of Nicolas Sanson's popular French world atlas of 1658 differed and, in addition, lines on plates contradicted the colouring and the national and continental maps were contradictory. The treatment of Alsace, Franche-Comté and Roussillon in these editions varied. Similar inconsistencies can be found in the maps produced by Pierre Du Val between 1663 and 1684. Nevertheless, there were innovations, such as the common practice by the end of the seventeenth century of distinguishing between traditional provincial borders and contemporary international frontiers by marking the latter within historically united provinces.

The problems that could still occur were illustrated during the crisis in 1762 when Peter III of Russia threatened war with Denmark in furtherance of the territorial claims of his Holstein-Gottorp dynasty. Titley, the British envoy in Copenhagen, reported in March 1762, 'A map of the Duchy of Holstein, wherein the Royal and Ducal possessions are distinctly marked, is, I believe, one of the desiderata of geography. I do not know that there is any such map extant'. Later in the month he obtained and sent a map that was certainly produced in about 1710 by John Homann (1664–1724), the Nuremberg cartographer who was made Imperial Geographer in 1716 and was one of the two leading German cartographers. This map in turn was based on one surveyed in 1638–48 by Johannes Mejer (1606–72) so that by the time Titley sent it the information was over 110 years old. The map was not particularly accurate: some of the locations in Mejer's original map had been approximate and based on observation rather than measurement. In 1763 a new large-scale survey, based on triangulation, was begun for administrative and taxation purposes, though it was not to be complete until 1806. Homann's colouring was based on the principles of the Hamburg scholar and cartographer Johannes Hübner (1668–1731), who is claimed to be the originator of the idea that the lands ruled by the same monarch or republic should be painted in the same colour. The purpose was to depict history rather than geography. Since the maps were intended to illustrate history, especially that of the princely dynasties, toponymy and, to an extent, topography were secondary, and quite often lesser towns and villages on Homann maps are identified only by the first letter of their name so as not to clutter the map and obscure the name of the territorial unit involved. Because of this purpose geographical accuracy was not seen as crucial, while error was sustained by the continued use of old plates. In the Empire, in particular, single maps, as opposed to specially composed atlases of base maps all showing the same area, were not a particularly good way of showing princely territorial rights. It was usually beyond the ingenuity of even the most skilful cartographer to indicate on one map alone areas of mixed jurisdictions, owing allegiance to different rulers for different aspects of their existence. The problem of the interpretation of treaties made single maps even more inadequate, while even in a major cartographic centre like Hamburg another British diplomat could report difficulties in obtaining maps of northern Europe and the Empire the following year.[4] Thus, as in most spheres, it is possible to stress both change and continuity on the subjects of maps and frontiers. Devices existed for the delimitation and depiction of linear frontiers but their use spread only gradually. Only in the Revolutionary and Napoleonic period were there the wholesale reorganizations of European frontiers, the sweeping aside of overlapping sovereignties, the reduction in the number of royal and princely rulers and the qualification of traditional territorial rights, which brought widespread dramatic changes in the nature of European frontiers, territoriality and political cartography.

ALLIANCES, ARMIES AND WAR

Alliances were the most common way in which rulers sought to achieve their political goals. No ruler in the competition of peacetime could afford to ignore the views of other rulers. However, coherent and lasting alliances were undermined by the disparate interests and views of rulers, and much diplomatic correspondence was devoted to complaints and remonstrations about the conduct of allies. Most alliances had scant support from any shared economic interests and little basis in popular support, popular being conceived of as the political nation. The Anglo-French alliance of 1716–31 and the successive Anglo-Austrian alliances had no basis in common cultural, economic or religious interests. Common cultural and religious characteristics could no more explain or sustain the Austro-French alliance of 1756–91 than they could prevent hostility between the two powers over the previous century. There were cultural and other affinities between the British and the Dutch but that did not prevent four Anglo-Dutch wars in 132 years.

If strains existed, they became worse at times of war. Most wars were fought by coalitions whose disparate aims were accentuated by the strains and opportunities of conflict. The fact that a compromise peace, rather than unconditional surrender, was generally the goal in warfare accentuated this situation because powers, allies or not, often could best hope to achieve their aims by unilateral negotiations. The agreed war aims of alliances were commonly not realized, either in war or negotiation.

The ability of armed forces to secure political objectives was limited despite their substantial growth in the early-modern period. In the late seventeenth and early eighteenth centuries the Austrian, French, Prussian and Russian armies and the British and French navies grew substantially, though second-rank powers also witnessed significant increases. Savoy-Piedmont's army grew from 8,700 in 1690 to over 24,000 in 1730 and 48,000 in 1748, though

[4] P. Barber and J. Black, 'Maps and the Complexities of Eighteenth-Century Europe's territorial Divisions: Holstein in 1762 '*Imago Mundi*' (forthcoming); BL. Add. 6861 f. 78.

its peacetime level was lower, 24,000 in 1778. The Prussian army, 80,000 in 1740 was, according to Frederick II, 188,000 in the peacetime year of 1781. These forces represented a considerable financial burden. In 1689 the army accounted for about one third of the total government expenditure of Savoy-Piedmont. By 1731, a year of peace, it accounted for close to one half of a budget twice as big. 75–80 per cent of Prussian revenues were spent on the army in the early 1780s and the French wartime budget of 1781 envisaged 25 per cent of their more substantial revenues being spent on the army, at a time of major naval expenditure. The substantial military growth of a number of powers and the absence of any marked technological or organizational edge, except increasingly between the Turks and their Christian neighbours, made military predominance on the continental, as opposed to the regional, scale impossible to achieve, though the British arguably had managed to achieve naval dominance in successive wars by 1747 and 1760. The absence of rapid communications for men or supplies was a major hindrance and modern fortresses helped defending powers. Rapid victory was not impossible, as the Swedish attack on Denmark in 1700 or the Prussian invasion of the United Provinces in 1787 indicated, but in land wars between major powers it was elusive. Austria appeared near to collapse in 1703–4 and 1741 but it survived thanks to domestic resilience and foreign assistance. Rulers could be driven by defeat to abandon their objectives, Philip V abandoning his Italian plans and dropping his chief minister Alberoni in 1720, or to be willing to surrender what had seemed vital interests, as Louis XIV was willing to do during the War of the Spanish Succession, but both were without allies. When monarchs fought as members of alliances it was difficult to translate victory, however stunning, into an equally clear political settlement. To translate military advantage into total victory was as difficult.

GREAT, SECOND-RANK AND MINOR POWERS

It is possible to organize a work on European international relations in this period in essentially two ways, chronological and thematic. Nor are the two necessarily incompatible especially if it is argued that the nature of international relations changed appreciably with time. Whichever method is employed there is a tendency to concentrate on the great powers and to study the period around the organizing theme of the rise of these powers. There is an understandable tendency, given shortages of space, to neglect the minor powers and to consider those in the second rank only in so far as they relate to the great ones. The definition of powers in this manner is impressionistic. There is no agreed typology and there are problems with evaluating the consequences of particular criteria, such as population, size, military force, princely rank or role as a diplomatic focus. However, some points can be suggested. Minor powers were militarily weak, diplomatically insignificant and not generally capable of initiating political moves that would substantially affect the second-rank and great powers. This category included all the German imperial free cities and ecclesiastical principalities and the vast majority of German and Italian territories. Though it was stronger, the Swiss confederation may be included as it played little role in international relations. These minor princes could be of consequence for dynastic reasons: the extinction of the Bavarian and Palatine branches of the Wittelsbach family increased the importance of their eventual successors, the Sülzbach and finally the Zweibrücken branches.

The second-rank powers varied considerably in consequence whatever criteria are adopted and their relative position altered chronologically. In addition, it is necessary to consider the specific political context. Whatever their respective strengths, Sardinia and Naples could play an independent role in Italy that was different from that of the Palatinate or Lorraine. In the seventeenth century the Baltic was dominated by second-rank powers each of them therefore of considerable consequence. The second-rank category can encompass Portugal, Savoy-Piedmont (Sardinia), Naples, Lorraine, the Palatinate, Bavaria, Hanover, Saxony, Denmark and Sweden. Prussia rose from this group in the eighteenth century, the United Provinces fell into it and Poland was removed from it. Within the category there were major differences in power and independent initiative. That would leave as major powers, Austria, Britain, France, Prussia, Russia, Spain and Turkey. Britain could not be thus classified until the 1690s when the British Isles was brought under central control, an effective system of public finance created and she began to take a major military and diplomatic role. Though Russia was already a major power she did not appear obviously such to the western European countries until after the defeat of Charles XII of Sweden in 1709 and the consequent conquest of the Baltic provinces. Prussia could not be thus classified until she had held Silesia against Austrian attempts to reconquer it in the 1740s. Spain was the largest colonial power in the world throughout the period and a considerable European territorial power until 1700. Her role and influence in eastern and northern European diplomacy were minor, but the same was true of Prussia and, until the late 1760s, Russia in the Mediterranean. Turkey was clearly a great power in the late seventeenth century, but in the following century, although her territorial extent was vast, not least in Europe, she was increasingly seen as a victim due to her failure to introduce governmental and military reforms.

The idea of minor powers as politically and militarily weak particularly describes the situation in Germany and Italy. In eastern Europe it is possible to point to Polish aristocratic families who were more powerful, not least in the size of their military forces, than many minor princes elsewhere and who followed policies accordingly, pursuing independent diplomatic initiatives in negotiations with foreign powers and using diplomatic methods in their political activities within Poland. Their feuds were like wars and when the houses of Tarlo and Poniatowski made peace they were solemnly reconciled in a convention of agreement. It was clear however, that such great houses as Radzivill or Sapieha, however independent they might be, were not sovereign: they did not function as states. What was less clear was the diplomatic status of a number of autonomous territories within the great eastern European empires including the khanate of the Crimea, the Danubian principalities (Wallachia and Moldavia), Transylvania, and though to a lesser extent as their independent actions were more clearly the result of rebellion, Hungary and the Ukraine. In 1750 the British envoy resolved to ignore the efforts of the Prussian government to treat a Crimean envoy as an accredited diplomat of equivalent rank on the grounds that he was not the representative of a sovereign body.

The autonomous principalities of eastern Europe were, with the exception of the khanate of the Crimea, essentially subdued in the period 1700–15, whereas in western Europe in this period, the picture was more diverse. Some second-rank powers, such as Bavaria and Lorraine, had their aspirations quashed, were overrun and only regained independence as the result of the intercession of the great powers they were allied with. Others, such as Savoy-Piedmont, Hanover and Prussia made important gains in the treaties of 1713–21 that ended the Spanish Succession and Great Northern wars. However, though these gains were considerable for the powers concerned and influenced the regional relationship between powers and thus more general European relations, they did not involve large areas of land. Only Russia and Austria gained substantial territories, as a result of the Great Northern and the Spanish Succession wars respectively. The Austrian gains were the result of dynastic claims, military success, an equivalence for the acceptance that a cadet Bourbon would succeed in Spain, and the death without sons of Joseph I (1705–11) so that the Habsburg claimant to the Spanish territories succeeded to Austria. These were the sole substantial territorial gains in the western half of Europe between 1679 and 1721; though there were several major dynastic gains, principally the Orangist and later Hanoverian succession in Britain and the Bourbon in Spain. Between 1721 and 1791 there were no comparable gains in western Europe. Naples, Sicily and Parma were acquired for the cadets of the Spanish Bourbons, the most substantial territorial changes, Tuscany by a cadet branch of the Habsburgs and Lorraine by France, while the extinction of several branches of the family united the Wittelsbach territories. However, none of these changes were comparable in their scale or effect to the Austrian and Russian gains in eastern Europe after 1683. The Prussian conquest of Silesia was important not only because of the wealth and size of the province but also because the repeated Austrian failure to defeat Prussia indicated a major shift in the power relationships in the Empire and eastern Europe. The Prussian gain indicated the importance of the relationship between domestic changes and foreign policy, for Silesia was not such a major gain as to lead automatically to Prussia acquiring the role that she did achieve under Frederick II.

Nevertheless, Prussia was the most problematic of the great powers, as indicated by the enormous costs, over half a century, of Prussian military preparedness, and by Frederick's anxieties about Austrian and, in particularly, Russian intentions. The problems she encountered suggest how difficult it was for a ruler to enlarge his holdings by territorial means, as opposed to dynastic succession. This arguably affected all the second-rank powers. In their diplomatic schemes and military activity they were dependent on the views of the major rulers, though they could hope to influence these. There were examples of major rulers who were in effect led into diplomatic initiatives as a result of the suggestions of weaker powers. The Saxons considerably influenced Austrian and British policies in the 1740s and 1750s. In addition, many rulers could become so committed to their allies, while at the same time lacking control over them, that the weaker allies affected their policies. Arguably this happened in Franco-Bavarian relations during the wars of the Spanish and Austrian successions. This pattern of dependence but some influence was repeated in the relationship between the second-rank and minor powers.

In both cases the situation was made more complex by the number of powers involved which commonly allowed weaker rulers to seek or receive assistance. In 1679 Louis XIV and the dukes of Brunswick blocked a Dano-Prussian attempt to coerce Hamburg. The failure to obtain a Spanish answer over the Tuscan succession led the Grand Duke to seek the intercession of Charles VI and George I in 1722. In 1748 the French offered Genoa support against possible Sardinian aggressive steps. In 1752 Frederick II could not believe that the Danes would attack Holstein because that would offend Russia. Three years later the ministers of the prince-archbishop of Salzburg, then in dispute with the elector of Bavaria over the profitable salt trade boasted of Austrian support. Small states' room for manoeuvre was therefore increased by tension between more powerful rulers. In 1715 Victor Amadeus II stressed the nature of the Austrian threat to France and called for the creation of an anti-Austrian league. In 1733 the Swedish envoy in London feared that any Anglo-French reconciliation would be bad, as their mutual security would lead them to have less concern for other powers such as Sweden. However differences between major rulers could create difficulties for lesser powers by leading the big powers to press for assistance and commitment, which could bring both hostile steps from other powers and neglect from allies once the commitment had been made. The Wittelsbach agent in The Hague warned in 1726 that Charles VI would show less care for the Wittelsbachs if they joined either him or the opposing Alliance of Hanover and he therefore urged a policy of neutrality. When French troops were let into Münster in 1757, the duke of Cumberland took possession of Paderborn which was ruled by the same prince-bishop. It was not, therefore, surprising that some rulers did not wish to commit themselves militarily or diplomatically.

Portugal was not involved in the Devolution, Dutch or Nine Years' conflicts in the late seventeenth century, and Denmark stayed out of the wars after the Great Northern War. Both Denmark and Sweden kept their involvement in the Nine Years' War as small as possible. The United Provinces negotiated with France a neutrality agreement for the Austrian Netherlands for the War of the Polish Succession, refused to become involved in the War of Jenkins' Ear and the Seven Years' War and delayed formal hostilities with France during the War of the Austrian Succession until 1747. Victor Amadeus II resisted pressure to commit himself during the confrontation between the Alliances of Hanover and Vienna in 1725–7. The British envoy in Lisbon wrote, in 1773, 'we have here so little connections with quarrelsome powers, that we are contented with the events, and do not trouble ourselves much with speculation: Jesuits and trade are the only objects of politics in this corner'. Eight years later the Bavarian foreign minister described his elector's system, 'to observe an exact neutrality whatever happens, in order to give ourselves time to breathe and for improvements that would put the Elector in a respectable state, not that he would ever abuse that, as he prefers with justice the description of pacific to that of warrior or conquering'.[5] It was certainly prudent not to offend major rulers, as Frederick II's forcible recruiting and intervention in law suits between Prussian and Saxon subjects indicated. These pacific hesitations could be repeated at the level of the minor rulers. Suspecting the duke of Modena of an anti-Bourbon understanding with Charles Emmanuel III of Sardinia, the French foreign minister, nevertheless, reflected in 1742, 'to some extent this is excusable, because he thinks the Sardinian party the strongest. Small princes are often in the situation of not knowing which side to turn to'.[6] That did not however prevent them from disputes with each other. They often rose over frontier and overlordship differences. In 1670–1, for example, the duke of Brunswick-Wolfenbüttel and the prince-bishop of Münster differed over the suzerainty of a Westphalian town, while the Imperial Free City of Cologne and the archbishop-elector of Cologne, whose territories did not include the city, clashed. Economic issues could be involved. In the early 1750s the archbishop-elector of Trier had a dispute with a local count over a bridge of boats while in the mid 1750s the small Italian city republic of Lucca complained of floods caused by river alterations in Tuscany.

The minor rulers tended to suffer more seriously at the hands of their powerful colleagues, especially in wartime. Forcible billeting, contributions and recruiting were then a general problem. Louis XIV broke his promises over the neutrality of Liège and seized the citadel there in 1675 declaring that he had only done it to better maintain the territory's neutrality. This was not uniquely cynical, for Louis's Dutch opponent behaved in much the same way. Hesse-Darmstadt was burdened with French winter quarters in 1744–5, the electorate of Mainz troubled by their exactions the following spring. In March

[5] Bedford RO. L. 30/14/410/4; Munich, Bayr. Ges. London, 24 June.
[6] AE. CP. Espagne 470 f. 49.

1748 the landgrave of Hesse-Cassel informed George II, who had sought permission for his Russian allies to cross Hesse, that his territories had been affected by the nearly continual march of troops. Ignoring the complaints of the princes of Anhalt, Frederick II sent in troops to obtain recruits, leading the Bavarian foreign minister to reflect in January 1773, 'it seems that the right of the strongest now determines all the moves of the great'.[7] Bullying and oppression was not restricted to military matters. It frequently characterized economic issues and it could be seen in ecclesiastical matters, such as the Habsburg attempt to dominate the appointment of prince-bishops in the early 1780s.

On 28 January 1749 the *Remembrancer*, a London newspaper, claimed that 'the power of peace and war . . . constitutes the greatness, independency and importance of states'. Later in the century a British traveller wrote of the small army of the margrave of Baden-Durlach, 'he has too just an understanding not to perceive that the greatest army he could possibly maintain, could be no defence to his dominions, situated as they are between the powerful states of France and Austria'.[8] The strength of the major rulers did not dismiss all their weaker counterparts to diplomatic and military nullity, but it cannot be said that most enjoyed the power of peace and war to any great extent. The manipulative policies of major rulers were often unsuccessful not least because of their rivalry. Major powers frequently bewailed the self-interest and perverseness of weaker states. Subsidies, for example, were generally used to further the policies of these states: they were not bought. Any detailed study of particular regions or years can only qualify any notion of the international relations of this period as being controlled by the great powers.

FOREIGN POLICY AND DOMESTIC CIRCUMSTANCES

The interrelationship of domestic circumstances with foreign policy and international success was a common theme in the diplomatic correspondence of the period. Considerable attention was devoted to these circumstances though it was generally not systematic and it concentrated on court politics and military matters to the detriment of a fuller assessment of the domestic situation. Thus, for example, the coverage of economic developments and social trends was generally very superficial. This is scarcely surprising as governments commonly were little better informed. In an age without, or at least with few, statistics information was sparse or unreliable and those at the capital were aware of the situation elsewhere only to a limited extent.

---

[7] Munich, Bayr. Ges. London 251.
[8] J. Moore, *A View of Society and Manners in France, Switzerland and Germany* (1779) I, 383.

If foreign policy was influenced by the subtle interplay of internal processes, this was not simply a matter of the functioning of a domestic political system and the international configuration of which the domestic system was a part. The strength of a state's finances and military forces, their government's ability to mobilize resources, was both crucial and seen to be so. It was objectively most important in wartime. The greater financial strength of Britain played a major role in her wars with France, not least in enabling her to fight both a war in America and an alliance of European enemies during the War of American Independence. In addition, the foreign perception of national strength was a constant factor of diplomatic importance. The role of 'reputation' was stressed by many diplomats, such as St Saphorin, George I's envoy in Vienna in 1722. Just as it was necessary for monarchs to have a reputation for honourable behaviour, firmness, justice and bravery so their territories had to be regarded as prosperous and militarily strong. A failure to be thus regarded could compromise a state's actual and potential value as an ally. In 1716 Victor Amadeus II's envoy in Paris reported that governmental and financial weakness would ensure that if France was ever obliged to fulfil the guarantees in the Peace of Utrecht, she would do so, slowly, feebly and with difficulty. Victor Amadeus was discouraged in his opposition to Austria by his envoy's reports that France was not only unwilling but unable to provide clear diplomatic support. Conversely, in 1726, the French envoy in Turin reported that French military preparations against the Alliance of Vienna had changed the Sardinian opinion of the state of France's finances. If second-rank powers could view the major states as potential patrons and allies not only with reference to their intentions but also with regard to their resources, the process worked both ways. In March 1744 the French foreign minister instructed the envoy to Charles VII to press him to create a more economical administration, so that he would be able to use French assistance more profitably and concentrate his expenses on the army. Nine years later the British envoy in Dresden was informed that Saxony must reform her government and finances in order for Austria to have a better opinion of her and seek her alliance.

The relationship between domestic circumstances and foreign policy was a complex one. It was possible to blame misconceived views or weak government for policies that were disliked when in fact it is more likely that they reflected an assessment of interests and needs. In the early 1750s Frederick II was scathing about what he saw as the consequence of France's failure to compete effectively with the Anglo-Austrian defensive system by gaining new allies and supporting her current allies, such as him, better. He attributed this to ministerial instability and governmental weakness. In March 1752 he predicted problems from the frequent changes of French ministers and instructed the Lord Marshal, his envoy in Paris, to press on the French the example of Louis XIV and his concern for foreign policy. That December the Lord Marshal reported that the French ministers sought tranquillity because they were disunited, the finances in a poor state, the populace irritated by the price of grain and their betters dissatisfied. In November 1753 Frederick complained that the Danes were being wooed from the Franco-Prussian system by reports of the poor state of the French army and finances, the weakness of her government and the political problems with the *Parlement* of Paris. The Lord Marshal also gave some weight to policy, attributing French passivity in part to the influence of Madame de Pompadour, Louis XV's mistress, her ascendancy he argued, depending on the continuance of peace. The Prussians, however, failed to consider the extent to which Louis XV and his ministers did not see themselves as obliged to commit themselves to Frederick's interests and views to the degree to which he expected. Frederick was particularly fond of ascribing the failure of powers to act as he believed they should to weakness and court intrigues. In March 1777 he attributed the French failure to act against the ambitious projects of Austria to the role of Marie-Antoinette, Joseph II's sister, and the complete weakness of French finances, which led him to describe France as a power only in title. Frederick argued that unless the finances were improved France would never be able to occupy the rank she had hitherto enjoyed, but he also asked whether it would be possible to encourage Louis XVI to develop an interest in mistresses in order to limit the influence of the queen. Frederick was informed that Louis was not interested in mistresses and, to a certain extent, his assessment of French policy was wrong. Financial problems did not prevent France from opposing Britain, Marie Antoinette did not lead Louis and Vergennes to support Joseph II over the Bavarian succession, the Bavarian exchange scheme or the opening of the Scheldt. Foreign observers might rightly assess domestic circumstances, but these were not necessarily directly linked to policy decisions.

This view can also be advanced with regard to Britain, a state whose constitution was very different to that of France. It appeared to be difficult to control a political system in which a powerful representative institution, the House of Commons, played a major part, including in foreign policy, not least through its financial role. Despite enjoying royal support, prominent ministers fell, such as Danby in 1678, Walpole in 1742 and Carteret in 1744, or encountered serious difficulties, such as Stanhope and Sunderland in 1718. Foreign relations could be affected by parliamentary criticism of the government, as in the attack on the Anglo-French alliance in 1730 over French repairs at Dunkirk, a potential privateering centre, and the attack on Pitt's anti-Russian policy in 1791. Poor relations between crown and Parliament could limit Britain's diplomatic choices. Charles II accepted French subsidies in his last years in large part because he did not wish to meet Parliament. William III found his English options affected by parliamentary impeachments arising from the Partition treaties.

However, contemporaries over-estimated British ministerial weakness and its effects on foreign policy. It may be that most of the aristocratic envoys of continental powers exaggerated the unpredictability of British politics and found it difficult to accept that monarchical power could be as great where it was constitutionally sharply limited as it could be where the theoretical and institutional restraints on it were less. There were certainly periods of marked ministerial and political instability, but there were also long and well-entrenched ministries, such as those of Henry Pelham, Lord North and William Pitt the younger. Ministerial stability required royal support as well as parliamentary management, and the crown wielded considerable influence in foreign policy, especially in peacetime, when parliamentary control over finance bore less direct weight on foreign policy. As Parliament was most concerned about commercial and colonial issues and the monarchs generally more interested in continental diplomacy, the diplomatic importance of the monarchy was further enhanced.

If foreign policies were influenced, but not dictated by domestic circumstances, it was, nevertheless considered worthwhile for diplomats to intervene in domestic politics. This intervention contributed another element to what was generally a highly complex mix of factors affecting policy.

The British envoy in Spain might report in June 1749, 'The secret of what passes here in such matters as are worth paying for, lies in a very narrow compass. The king, the queen, and their two ministers', and other diplomats could make similar reports, but that did not imply that these small groups were oblivious of wider domestic circumstances, any more than that they only concerned themselves with the views of similar small groups abroad. Just as monarchs and ministers were concerned with the military and financial strength and political stability of foreign powers, so they were aware of the importance of their own. However, these issues, which were most important in periods of war and brinkmanship, did not mean that diplomacy was a simple measure of power. Power and authority were difficult to assess and the effect of multi-state diplomacy was to enhance the options for and role of foreign policy. Power aroused opposition as much as compliance. Contemporaries had to consider the impact of domestic circumstances without having any sure guides as to how to assess them or gauge their likely effect.

CONCLUSION

'How can we know what may determine the course of that flood of power, which is now in a state of fluctuation, or seems driven to different points by different impulses', asked Henry Pelham in the House of Commons in 1741. Mutual interests and systems appeared to provide no guide. Both Puysieulx and Frederick II commented on the shared nature of French and Prussian interests in 1749, Frederick telling his envoy in London that these reciprocal interests were so solid, natural and durable that neither could leave the other unless the European system changed. It did and eight years later at Rossbach

Frederick destroyed French military reputation and the prestige of her monarch. In 1773 an experienced British diplomat complained 'there is no real system anywhere, no grand bond of union and therefore not knowing who and who is together, every court stands upon his own bottom, and lives from hand to mouth without any great principle of policy'. Twelve years later a British official wrote of 'these strange disjointed times. Where there is no system, but that of striving to . . . overreach. Surely things must mend, and we shall again see a right understanding in those who ought to form a balance for the preservation of mankind, and not for the destruction of those they are born to protect and render happy merely for the purpose of gratifying their own ambition'. Kaunitz criticized Frederick II for lacking a system, but his theorizing methods did not prevent him from following an indefinite and at times confused policy during the period 1768–74, when the number of independent variables he had to contend with, not least Maria Theresa and Joseph II, defied the creation and implementation of any predictive analysis.

If the situation remained kaleidoscopic there were other constants, including the importance of dynastic and personal honour, and the close relationship between domestic and international strength. Religion became less and trade, especially colonial trade, more important, though neither trend should be exaggerated, and the response to revolutionary France was to indicate the continued strength of popular religiosity. The military and diplomatic gaps between the major and the minor powers grew, although they had already been prominent in 1679. What was still true at the end, as at the beginning of the period, was the importance of international relations. In the last five years before the beginning of the revolutionary wars, Austria, Russia, Sweden and Turkey were involved in conflict, and Britain, Denmark, Prussia and Spain close to war. The fate of Poland had in effect been determined. The revolutionary wars were to add a striking ideological aspect to international tension and conflict, but the revolutionary period simply confirmed what was already apparent, the interrelationship of political developments in different countries and the centrality of international relations.

Bibliography

This bibliography is intended as a guide to further reading. In light of student demand it is restricted to works in English. The stress is on recent work and books. Articles, older and other work and literature in foreign languages can be approached through the bibliographies and footnotes of the works listed. Books are published in London, unless otherwise stated.

GENERAL WORKS

M. S. Anderson, *Europe in the Eighteenth Century* (3rd edition, 1987).
M. S. Anderson, *War and Society in Europe of the Old Regime, 1618–1789* (1988).
J. Black, *Natural and Necessary Enemies, Anglo-French Relations in the Eighteenth Century* (1986).
J. Black (ed.), *The Origins of War in Early Modern Europe* (Edinburgh, 1987).
J. Black, *Europe in the Eighteenth Century, 1700–89* (1990).
The New Cambridge Modern History volumes 5–8 and volume 14 (atlas).
W. Doyle, *The Old European Order 1660–1800* (Oxford, 1978).
P. Kennedy, *The Rise and Fall of the Great Powers* (1988).
D. McKay and H. M. Scott, *The Rise of the Great Powers, 1648–1815* (1983).
J. Stoye, *Europe Unfolding, 1648–1688* (1969).

I

Eastern Europe

M. S. Anderson, *Peter the Great* (1978).
T. M. Barker, *Double Eagle and Crescent* (Albany, 1967).
C. Duffy, *Russia's Military Way to the West* (1981).
C. Ingrao, *In Quest and Crisis: Emperor Joseph I and the Habsburg Monarchy* (West Lafayette, Indiana, 1979).
P. Longworth, *Alexis, Tsar of all the Russians* (1984).
D. McKay, *Prince Eugene of Savoy* (1977).
W. H. McNeill, *Europe's Steppe Frontier, 1500–1800* (Chicago, 1964).
J. P. Spielman, *Leopold I* (1976).
J. Stoye, *The Siege of Vienna* (1964).

O. Subtelny, *Domination of Eastern Europe, Native Nobilities and Foreign Absolutism 1500–1715* (Gloucester, 1986).
B. Sumner, *Peter the Great and the Ottoman Empire* (Oxford, 1950).

The Baltic

R. M. Hatton, *Charles XII of Sweden* (1968).
L. R. Lewitter, 'Russia, Poland and the Baltic, 1697–1721' *Historical Journal* (1968).
J. J. Murray, *George I, the Baltic and the Whig Split of 1717* (1969).
M. Roberts (ed.), *Sweden's Age of Greatness, 1632–1718* (1973).
M. Roberts, *The Swedish Imperial Experience, 1560–1718* (Cambridge, 1979).

Louis XIV's Foreign Policy and Western Europe

Louis XIV et L'Europe – special issue of *XVII Siècle* 123 (1979).
J. S. Bromley and R. M. Hatton (eds), *William III and Louis XIV* (Liverpool, 1967).
C. J. Ekberg, *The Failure of Louis XIV's Dutch War* (Chapel Hill, North Carolina, 1979).
P. Goubert, *Louis XIV and Twenty Million Frenchmen* (1970).
R. M. Hatton (ed.), *Louis XIV and Europe* (1976).
R. M. Hatton, 'Louis XIV: Recent gains in historical knowledge' *Journal of Modern History* (1973).
J. T. O'Connor, *Negotiator out of Season: the Career of W.E. v. Fürstenberg, 1629–1704* (Athens, Georgia, 1978).
R. Place, 'The Self-deception of the Strong: France on the Eve of the War of The League of Augsburg' *French Historical Studies* (1970).
P. Sonnino, 'The Origins of Louis XIV's Wars' in Black (ed.), *Origins of Wars*.
R. A. Stradling, *Europe and the Decline of Spain: a study of the Spanish System, 1580–1720* (1981).
G. Symcox, *The Crisis of French Naval Power, 1688–97* (The Hague, 1974).
G. Symcox, *Victor Amadeus II. Absolutism in the Savoyard State 1675–1730* (1983).

Britain and the Netherlands

S. Baxter, *William III* (1966).
J. Black (ed.), *Knights Errant and True Englishmen, British Foreign Policy 1660–1800* (Edinburgh, 1989).
A. C. Carter, *Neutrality or Commitment: the evolution of Dutch Foreign Policy, 1667–1795* (1975).
P. Geyl, *The Netherlands in the Seventeenth Century, II: 1648–1715* (1964).
G. C. Gibbs, 'The Revolution in foreign policy' in G. Holmes (ed.), *Britain after the Glorious Revolution, 1688–1714* (1969).
J. B. Hattendorf, *England in the War of the Spanish Succession* (1987).
J. R. Jones, *Britain and Europe in the Seventeenth Century* (1966).
J. R. Jones, *Britain and the World, 1649–1815* (1980).
H. H. Rowen, *The Princes of Orange* (Cambridge, 1988).
J. M. Smit, 'The Netherlands and Europe in the seventeenth and eighteenth centuries' in J. S. Bromley and E. H. Kossmann (eds) *Britain and the Netherlands in Europe and Asia* (1968).

II

Austria, Prussia, Russia and Sweden

R. Browning, 'The British orientation of Austrian foreign policy 1749–54' *Central European History* (1968).

H. Butterfield, *The Reconstruction of an Historical Episode* (Glasgow, 1951).

D. B. Horn, 'The Diplomatic revolution' in *New Cambridge Modern History* 7.

D. B. Horn, *Frederick the Great and the Rise of Prussia* (1964).

C. W. Ingrao, 'The Pragmatic Sanction and the Theresian Succession' in W. J. McGill (ed.), *Theresian Austria* (Washington, 1981).

H. H. Kaplan, *Russia and the Outbreak of the Seven Years' War* (Berkeley, 1968).

W. J. McGill, 'The Roots of Policy: Kaunitz in Italy and the Netherlands, 1742–1746' *Central European History* (1968).

W. J. McGill, 'The Roots of Policy: Kaunitz in Vienna and Versailles 1749–1753' *Journal of Modern History* (1971).

L. J. Oliva, *Misalliance: a Study of French Policy in Russia during the Seven Years' War* (New York, 1964).

M. Roberts, *The Age of Liberty, Sweden 1719–1772* (Cambridge, 1986).

K. A. Roider, *The Reluctant Ally: Austria's Policy in the Austro-Turkish War, 1737–1739* (Baton Rouge, 1972).

K. W. Schweizer, *England, Prussia and the Seven Years War* (Lewiston, New York, 1989).

Western Europe

J. M. Black, *British Foreign Policy in the Age of Walpole* (Edinburgh, 1985).

J. M. Black, 'French Foreign Policy during the Administration of Cardinal Fleury Reassessed' *English Historical Review* (1988).

J. M. Black, 'The Problems of a small state: Bavaria and Britain in the second quarter of the eighteenth century' *European History Quarterly* (1989).

R. Browning, *The Duke of Newcastle* (New Haven, 1975).

R. Butler, *Choiseul* I (Oxford, 1980).

A. C. Carter, *The Dutch Republic in Europe in the Seven Years War* (1971).

T. R. Clayton, 'The Duke of Newcastle . . . and the American Origins of the Seven Years War' *Historical Journal* (1981).

S. Conn, *Gibraltar in British Diplomacy in the Eighteenth Century* (New Haven, 1942).

H. Dunthorne, 'Prince and Republic: The House of Orange in Dutch and Anglo-Dutch politics during the first half of the eighteenth century' in J. M. Black and K. W. Schweizer (eds), *Essays in European History in Honour of Ragnhild Hatton* (Lennoxville, Quebec, 1985).

G. S. Graham, *Empire of the North Atlantic: the Maritime Struggle for North America* (Toronto, 1950).

R. Hatton, *George I: Elector and King* (1978).

D. B. Horn, 'The Duke of Newcastle and the origins of the Diplomatic Revolution' in J. H. Elliott and H. G. Koenigsberger (eds), *The Diversity of History* (1970).

R. Lodge, *Great Britain and Prussia in the Eighteenth Century* (Oxford, 1923).

J. O. McLachlan, *Trade and Peace with Old Spain 1667–1750* (Cambridge, 1940).

W. Mediger, 'Great Britain, Hanover and the rise of Prussia' in R. M. Hatton and M. S. Anderson (eds), *Studies in Diplomatic History* (1970).

R. Middleton, *The Bells of Victory, The Pitt-Newcastle Ministry and the Conduct of the Seven Years' War 1757–1762* (Cambridge, 1985).

R. Pares, *War and Trade in the West Indies 1739–1763* (Oxford, 1936).

R. Pares, 'American versus continental warfare, 1739–1763' *English Historical Review* (1936).

G. Quazza, 'Italy's role in the European problems of the first half of the eighteenth century' in R. M. Hatton and M. S. Anderson (eds.), *Studies in Diplomatic History* (1970).

Z. E. Rashed, *The Peace of Paris 1763* (Liverpool, 1951).

M. Savelle, *The Origins of American Diplomacy: the International History of Anglo-America 1492–1763* (New York, 1967).

J. H. Shennan, *Philippe Duke of Orléans, Regent of France, 1715–23* (1979).

A. M. Wilson, *French Foreign Policy during the Administration of Cardinal Fleury, 1726–1743* (Cambridge, Mass. 1936).

III

Eastern Europe

M. S. Anderson, 'European Diplomatic Relations 1763–90' *New Cambridge Modern History* 8.

M. S. Anderson, 'The Great Powers and the Russian Annexation of the Crimea, 1783–4' *Slavonic and East European Review* (1958–9).

H. A. Barton, 'Russia and the problem of Sweden-Finland, 1721–1809' *East European Quarterly* (1972).

H. A. Barton, 'Gustav III of Sweden and the East Baltic, 1771–1792' *Journal of Baltic Studies* (1976).

P. P. Bernard, *Joseph II and Bavaria* (The Hague, 1965).

A. W. Fisher, *The Russian Annexation of the Crimea 1772–1783* (Cambridge, 1970).

D. M. Griffiths, 'The rise and fall of the Northern System' *Canadian-American Slavic Studies* (1970).

J. Lojek, 'The international crisis of 1791: Poland between the Triple Alliance and Russia' *East-Central Europe* (1975).

J. Lojek, 'Catherine II's armed intervention in Poland . . . 1791–2' *Canadian-American Slavic Studies* (1970).

R. H. Lord, *The Second Partition of Poland* (Cambridge, Mass., 1915).

I. de Madariaga, *Russia in the Age of Catherine the Great* (1981).

R. J. Misiunas, 'The Baltic Question after Nystad' *Baltic History* (1974).

M. Raeff (ed.), *Catherine the Great: a Profile* (1972).

K. A. Roider, 'Kaunitz, Joseph II and the Turkish War' *Slavonic and East European Review* (1958–9).

K. A. Roider, *Baron Thugut and Austria's Response to the French Revolution* (Princeton, 1987).

H. M. Scott, 'Frederick II, the Ottoman Empire and the origins of the Russo-Prussian alliance of April 1764' *European Studies Review* (1977).

A Sorel, *The Eastern Question in the Eighteenth Century* (1898).

J. Topolski, 'Reflections on the first partition of Poland (1772)' *Acta Poloniae Historica* (1973).

Western Europe

T. C. W. Blanning, *The Origins of the French Revolutionary Wars* (1986).

J. H. Clapham, *The Causes of the War of 1792* (Cambridge, 1899).

A. Cobban, *Ambassadors and Secret Agents. The Diplomacy of the First Earl of Marlborough at the Hague* (1954).

J. R. Dull, *The French Navy and American Independence* (Princeton, 1975).

J. R. Dull, *A Diplomatic History of the American Revolution* (New Haven, 1985).

J. Ehrman, *The British Government and Commercial Negotiations with Europe, 1783–93* (Cambridge, 1962).

J. Ehrman, *The Younger Pitt: The Years of Acclaim* (1969).

J. Ehrman, *The Younger Pitt. The Reluctant Transition* (1983).

H. V. Evans, 'The Nootka Sound controversy in Anglo-French diplomacy – 1790' *Journal of Modern History* (1974).

V. T. Harlow, *The Founding of the Second British Empire 1763–1793, i. Discovery and Revolution* (1952).

W. O. Henderson, 'The Anglo-French Commercial Treaty of 1786' *Economic History Review* (1957–8).

P. Mackesy, *The War for America, 1775–1783* (Oxford, 1964).

I. de Madariaga, *Britain, Russia and the Armed Neutrality of 1780* (1962).

O. T. Murphy, *Charles Gravier, Comte de Vergennes: French Diplomacy in the Age of Revolution, 1719–1787* (Albany, New York, 1982).

J. F. Ramsey, *Anglo-French Relations 1763–70: A Study of Choiseul's Foreign Policy* (Berkeley, 1939).

M. Roberts, 'Great Britain and the Swedish revolution, 1772–3' *Historical Journal* (1964)

M. Roberts, *British Diplomacy and Swedish Politics, 1758–1773* (1980).

H. M. Scott, 'The importance of Bourbon naval reconstruction to the strategy of Choiseul after the Seven Years War' *International History Review* (1979).

N. Tracy, *Navies, Deterrence and American Independence: Britain and Seapower in the 1760s and 1770s* (Vancouver, 1988).

IV

M. S. Anderson, 'Eighteenth-century theories of the balance of power' in R. M. Hatton and Anderson (eds.), *Studies in Diplomatic History* (1970).

J. M. Black, 'The theory of the balance of power in the first half of the eighteenth century' *Review of International Studies* (1983).

P. E. Chamley, 'The Conflict between Montesquieu and Hume: a Study of the Origins of Adam Smith's Universalism', in A. S. Skinner and T. Wilson (eds.), *Essays on Adam Smith* (1975).

Diplomatic Thought 1648–1815, special issue of *Studies in History and Politics* (1981–2).

F. Gilbert, *To the Farewell Address: Ideas of early American Foreign Policy* (Princeton, 1961).

R. M. Hatton, *War and Peace, 1680–1720* (1969).

P. C. Howe, 'Revolutionary Perspectives on Old Regime Foreign Policy' *Consortium on Revolutionary Europe, Proceedings* (1987).

H. Mason, 'Voltaire and War' *British Journal for Eighteenth-Century Studies* (1981).

H. Meyer, *Voltaire on War and Peace Studies on Voltaire* (Oxford, 1976).

R. Niklaus, 'The Pursuit of Peace in the Enlightenment' *Essay on Diderot and the Enlightenment in Honor of Otis Fellows* (Geneva, 1974).

R. W. Olson, *The Siege of Mosul and Ottoman-Persian Relations 1718–1743* (Bloomington, Indiana, 1975).

M. L. Perkins, 'Montesquieu on national power and international rivalry' *Studies on Voltaire* (Oxford, 1985).

F. S. Ruddy, *International Law in the Enlightenment. The Background of Emmerich de Vattel's Le Droit des Gens* (Dobbs Ferry, New York, 1975).

E. V. Souleyman, *The Vision of World Peace in Seventeenth and Eighteenth-Century France* (New York, 1941).

G. Symcox (ed.), *War, Diplomacy and Imperialism, 1618–1763* (New York, 1973).

M. Wright (ed.), *Theory and Practice of the Balance of Power 1486–1914* (1975).

V

D. Altbauer, 'The Diplomats of Peter the Great' *Jahrbücher für Geschichte Osteuropas* (1980).

T. M. Barker, *Army, Aristocracy, Monarchy: Essays on War, Society, and Government in Austria, 1618–1780* (Boulder, Colorado, 1982).

J. Black and P. Woodfine (eds), *The British Navy and the use of Naval Power in the Eighteenth Century* (Leicester, 1988).

D. Chandler, *The Art of Warfare in the Age of Marlborough* (1976).

J. Childs, *Armies and Warfare in Europe, 1648–1789* (Manchester, 1982).

A Corvisier, *Armies and Societies in Europe, 1484–1789* (Bloomington, Indiana, 1979).

C. Duffy, *The Military Life of Frederick the Great* (1986).

C. Duffy, *The Military Experience in the Age of Reason* (1987).

J. Dull, *Franklin the Diplomat: the French Mission* (Philadelphia, 1982).

D. B. Horn, *The British Diplomatic Service, 1689–1789* (Oxford, 1961).

H. M. A. Keens-Soper, 'The French Political Academy, 1712: a School for Ambassadors' *European Studies Review* (1972).

H. M. A. Keens Soper and K. W. Schweizer (ed.), F. de Callières, *The Art of Diplomacy* (Leicester, 1983).

J. H. L. Keep, *Soldiers of the Tsar: Army and Society in Russia, 1462–1874* (Oxford, 1985).

J. Klaits, 'Men of Letters and Political Reform in France at the end of the reign of Louis XIV' *Journal of Modern History* (1971).

J. Luvaas, (ed.), *Frederick the Great on the Art of War* (1966).

O. T. Murphy, 'Charles Gravier de Vergennes: profile of an old regime diplomat' *Political Science Quarterly* (1968).

P. Paret, *Yorck and the Era of Reform* (Princeton, 1966).

G. Parker, *The Military Revolution, Military innovation and the rise of the West, 1500–1800* (Cambridge, 1988).

J. C. Riley, *The Seven Years' War and the Old Regime in France. The Economic and Financial Toll* (Princeton, 1986).

W. Roosen, *The Age of Louis XIV. The Rise of Modern Diplomacy* (Cambridge, Mass., 1976).

INDEX

Dates after monarchs and ministers are the years of their reign